P9-EJH-759

The publisher gratefully acknowledges the
generous support of the Humanities Endowment Fund
of the University of California Press Foundation.

THE FIRESIDE CONVERSATIONS

THE FIRESIDE CONVERSATIONS

America Responds to FDR during the Great Depression

LAWRENCE W. LEVINE
CORNELIA R. LEVINE

Foreword by Michael Kazin

University of California Press

BERKELEY   LOS ANGELES   LONDON

University of California Press, one of the most distinguished
university presses in the United States, enriches lives around the world
by advancing scholarship in the humanities, social sciences, and
natural sciences. Its activities are supported by the UC Press Foundation
and by philanthropic contributions from individuals and institutions.
For more information, visit www.ucpress.edu.

University of California Press
Berkeley and Los Angeles, California

University of California Press, Ltd.
London, England

© 2002, 2010 by Lawrence W. Levine and Cornelia R. Levine

Selected letters originally published in *The People and the President,*
© 2002 by Lawrence W. Levine and Cornelia R. Levine

Library of Congress Cataloging-in-Publication Data
Levine, Lawrence W.
[People and the president. Selections]
The fireside conversations : America responds to FDR during the Great Depression /
Lawrence W. Levine, Cornelia R. Levine ; foreword by Michael Kazin.
p.   cm.
"Selected letters originally published in The people and
the president, 2002 by Beacon Press"—T.p. verso.
Includes bibliographical references.
ISBN 978-0-520-26554-7 (alk. paper)
1. United States—Politics and government—1933-1945. 2. United States—
Social conditions—1933-1945. 3. New Deal, 1933-1939. 4. Roosevelt, Franklin D.
(Franklin Delano), 1882-1945. 5. United States—Politics and government—
1933-1945—Sources. 6. United States—Social conditions—1933-1945—Sources.
7. New Deal, 1933-1939—Sources. 8. Roosevelt, Franklin D. (Franklin Delano),
1882-1945—Correspondence. 9. Presidents—United States—Correspondence.
10. American letters. I. Levine, Cornelia R.
II. Title.
E806.L479   2010
973.917—dc22
2010014862

This book is printed on Cascades Enviro 100, a 100% postconsumer waste,
recycled, de-inked fiber. FSC recycled certified and processed chlorine free.
It is acid free, Ecologo certified, and manufactured by BioGas energy.

For Our Grandchildren

STEPHANIE

BENJAMIN

and

JONAH

Who Continue Our Education

CONTENTS

FOREWORD

THIS REMARKABLE BOOK demonstrates the power one gifted voice can wield during a time of national calamity. It is no mystery why Franklin Roosevelt's Fireside Chats elicited so much mail or why they remain one of the primary ways in which Americans remember the Great Depression. Like Dorothea Lange's photo of the "Migrant Mother," Yip Harburg's lyric "Brother, Can You Spare a Dime," and John Steinbeck's *Grapes of Wrath,* the Chats expressed an acutely crafted sense of empathy for a people whose misfortune was no fault of their own. More than eighty years after the stock market crash of 1929, each of these artifacts seems to embody the suffering of that era, the ways in which Americans endured hard times, and the means with which some battled the forces they believed had caused or exacerbated them.

However, the president's task was more complicated than the one talented artists and writers set for themselves. FDR was, after all, a politician. He had to reassure his listeners that both the economy and the federal government were essentially stable. He had to persuade them to support New Deal initiatives that regulated business and increased the powers of the state far beyond what previous administrations had attempted. And he had to promote his own candidacy for reelection and the campaigns of his fellow Democrats—without making either explicit partisan appeals or attacks. FDR's rhetorical mastery helped him score one electoral victory after another. No other man served so long in the White House—and he died barely a month after his fourth term began.

As the Levines point out in their introduction, Roosevelt was fortunate to serve in office during the heyday of radio, when the broadcasts most people tuned into on sets that resembled large pieces of furniture came to surpass the political influence of every other medium. During the Depression, most Americans read a daily paper and went to the movies as often as their incomes allowed. But only on the radio could a political figure sway and mobilize a majority of citizens, at the same time. "The lower a person's economic status," observes the historian Lizabeth Cohen, "the more likely he or she preferred radio over print." National broadcasts encouraged listeners to follow the lead of a seductive voice electronically transmitted, instead of a variety of more humble spokespeople in their own localities whom they could see and with whom they could easily argue.[1]

The new medium had the potential to do great harm as well as to aid those who sincerely advocated for the greater good. Adolph Hitler, who was sworn in as German chancellor just a month before FDR was inaugurated as president, used the radio to stoke Germans with confidence that, under his leadership, they could defeat Jews and other non-"Aryans" who had kept them from fulfilling their national and racial destiny. Benito Mussolini closely studied the emotions of crowds and understood how to move them with what a biographer calls "simple, oft-repeated statements, with little obvious artifice and employing a small vocabulary." In the United States, Father Charles Coughlin gained an audience of millions with mellifluous jabs at "international bankers" and a president he accused of being "anti-God" and "bent on communistic revolution."[2]

Although FDR's most bitter foes accused him of dictatorial ambitions, he employed the radio to advance democracy, not to dismantle it. At a time when many European nations were moving sharply to the right and most leftists were praising Stalin's rule in the USSR, the Roosevelt administration helped millions of workers to organize unions, enacted benefit plans for seniors and the unemployed, and protected the savings and investments of every citizen—without changing a single sentence of the Constitution, ratified 150 years before.

However, as a solution to the Depression, his New Deal was far from an unmitigated triumph. With the aid of government spending, the economy rebounded somewhat during the mid-1930s, but the New Deal never created enough jobs—public or private—to end chronic unemployment. Only the industrial boom stimulated by World War II accomplished that. In Congress, a tacit coalition between most Democrats from the rural South and West and nearly all Republicans kept agricultural workers—a large number of whom were black, Latino, or Asian—from enjoying the protections of either Social Security or the Wagner Act—the landmark labor law passed in 1935 that enabled unions to gain a strong foothold in factories, mines, and docks. When FDR died, he bequeathed an incomplete welfare state whose benefits were disproportionately enjoyed by white Americans.[3]

Yet Roosevelt did give millions of Americans a sense that they had a friend running the government—and that, as a result, the government would listen to them. The textile worker from North Carolina who told a reporter that FDR was "the only man we ever had in the White House who would understand that my boss is a sonofabitch" was unintentionally bearing witness to a sea change in American politics. The letters the Levines reproduce in this volume testify to that change. Never before had so many wage earners, small farmers, and their families allowed themselves to expect so much from the federal government. Before the Depression, Americans assumed that officeholders in Washington, D.C., would do little more than make sure the mail was delivered on time, dole out a small pension to military veterans, and defend the nation in time of war. Nearly every other task fell to state and local governments, which also collected the lion's share of taxes. But FDR's invitation to "tell me your troubles"—and the programs he sponsored that were intended to alleviate them—left that era firmly in the past.[4]

In the short run, his well-earned reputation for empathy yielded a significant political benefit: it enabled FDR and his party to co-opt a variety of populist movements that fed off the anger bred of economic collapse. Unemployed veterans demanded immediate payment of a bonus for their wartime service. Industrial wage earners went on strike and occupied their factories; millions signed up with new unions, some of which were led by Communists and Socialists. Louisiana Senator Huey Long promised to make "every man a king" by confiscating large fortunes and using the windfall to double the median family income. The liberal humorist Will Rogers—the Jon Stewart of his day—put the populist argument in words people raised on farms could appreciate: "All the feed is going into one manger, and the stock on the other side of the stall ain't getting a thing. . . . We got it, but we don't know how to split it up."[5]

All this worried the captains of the New Deal. Harold Ickes—the Interior Secretary and one of Roosevelt's closest advisers—wrote in his diary, "The country is much more radical than the administration." One opinion poll in 1935 found that Huey Long would draw 11 percent of the vote if he ran a third-party campaign for president. "I am fighting communism, Huey Longism, Coughlinism," FDR told a reporter. Although many of the "isms" he listed were not on speaking terms with one another, it was not certain that the president and his allies would win.

Of course, they did triumph: Roosevelt won reelection by a landslide in 1936 and, in so doing, crafted a liberal coalition that remained largely intact for the following three decades. He did so with a deft combination of populist rhetoric and programs that convinced most discontented Americans that the government was truly on their side. Running for a second term,

Roosevelt bashed "the privileged princes of these new economic dynasties" who "reached out for control over government itself." Such talk didn't end mass unemployment or alleviate the poverty of millions. Yet by the time the United States entered World War II, more of the feed was making its way into the stalls where most Americans lived.

As a consequence, even sixty-five years after his death, Roosevelt is still the standard by which Americans judge their presidents. Voters hate to pay taxes, and most routinely tell pollsters the government is too big and spends too much of their money. But they loyally support and depend upon the biggest government initiatives those revenues make possible, most of which either were first enacted when FDR was in office (Social Security, the Wages and Hours Act, bank deposit insurance) or were inspired by his example (Medicare, Medicaid, and the Environmental Protection Agency). Libertarian conservatives rail at "the nanny state," but no conservative president has attempted to repeal a single one of these programs. To do so would have courted his doom. In the White House, Ronald Reagan, who began his political life as a New Deal Democrat, liked to quote FDR to signify that he, too, was engaged in transforming a hapless government that no longer served ordinary people. It is fitting that FDR is the only chief executive since Lincoln to have a memorial placed in the heart of the nation's capital. Like the humble dime that bears his likeness, he belongs to the quotidian life of his country.

* * *

The financial crisis that broke in 2008 and the deep recession that followed it have revived interest in the Great Depression—and stirred analogies between FDR and Barack Obama, who also owed his lopsided victory, in large part, to repudiation of the probusiness Republican who preceded him in office. Of course, the prepresidential biographies of Franklin Roosevelt and Barack Obama are wildly dissimilar: one man came from landed gentry, or as close as one could get to such a class in industrial America; the other man had an absentee African father and spent his teenage years living with grandparents who sometimes had to rely on food stamps.

The contrasts between the society of the 1930s and the contemporary one are nearly as stark. The Great Depression was the crisis of a manufacturing and farming economy that depended chiefly on a domestic market. An unbridgeable chasm then existed, socially and psychologically, between financiers and industrialists and most other Americans. In the 1930s, the average factory worker earned a weekly wage of about $24; some steelworkers routinely walked to work barefoot to conserve the leather on the single pair of shoes they owned. Fewer than 5 percent of Americans invested in the stock market when the 1929 crash hit, and fewer than half owned their own homes. Now, most citizens own stock, if only indirectly through their pension funds. Until the onset of the housing crisis, two-thirds owned a home or condominium. Despite their economic woes, the majority of Americans pride themselves on being "middle-class." The nation in which most breadwinners worked with their hands as long as they were able for only a modest wage and no fringe benefits seems quite far away.[6]

The political context of the thirties was quite different as well. The coalition that backed FDR was one based almost entirely on shared economic interests. Southern planters, working-class immigrants from Europe, and, beginning with the 1936 election, black voters both North and South disagreed about religion, race, and attitudes toward moral issues—the prohibition of selling alcoholic beverages being the most salient at the time. But they all blamed "big business" and its friends in the Republican Party for their plight. Seventy-five years later, the Democratic coalition is united more by cultural affinities and political loathings than economic ones. In the 2008 election, Obama did best among voters who held graduate degrees and those who lacked even a high-school diploma. What brought these disparate groups together was their affection for an eloquent candidate "with a funny name" and a fierce hostility toward the deeds of George W. Bush.

There is one significant way in which future historians may view Obama as akin to FDR: Roosevelt was a transformative president, the main architect of a new political era; Obama hopes to become another member of that small, ultra-exclusive club. In his analysis of the history of the presidency, political scientist Stephen Skowronek argues that only five chief executives—Jefferson, Jackson, Lincoln, FDR, and Reagan—have truly "reconstructed" the American political universe. All did so in a similar context. Each man had the good fortune to have succeeded a president who was an utter failure and whose party coalition was unraveling. Each was elected with a campaign that resembled a mass movement and was then able to convert that movement into the engine of a new electoral coalition that dominated American politics for a generation or more.[7]

It is too early to know whether Obama will be able to transform the nation's politics and its policies—or will become the victim of a system that resists necessary reforms. There are, however, two ways in which he already resembles FDR. His 2008 campaign proved him to be a master of a new medium of political communication—the Internet instead of the radio. And in his best speeches and press conferences, Obama has demonstrated an ability to appreciate both the longing of Americans for a government that cares about their problems and can help to solve them and their deep skepticism that the political class is capable of fulfilling that promise. To become a transformative president, Obama will have to keep expressing his empathy, in sincere and well-chosen words. He will also have to defeat a conservative opposition that is larger and better mobilized than the dispirited one that failed to defeat FDR or thwart the New Deal.

*　　*　　*

Empathy was also the quality Larry Levine prized most in both the writing and teaching of history. Soon after the publication of his first book, about the last decade of William Jennings Bryan's life, Larry wrote an essay on what led him to choose that subject and to understand Bryan and his followers the way he did. Entitled "The Historian and the Culture Gap," it begins:

> At some point in his studies (for many historians at *all* points), the historian is faced with a situation where there is little continuity or connection between his own cultural conditioning and expectations and that of his subjects. He is faced with a culture gap that must be bridged both by painstaking historical reconstruction and by a series of imaginative leaps that allow him to perform the central act of empathy—figuratively, to crawl into the skins of his subjects. . . . It is, in fact, the primary function of the historian and gives the study of history much of its excitement and importance.[8]

I cannot think of a more useful, more humane observation about our craft. Empathy is easy to proclaim but quite difficult to practice consistently. For all our good intentions, historians invariably slip in a few paragraphs or sentences or turns of phrase that put down our subjects for failing to think and act as they *should* have—to be as enlightened as we imagine ourselves to be.

Larry understood that historians who have insufficient empathy for their subjects are not just guilty of condescension. They usually produce flawed history: either they view historical actors inhabiting one small, cramped dimension of existence, or they see them as crushed beneath structures far too mighty for them to grasp or change.

Larry's work demonstrates the profound error of this way of thinking. In glorious detail and vivid prose, he proved that the small-town folks who admired Bryan, the black men and women who turned their suffering and their hopes into great music and humor, the audiences who turned William Shakespeare into a popular American playwright, and the millions who listened to FDR's Fireside Chats were creative and complex individuals. They were capable of bigotry and violence, to be sure, but they also knew how to make sense of their lives in cultural terms, and the cultures they built became vital resources for democratizing America. Larry's work had a tremendous impact, one attested to by the numerous awards he received and the high offices he held in his profession.

But he was never working alone. Larry was acutely conscious that he belonged to a new generation of historians; trained in the 1950s and 1960s, they transformed the way we now understand the American people and their constantly evolving past. Larry and his intellectual comrades eagerly explored and debated the impact and meaning of the diverse cultures of America, in part because they represented that cultural diversity themselves. They were not the first historians to spring from immigrant and non-Protestant backgrounds. But they were the generation that shaped the way history is taught in most colleges and many high schools today.

In the laborious research that went into *The Fireside Conversations,* Larry also had the advantage of collaborating with a partner who shared his opinions, his work habits, and his life. Together, Cornelia and he read tens of thousands of letters, drawn from the millions that were written to FDR during his long years in the White House. They decided to limit their scope to correspondence received during the two weeks following each Fireside Chat. As Cornelia writes, the Chats "were specifically crafted . . . to appeal to ordinary citizens." Sitting side by side at a long table at the FDR Library in Hyde Park, New York, the couple would occasionally "share a letter that was too good not to be savored right away. It usually involved some funny phrasing or imaginative spelling."[9]

Larry Levine didn't just practice empathy in his writings. He was also an empathetic teacher. In a 1997 interview with Sheldon Hackney, who was then head of the National Endowment for the Humanities, Larry confessed:

> I am a person of very strong beliefs. . . . I have very strong feelings and I have acted on them, probably not as often as I ought to have. . . . But I decided a long time ago that . . . my function in the classroom was not to promulgate beliefs. You learn as a scholar and teacher that if you argue with the dead and you don't win the argument, you're a fool, so I decided that arguing with the dead wasn't what I wanted to do. And the same thing is true of arguing with the living when the living have less power than you. You can force your ideas on them—that wasn't my goal. So, always admitting what my own ideas were, I tried to teach them with balance and to leave room for other ideas.[10]

That wisdom is the essence of good teaching. It is also the core of what makes good citizens—men and women who not only feel confident about expressing their own opinions and needs but also show respect for the needs and judgments of people who have less power than they do. That is what FDR was trying to do with his Fireside Chats, and he largely succeeded. The same can be said for Larry and Cornelia Levine. In that sense, they and the old Dutchman from Hyde Park were kinsmen. And their truths go marching on.

—Michael Kazin

INTRODUCTION

You have no fireplace? How do you listen to the President's speeches?

Groucho Marx, Room Service (1935)

Radio sets were not then very powerful, and there was always static. Families had to sit near the set, with someone always fiddling with the knobs. It was like sitting around a hearth, with someone poking the fire; and to that hearth came the crackling voices of Winston Churchill, or George Burns and Gracie Allen, and of FDR. The fireside chats . . . It was not FDR who was at his fireside . . . it was we who were at our firesides.

Henry Fairlie, New Republic, January 27, 1982

THE ADVENT OF RADIO in the 1920s and especially the 1930s changed things indelibly. It was what the novelist Margaret Atwood has called one of those "definitive moments, moments we use as references, because they break our sense of continuity, they change the direction of time. We can look at these events and we can say that after them things were never the same again."[1] Radio, of course, was the first form of mass media that had the quality of simultaneity, creating what Hadley Cantril called "the largest grouping of people ever known."[2] In a series of articles she wrote on radio for the *New York Times Magazine* in the spring of 1932, the political correspondent Anne O'Hare McCormick spoke of "this incredible audience," "millions of ears contracted into one ear and cocked at the same moment to the same sound."[3] In their 1935 book, *The Psychology of Radio*, Hadley Cantril and Gordon Allport estimated that "our countrymen spend approximately 150,000,000 hours a week before the [movie] screen, but nearly 1,000,000,000 hours before the [radio] loud-speaker." Radio, they maintained, is "the greatest single democratizing agent since the invention of printing."[4] Lew Sarett and William Trufant Foster compared radio to the ancient Greek Acropolis: "a place from which the Elders might speak to all the citizens at once."[5]

Contemporaries grasped the force and significance of radio very early. Though they often made the mistake of equating the populist potential of radio with democracy — a parallel the career of Adolf Hitler alone should have disabused them of — they nevertheless comprehended radio's enormous capacity to reach and affect people in numbers and ways formerly inconceivable. The memories of those who experienced the Great Depression and the war that followed it were commonly and often inextricably bound to the radio. Thus the poet Maxine Kumin remembering Pearl Harbor:

> The Day
> of Infamy, Roosevelt called it. I was
> a young girl listening to the radio
> on a Sunday of hard weather . . .[6]

Though listening to radio quickly became a common experience, for many it remained somehow magical. V. T. Chastain recalled that his father had the first radio in Holly Springs, South Carolina: "Neighbors from all around congregated at our house to see and hear the amazing radio! One man I remember in particular really enjoyed a certain musical rendition, and he told Dad, 'Make 'em play that one again, Wade.' Nothing Dad could say would convince him that the musicians were in Greenville and not somewhere, somehow, inside that box!" Evelyn Tomason remembered her grandfather in the early 1930s listening to local election returns and suddenly holding his hand up high, asking the radio: "Repeat that please!" In 1934 Gus Wentz looked "into the back of the radio to try to see the 'little people' in there," and Trina Nochisaki couldn't remember "how many times I tried to sneak up on the real little people I just *knew* lived in the radio — if only I could catch them unawares."[7]

The millions of Americans who heard the first Fireside Chat on March 12, 1933, certainly didn't think FDR was one of those tiny people nestled within their radios, but radio was still such a new force that they did feel his presence in a manner so novel and extraordinary to them that we — to whom the wonders of radio, television, and the computer have become so familiar — have to make a leap of empathy to appreciate what they experienced. Myra King Whitson of Houston, who described herself as a mother "with young mouths to feed, young minds to educate, young fears to quiet," who had been living through what she called a "long nightmare," thanked FDR for "your talk last night, when our radio seemed to bring you to us in person — there is a deep happiness — a feeling that we have a real share in our government, and that our government is making our welfare its chief concern."[8] The mayor of Richland Center, Wisconsin, informed Roosevelt, "An old friend said to me this morning 'I almost wept during the President's talk last night, it seemed he was sitting by my side talking in plain simple words to me.' "[9]

The mystique of the Chats lasted far beyond the initial one. "Listening to you," Nathan Weldon wrote in 1935, "I could feel the prescence of your honest sincerity in the room. I found myself answering you, nodding to you, chatting to you, and agreeing with you."[10] Five years later, Florence Gunnar Nelson wrote: "With only the lighted dial of our radio for illumination, a feeling of deep gratitude came over me. With no lites to disclose my surroundings I might imagine myself in the same room — at the same fireside as our great President Roosevelt, listening to his stirring words."[11]

FDR received these letters from a wide spectrum of the American people — farmers, businessmen, salesmen, housewives, doctors, nurses, teachers, entertainers, ministers, priests, and rabbis, retired people, the unemployed, students, lawyers, workers, union leaders and members, local and state government officials of all kinds, members of a wide variety of ethnic organizations and clubs, residents of large urban centers, small towns, and villages, Democrats as well as large numbers of Republicans, and not a few Socialists and Communists, people from all sections of the country — responding to their President in a period of deep domestic, and ultimately international, crisis.*

They jotted their thoughts down on every imaginable kind of paper, from formal stationery to lined notebook pages, from three-by-five-inch filing cards to the backs of business cards, from scraps of paper to gaudy greeting cards. They enclosed editorials, articles, cartoons, and pamphlets

---

*Studies of radio in the 1930s indicated that while the wealthy owned disproportionately more radios, middle- and lower-income groups listened more frequently and wrote more mail to radio stations and personalities than higher-income groups. A study of the mail Roosevelt received during a five-day period in March 1934 confirms these findings: 46 percent of his letters were from laborers, 17 percent from businessmen, 15 percent from farmers, 14 percent from clerical workers, 3 percent from professionals, 1 percent from government officials, 1 percent from students, 1 percent from children, and 2 percent from organizations (Leila Sussmann, *Dear FDR: A Study of Political Letter Writing* [Totowa, N.J.: Bedminster Press, 1963], 141).

they thought the President should see, as well as poems, drawings, photos, stories, jokes, and recipes they wanted to share with him. Their letters allow us to approach FDR and the New Deal through the eyes of contemporaries who viewed what was transpiring in Washington from outside the centers of power, to be sure, but who felt its effects at first hand and who responded to their President with gratitude and censure, criticism and advice. Here is the *other*, less known and less understood side of radio: the audience.

Radio inspired and encouraged this correspondence; it was one of the prime modern forces that helped to circumvent the structural barriers the Founders had erected to insulate the federal government from direct popular influence. By the Great Depression, and especially during the Great Depression, communication between the public and its national leaders had become a much more immediate process. As a number of scholars have observed, the written word was increasingly replaced by the spoken word. Radio certainly stimulated the rise of what has been called the "rhetorical presidency," in which FDR used his speeches as "events" in and of themselves in an attempt to communicate with the public over the heads of the legislature and the newspapers.[12]

But while radio undeniably elevated the centrality of the spoken word, it also greatly stimulated the importance of the written word in the form of the growing stream of letters from listeners. "The mail room in a big broadcasting station is the most amazing exhibit in the whole radio show," Anne O'Hare McCormick observed. "It is a human document in endless volumes, an orgy of the kind of old-fashioned letter writing the social historian saw vanish with the horse and the darning egg."[13] Radio stations, which in their formative years had no other means to measure the size and attitudes of their audiences, literally trained their listeners to write letters by constantly urging them to send in their opinions and responses to programs. In the early 1930s, about two-thirds of NBC programs requested listeners to write in. The success of these appeals is clear. NBC received 383,000 letters in 1926; 775,000 in 1928; 1 million in 1929; 2 million in 1930; 7 million in 1931. CBS was even more successful, receiving 12.6 million letters from its listeners in 1931 alone.[14] When, in January 1931, the Catholic priest Father Coughlin, who was to build his extremely popular Sunday radio talks into a national dissident movement, asked his listeners to endorse his speeches by writing to the broadcasting stations, there was a deluge of

485,252 letters.[15] "Listening-in for a decade," a *Times* reporter observed in 1932, "has created a habit of letter-writing."[16]

FDR was a central part of this process. Roosevelt's radio speeches helped make participants — even activists — out of his audience. When in the midst of one address Roosevelt invited his audience to "tell me your troubles," Ira Smith, the White House Chief of Mails, testified that large numbers of people "believed that he was speaking to them personally and immediately wrote him a letter. It was months before we managed to swim out of *that* flood of mail." The letters came in so fast, Smith remembered, that "within a week I had some 450,000 letters stacked all over the office."[17] Precisely the same happened after FDR's Fireside Chat of July 24, 1933, in which he asked employers — "the big fellows and the little fellows" — who intended to participate in the National Recovery Administration "to write or telegraph to me personally at the White House." "The response to that was immediate and perfectly overwhelming," according to Hugh Johnson, the head of the NRA. "Telegrams and letters by the tens of thousands poured into Washington for days. No such volume of mail had ever been received by the government."[18] The flood of letters delighted Roosevelt. He told reporters that the great volume of mail demonstrated "an increasing and wholesome reawakening of public interest in the affairs of government" — a statement that could only encourage people to continue writing to him.[19] Whenever the influx of letters decreased, Ira Smith recalled, "we could expect to hear from him or one of his secretaries, who wanted to know what was the matter — was the President losing his grip on the public?"[20]

FDR especially valued these letters because, as he informed his adviser Louis Howe, who supervised the President's correspondence both before and directly after he became President, personal mail from everyday folks, who tended to express their convictions honestly, constituted the "most perfect index to the state of mind of the people."[21] Thus FDR insisted that the letters he received be read and answered. Personal letters from the President's family and friends were sent unopened to his office. The bulk of the correspondence was opened and read by clerks, who forwarded the substantial number of specific queries and requests to appropriate departmental and agency offices, such as the Federal Emergency Relief Administration (FERA), the Works Progress Administration (WPA), and the Department of Agriculture, which were directed to read and respond to them.[22] The remainder were read and answered by presidential secretaries and assistants within the White House itself, and FDR seems to have stayed very much within the loop.

The President, Ira Smith noted, "does see a good many letters, and the summaries and other data that are supplied him make it possible for him to keep a close tab on public opinion and on the problems that are uppermost in the minds of ordinary people."[23] FDR, Howe recorded, "likes to see a cross section of the daily mail, and not infrequently answers, himself, some of the letters contained in this batch. . . . I have seen him spend precious moments poring over letters scribbled on butcher paper or ruled pages torn from a cheap pad, often directing special attention or replies to the writers of such letters."[24] During such particularly trying moments as the struggle over the Supreme Court, the 1937 recession, American intervention in the European war, the question of whether to run for a third term, FDR relied on what were known as "mail briefs" — analyses of his mail by his staff that gave him a pro and con breakdown with excerpts from each group — to help him grasp public feeling. Lela Stiles, who chose the excerpts FDR would see, maintained that she did not spare the President's feelings even when the opposing letters grew bitter.[25]

Eleanor Roosevelt also received a considerable mail — over three hundred thousand letters in 1933 alone — which, she wrote, "often kept me busy far into the night." She insisted that all the letters be answered by her staff or herself since "the times were too serious and the requests too desperate" to send mere form replies. She made a practice of sharing her more interesting letters with her husband: "I always prepared small piles of my letters for him." These she often placed on the table next to his bed: "I learned to save anything I wanted to tell him till he was in bed, for that was likely to be the only quiet time in the whole day."[26] Some of her correspondents counted on just such behavior on her part. As one woman wrote: "Centuries back Catholics prayed to the Virgin Mary because they thought she might intercede with a diety who could not take time to hear every petitioner. In some such spirit we turn to you."[27] Albert Moreau's letter to FDR was addressed to Eleanor Roosevelt "because I know our dear President is to busy to read these letters but I hope you will tell him how we stand with him."[28]

If Eleanor Roosevelt tried her best to avoid form replies to her correspondents, her husband, whose volume of mail was much larger, didn't have that luxury. The names of those presidential assistants and secretaries who signed the replies — Louis McHenry Howe, Marguerite (Missy) LeHand, Stephen Early, Marvin McIntyre, Grace Tully, Major General Edwin M. (Pa) Watson, and for a time FDR's son James — were generally known to the public, which doubtless pleased his correspondents and reassured them that their letters were not being ignored. "I have written to you twice before and got a repley at once," Margie DeBett informed FDR with obvious pleasure in 1934.[29] The replies, however, were often formulaic. In 1941 C. V. Easterwood began his letter to FDR by congratulating him "on your speech last night" and then went on to demand that workers who went on strike be drafted into the army or sent to a concentration camp. He was answered by Edwin Watson, who skipped the substance of the letter and wrote simply: "Thank you very much in the President's behalf for your kind message of congratulations in reference to his recent radio address."[30]

Within this formulaic structure there could be varying touches of a personal answer. When Charles Fisher wrote FDR in December of 1940: "Altho I am colored & am out of the conscription age at present, you will find me ready to serve anytime men of my age are needed, either in peace or in war," Stephen Early responded with the usual: "Your letter of December twenty-ninth has been received and will be brought to the President's attention," and then added, "Meanwhile, I know he would want me to thank you for this evidence of your loyalty and good will."[31] On another occasion, Edwin Watson wrote Mary Jester, "What you say concerning your son who is a member of the armed forces has been noted with appreciative understanding and the President wants you to know how profoundly conscious he is of your pride in your boy and his service to our country's cause."[32] Ten-year-old Velma Hess's letter inviting FDR to visit her family in Martinsburg, West Virginia, was answered by Grace Tully, who thanked her for her "nice little letter," and added "the President's grateful thanks to your mother for remembrance in prayer," but ignored the invitation to visit.[33]

While his correspondents had little chance of hearing from FDR directly, some came close. Robert Woolley's opening comment in his letter to FDR, "This note may never reach you personally. Just the same I am deriving a world of satisfaction from writing it," received this response from Stephen Early: "Permit me first to assure you that the President did read your letter of May twenty-eighth and derived as much satisfaction from reading it as you did in writing it."[34] Some writers addressed their letters directly to one of the President's secretaries and occasionally obtained the results they were aiming at. Marvin McIntyre responded to one such letter from Detroit: "Your expressions of faith were such that I took the liberty of showing it to the President. He found it extremely interesting and asked me to express his thanks."[35] Although all the letters were read, only the positive ones received replies, as J. T. Cannon of Philadelphia discovered when he tried a little experiment: he sent a number of positive letters to the President and received prompt acknowledgments. "On the other hand, not once did I get a reply from a letter of criticism, nor do I know of anyone else that ever did."[36]*

The attempts of Franklin and Eleanor Roosevelt to respond to their millions of correspondents were often imperfect and perfunctory, but they nevertheless intensified the profound feelings of connection Americans felt toward them. This was affirmed by Lorena Hickock, who traveled through the nation during the early years of the New Deal describing the conditions she found to FDR's relief administrator, Harry Hopkins. Reporting on Alabama in the spring of 1934, she commented on "the number of letters you see around over the President's and Mrs. Roosevelt's signatures. They are seldom anything more than the briefest and most formal acknowledgment of a letter. . . . But I doubt if any other President — or his wife — has ever been so punctilious about acknowledging letters. And these people take them all very seriously, as establishing a personal relation."[37]

In letter after letter, the President's correspondents informed him — often with enclosed copies — of the letters they sent to their Representatives and Senators demanding that they support New Deal policies. FDR directly encouraged this development. According to the *New York Times,* by the beginning of 1934 members of Congress were receiving fifty thousand letters a day, forty thousand addressed to Representatives and ten thousand to Senators.[38] A year later the *Times* described the "stooped shoulders" of the twenty-four postmen who handled the "bulging mail-

---

*Our own research in the responses to the Fireside Chats confirmed Mr. Cannon's impressions. The letters replying to the Fireside Chats are organized in the FDR Library by the date of the Chat to which they are responding, the names of the respondents in alphabetical order, and whether they are pro or con. The latter, of course, could have been ascertained only if the letters were read. Other signs that they were read include underlinings and other markings by FDR's staff directly on the letters as well as a notation of the date of the acknowledgment, if any. The negative letters went unacknowledged, though they were neither uncounted nor destroyed, as at least one of FDR's correspondents feared (Mrs. Walter S. Cooke, Worcester, Massachusetts, to FDR, March 10, 1937).

sacks" containing eighty-five thousand letters a day — forty thousand incoming and forty-five thousand outgoing — that made their way through the post office of the U.S. Senate alone.[39] In 1934 Senator Simeon Fess, Republican of Ohio, demonstrated what he called this "enormous" volume of mail by bringing to the Senate floor the letters and telegrams he had received during the past twelve hours, the bulk of which urged him to support the President's monetary policies. "Some of the letters," he informed his colleagues, "even ask us totally to abdicate all responsibility of expressing judgment and vote as rubber stamps."[40] Fess's experience was typical. "The name that appears in the letters more often than any other," a press report concluded, "is that of President Roosevelt. Senators and Representatives, regardless of party affiliation, are urged to 'stand by the President,' and are threatened with defeat at the polls if they fail to support his recovery program."[41]

As the first year of the New Deal wound down, the journalist Stanley High marveled at the ways in which it had made "the average, garden-variety American voter Washington-conscious," brought the government and its people closer to each other than ever before, and turned the entire nation into something resembling a New England town meeting. "It is probable," he observed, "that in the last twelve months more hitherto inarticulate American citizens have 'taken their pens in hand' for political purposes than during any such period in our whole history." For this he credited the President: "The spirit, even more than the content, of his 'My Friends' speeches was something new in the annals of our democracy. There is a latch-string-is-always-out quality about them. They invite familiarity." The country, High concluded, "sends its orders to its Congressmen. But it talks things over with its President."[42] If the extraordinary number of letters arriving at the White House were any indication, another journalist noted, "more Americans are awakened to their public duty and quickened with the sense of social responsibility than at any other time in recent history. The whole land appears to be thinking, [and] wanting to help the President to think."[43]

At the very least, FDR helped to school people in the significance and legitimacy of writing freely to the head of their government and other elected officials, an activity that really began in a significant way during the Great Depression and continues vigorously to this day. "When I first went to work at the White House," Ira Smith has testified, "President McKinley was getting an average of perhaps 100 letters a day, and there were frequent complaints that something would have to be done about such an avalanche of mail. . . . In President Hoover's time, the mail averaged about 800 a day, and during the New Deal it averaged about 8000 a day, with peak days on which we would go down under a count of 150,000 letters and parcels. . . . The mere physical handling of the mail required a staff that grew from one man — myself — to twenty-two regularly employed persons and in emergencies to seventy persons."[44] Leila Sussmann calculated that during the Civil War Lincoln received 44 letters annually for every 10,000 literate adults in the nation, during World War One Wilson received 47, and during the Great Depression FDR received 160.[45] On December 16, 1933, the White House announced that it would institute a night shift for the first time in its history in order to handle the unprecedented volume of mail.[46]

Louis Howe told the readers of a national magazine that his recurrent nightmare "finds me in an airplane, high up, so that the whole map of the United States lies spread out beneath me. . . . It appears to be covered with a white blanket flowing toward one point. As the airplane descends, I find to my horror that the white blanket consists of letters — letters from every part of the country — and their ultimate destination is the White House."[47] As with most dreams, Howe's embodied elements of barely disguised reality. Franklin Roosevelt, with the indispensable aid of radio, was presiding over a revolution in mass political letter writing.

FDR not only stimulated an enormous increase in the number of letters sent to the President, but he used this correspondence innovatively to pressure his opponents inside and outside the Congress and to justify his actions. "All we have to do," he told his advisers during one legislative battle, "is to let the flood of mail settle on Congress . . . and the opposition will be beating a path to the White House door."[48] Above all, he employed his enormous correspondence to fathom the attitudes of the American people and to free himself of the dependency previous Presidents had upon members of Congress to learn what their constituents were thinking. FDR was convinced that he possessed an independent pipeline to the public far more extensive than anyone in Congress, and he used it to help shape and implement his program. Nor did Roosevelt feel, as many of his predecessors had, dependent on newspaper reporters to help him keep his finger on the pulse of the people. "I am more closely in touch with public opinion in the United States than any individual in this room," he told a group of newspaper editors. "I get a better cross section of opinion."[49] There was, Eleanor Roosevelt recalled after the President's death, "a real dialogue between

Franklin and the people. He would read samplings of his mail. . . . He always knew what the reaction was to what he was doing, and he could respond to that reaction."[50]

Sam Rosenman, one of the President's principal speechwriters, gives a number of instances of the impact of mail upon FDR. After a Chicago speech in 1937 in which the President stated that an "epidemic of world lawlessness" was spreading and made an analogy with epidemics of physical disease, which were dealt with by quarantine "in order to protect the health of the community," he received such a negative flood of antiwar telegrams opposing what became known as his "quarantine the aggressors" speech that he was forced to back down at his press conference the very next day.[51] "It's a terrible thing," he remarked to Rosenman, "to look over your shoulder when you are trying to lead — and to find no one there." Conversely, Rosenman cites the President's May 26, 1940, Fireside Chat calling for enhanced American military preparedness as receiving such a positive response that it emboldened FDR to go to Congress just five days later requesting additional appropriations for national defense.[52] During the first six months of 1940, FDR asked for daily mail briefs on what his correspondents thought about his seeking a third term and discovered, according to Leila Sussmann, that "the letter-writers were overwhelmingly in favor of his running again and that among them, the objection to breaking the two-term tradition carried little weight."[53] In the final year of the war, FDR received many letters revealing the public's fear of renewed economic depression and hardship when peace returned. He sent such letters on to Rosenman as "speech suggestions" and did in fact include these matters both in his speeches and in his plans for peacetime reconstruction.[54]

One of the most common requests in his letters was that FDR deliver his Fireside Chats more frequently: monthly or even weekly. Charles Flaig of Richmond, Indiana, was typical: "I hope you will come before the people oftener. Since 80% of the press, magazines and their other loud speakers are daily vomiting out their hate and criticism against you, it is confusing many people and clouding the real facts and issues. Our only salvation is the radio, we must use it often."[55]

FDR certainly agreed that radio had become essential to American democracy. In an address he gave as governor of New York at the beginning of 1929, he estimated that "whereas five years ago ninety-nine out of one hundred people took their arguments from the editorials and the news columns of the daily press, today at least half of the voters sitting at their own firesides listen to the actual words of the political leaders on both sides and make their decision on what they hear rather than what they read."[56] Accordingly, he supported the efforts of those within his administration who wanted to produce public service and educational radio shows for the networks. By 1939 there were forty-two different New Deal agencies, bureaus, and departments engaging in radio programming, ranging from the Department of Agriculture's "Farm and Home Hour," the Public Health Service's "Help Yourself to Health," and the Children's Bureau's "Your Child" to dramatizations by the Social Security Board and the Federal Housing Administration explaining their services. The Department of the Interior had its own weekly drama series, "What Price America," highlighting the nation's battle to control and conserve its natural resources, and the Office of Education series "Americans All — Immigrants All" explored the roles played by different religions, races, and nationalities in America's cultural and economic life. Then there were the Federal Theatre Project's radio productions of famous plays, including a series of Shakespearean dramas. The public responded to many of these programs exactly as it responded to the Fireside Chats: with a barrage of letters. The Office of Education — the federal agency producing the largest number of radio programs until Congress cut its budget in 1940 — received four hundred thousand letters in 1937, eight hundred thousand in 1939, and almost a million in 1940.[57]

The President, of course, was the undisputed star of the New Deal's broadcasting endeavors. Nevertheless, he resolutely refused to heed pleas that he himself use radio more often. After his election in 1932 but before he had taken office, the president of NBC offered him airtime and urged him to speak to the people fifteen to twenty minutes once a week. FDR responded: "I fully expect to give personal talks from time to time on all kinds of subjects of national interest, but I do not believe that it would be advisable to make one each week."[58] It was a position from which he never deviated. "Sometimes I wish I could carry out your thought of more frequent talking on the air on my part," he wrote Russell Leffingwell in March of 1942, "but the one thing I dread is that my talks should be so frequent as to lose their effectiveness."[59] A week later he wrote Mary Norton: "For the sake of not becoming a platitude to the public, I ought not to appear oftener. . . . I am inclined to think that in England Churchill, for a while, talked too much, and I don't want to do that."[60]

Thus, in spite of his striking radio successes, he continued to use the radio format sparingly: only thirty-one Fireside Chats from March 1933 to

January 1945, and these were not evenly spread out but tended to come in clusters during periods of crisis. Accordingly, the Chats became significant and widely anticipated events. Belle Conwell of Birmingham, Alabama, assured FDR: "I must tell you that when it is announced that the President is to speak, we fore-go any engagements to be at home. It is akin to a visit with a good friend."[61] "I would not have missed hearing it for anything," B.J. Campbell of Memphis wrote. "Mrs. Campbell and me were invited to an egg nog party so in order to hear it I phoned our host and he said go ahead. I have postponed the party until after the President's message."[62]

The Administration created suspense by refusing to divulge the subjects the President would include and only gradually and grudgingly giving out any details of the coming broadcast, thus making the contents of his Chats national news before and not merely after he gave them. On May 13, 1941, for example, the *New York Times* announced that FDR would deliver a Fireside Chat on May 27 and noted, "The Executive seldom makes fireside chats except upon important matters." On May 23 it announced: "The President spent four hours today working on his speech." The next day it gave the list of those who would constitute FDR's small — and very silent — live audience and specified the local stations that would carry the Chat. On May 25 a *Times* headline, referring to press secretary Stephen Early, proclaimed: "ROOSEVELT SPEECH WON'T PLEASE FOES OF DEMOCRACY, SAYS EARLY," and the paper spent considerable space speculating on what the President would say. On the morning of the speech, the *Times* reported that FDR "was devoting more time to preparation of this speech than to any previous address he had made to the American people" and that according to White House sources "the President's speech would be one of the most important he ever made."[63] Radio stations treated the Chats as important events by giving the President free airtime and by rebroadcasting them the next day "for the benefit of those unable to hear it at the regular time."[64] Similarly, newspapers all over the country summarized and often printed the Chats in full or part.[65]

Those who did not own radios wrote him of their sense of deprivation. "I wish I had a small Radio in my lonely Furnish Room," Elizabeth Berg wrote from New York City, "so I could hear your Talk. I Receive so little Money for Rent and Food. so I cant Buy any."[66] Walter Edison of Oakland, California, was one of the many who wrote for a transcript of a Fireside Chat, explaining, "I can't afford a radio or well afford buying a newspaper with it published in as I'm on un-employables inadequate relief."[67]

For Roosevelt, the radio turned out to be very much a two-edged sword. While many letters were characterized by adulation and compared Roosevelt to biblical figures (Moses, Gideon, Solomon, Jesus, even God) or famous secular leaders (Caesar, Washington, Wilson, and especially Abraham Lincoln), there was also a frankness and a willingness to push FDR in directions he didn't seem to be embracing with enough will or decisiveness, or to urge him to move with more deliberateness and caution. He was besieged with advice concerning his economic and social programs, alerting him to defects, counseling him to alter or supplement his approaches, warning him of conditions his advisers were ignoring, or simply praising his efforts. There was no dearth of voluntary advisers anxious to have the President peruse their solutions for the crisis. "Plans, plans, and plans," Louis Howe exclaimed in 1934. "Some two pages long, some thick manuscripts handsomely bound and carefully indexed; every day brings a flood of them to the White House door."[68]

When FDR took a serious misstep, as many felt he did when he tried to "pack" the Supreme Court or involve the United States in the European conflict, numerous supporters wrote him anguished letters of reproach, pleading with him to adhere to his own principles and the historic American system. On the Court issue, for example, Paul Barrett of Philadelphia informed FDR: "Your remarks filled me with a deep sense of sorrow and chagrin," and a group of stenographers implored him: "Don't throw over our love and loyalty for a stubborn idea. . . . Don't sell us out in order to personally triumph over a few political enemies."[69] And of course there were those who never pretended to be his admirers and kept up a drumbeat of rancorous opposition in their responses to his Fireside Chats: "PLEASE GET OFF THE AIR WE WANT TO HEAR OUR FAVORITE PROGRAM," A. M. Tebbetts of St. Louis, Missouri, telegraphed in 1941.[70] A New Jersey resident felt it necessary to inform the President: "I wouldn't urinate on you if you were burning at the stake."[71]

It has been said of Father Coughlin that he "built an electronic neighborhood."[72] This describes precisely what FDR did as well, and unlike Coughlin, whose reign as the "radio priest" was relatively brief, the President was able to maintain his neighborhood through the long years of depression and war. FDR's creation of a new form of public discourse flowered in the years of his presidency but had its origins during his governorship of New York from 1928 to 1932, when, as he wrote in 1938, "it was often necessary for me to appeal for public support over the heads of the Legislature and sometimes over the almost united opposition of the newspapers of the State. . . . The use of the radio by me in those days not only to appeal directly to the people, but also to describe fully the facts about the legislation which were not always given by many press reports, was the beginning of similar use of the radio by me as President in what have come to be known as 'Fireside Chats.' The radio has proved to be a direct contact with the people which was available to only two presidents before me. It has been invaluable as a means of public approach."[73] The day before his initial Fireside Chat, FDR explained its purpose in a statement issued from the White House: "The Constitution has laid upon me the duty of conveying the condition of the country to the Congress assembled at Washington. I believe I have a like duty to convey to the people themselves a clear picture of the situation at Washington itself whenever there is danger of any confusion as to what the Government is undertaking."[74]

The aims and purposes of the Fireside Chats remained the same as the gubernatorial chats. What changes there were emanated primarily from Roosevelt's increasingly sophisticated use of radio. He simply got better and better at it. What has not been stressed sufficiently is how much FDR *needed* radio. Radio began to develop as a major genre of communication in the 1920s, during the very years when Roosevelt suffered the devastating effects of polio. Radio offered enormous compensation for that illness since it allowed Roosevelt to reach the American people with his *voice*. This is not to minimize the extent to which FDR continued to travel as President — by railroad alone he made 399 trips logging over half a million miles, and he put in many more miles by air, sea, and auto — speaking in person with aggregations of people large and small, something he loved to do and did with superb skill.[75] But polio prevented him from moving among and mingling with people. Radio allowed him to enter people's homes, their neighborhoods, their lives. Without radio, he undoubtedly would have had a markedly different political career than the one he did have.

Many of FDR's political and official speeches, such as his four Inaugural Addresses and many of his Annual Messages, were carried on the radio, but each one of the Fireside Chats was designed from the beginning as a *radio* address. FDR and his speechwriters worked diligently to make these speeches accessible and comprehensible to as large an audience as possible. Indeed, FDR adopted so basic a vocabulary that 70 percent of his words were among the five hundred most commonly used words in the English vocabulary and 80 percent were among the one thousand most commonly used words.[76] The Fireside Chats were relatively brief, ranging from fifteen to forty-five minutes and averaging twenty-six minutes in length. They emanated from the White House or, in two instances, from FDR's home in Hyde Park, New York. They were broadcast on all the national networks, most often on Sundays, Mondays, and Tuesdays at around ten in the evening, Eastern Time — when Easterners were still awake and people in other parts of the country were already home from their day's activities — in order to attract a peak national audience. Each Chat was generally devoted to a single subject or to a small cluster of related subjects. Roosevelt's purpose in these Chats was not to make ringing statements for posterity but to speak in a face-to-face style.

In his initial Chat, it was FDR's intention to demystify a banking system shrouded in enigma to a people enveloped by anxiety.[77] Thus his first Fireside Chat, delivered in the midst of a momentous crisis that could have altered the American political system fundamentally, began conversationally with FDR speaking "for a few minutes" about banking to "the comparatively few who understand the mechanics of banking, but more particularly with the overwhelming majority of you who use banks for the making of deposits and the drawing of checks. I want to tell you what has been done in the last few days, and why it was done, and what the next steps are going to be." This patient, gentle tone prevailed throughout and turned to mild exhortation only at the conclusion: "You people must have faith; you must not be stampeded by rumors or guesses. Let us unite in banishing fear."[78]

FDR's delivery fit seamlessly with the simplicity and accessibility of his words. He spoke calmly, slowly, usually not much more than 100 to 120 words per minute, some 30 percent less than was common in radio broadcasts — at the other end of the spectrum the news commentator Walter Winchell spoke 200 words per minute — and when the situation was particularly grave, as in his Fireside Chat following the attack on Pearl Harbor, he dropped the pace to 88 words per minute. This unusually deliberate pace allowed FDR to pay attention to his phrasing, his pauses, and his vocal pacing, all of which he became a master at — elongating and prolonging his vowels and consonants, using silences effectively, varying his emphases and the modulation of his tenor voice. How deeply Roosevelt cared about these matters was made evident both before and after he delivered a Chat. He would read a draft out loud, Robert Sherwood reported, "to see how it sounded and to detect any tongue-twisting phrases that would be difficult on the radio." At the close of his Fireside Chats he would eagerly query the radio announcers and technicians in the room: "Was I all right?" "Did I go too fast?" "Did I put too much emphasis on this point?" "Did I slur over that word?"[79] He displayed precisely the same attitude toward the cameramen who shot portions of the Chats for the movie newsreels, asking them: "How did that go? Need another take?" and using professional terms like "take," "cut," "footage," "fadeout."[80]

"I am not an expert on radio technique," Felix Ury wrote FDR in 1937, "but . . . I can honestly say from my own point of view that your delivery last night over the radio was your 'Masterpiece'. You were just right — not too fast or not too slow and your tone was one of genuine sincerity . . . from the heart."[81] "The thing which impressed me, and inspired me to send this letter," W. M. Holmberg wrote during the war, "was the calm confidence and strength of your voice which carried a real message of assurance of ultimate victory for the United Nations."[82] Glowing reviews of FDR's voice were not confined to his radio audiences. John Carlile, who worked as a voice expert for CBS, characterized the President's voice as revealing "sincerity, good-will and kindliness, determination, conviction, strength, courage and abounding happiness."[83] "Like his picture," Professor Jane Zimmerman of Columbia University's Teachers College asserted, "his voice gives the impression of a genial smile."[84] "His tone and manner were as near perfection as any one can come over the radio," the *New York Times* proclaimed on its editorial page after FDR's Chat in April 1935.[85] "His voice lent itself remarkably to the radio," Eleanor Roosevelt later wrote. "It was a natural gift, for in his whole life he never had a lesson in diction or public speaking. His voice unquestionably helped him to make the people of the country feel that they were an intelligent and understanding part of every government undertaking during his administration."[86]

What is more difficult to describe about his delivery was its spirit and tone. This patrician from the Hudson River Valley had mastered the art of conversational speaking over the radio to a diverse audience of tens of millions of people — as many as 83 percent of those who owned radios tuned in to his Chats on at least two occasions.[87] Harry Butcher, the CBS official who coined the term "Fireside Chats," was told by the President "that he thought of his radio talks as himself sitting in the White House and talking to one person in his own home. To make this picture more simple for himself, the President said he picked some object on the mantel and imagined, while dictating or working on a draft of his 'chat,' that object to be the person to whom he was speaking."[88] FDR was obviously able to bring that conception into the actual broadcast of the Chats. Even someone as conditioned to political oratory as the radio correspondent Richard Strout testified: "You felt he was there talking to you, not to 50 million others, but to you personally."[89]

FDR also knew precisely how to set the right informal tone in the makeshift White House studio from which the Fireside Chats were broadcast and which was filled with presidential aides, secret servicemen, invited guests, radio technicians, newspaper reporters, photographers, and newsreel cameramen. Two minutes before he went on the air with his second Chat, he looked up from his text, which he had been perusing one last time, observed the silent, tense gathering and broke the nervous pall that enveloped the room by announcing with a broad smile: "If anybody has to sneeze, he'd better do it now!"[90]

The open but restrained quality of FDR's initial Chat, which Raymond Moley, his close adviser during his first term, called "as simple and moving as any presidential utterance in the history of this country,"[91] belied the intense preparation that went into it and all of his subsequent Fireside Chats. The Fireside Chats, Eleanor Roosevelt testified, "entailed a great deal of work on Franklin's part. . . . I have known . . . Franklin to take a speech that had almost reached the final stages and tear it up and dictate it from the beginning, because he felt the others had not made it clear enough for the layman to understand. Franklin had a gift for simplification."[92] Robert Sherwood, the playwright who worked on Roosevelt's speeches, observed that FDR "knew that all of those words would constitute the bulk of the estate that he would leave to posterity," and thus "utmost importance was attached to his public utterances and utmost care exercised in their preparation."[93]

FDR himself made it clear how hard he worked on his Fireside Chats to make them sound like simple conversation. In a letter to one of those urging him to give more Fireside Chats, FDR wrote: "I suppose you know that every time I talk over the air it means four or five days of long, overtime work in the preparation of what I say."[94] He explained on another occasion: "I usually take the various drafts and suggestions which have been submitted to me and also the material which has been accumulated in the speech file on various subjects, read them carefully, lay them aside, and then dictate my own draft. . . . On some of my speeches I have prepared as many as five or six successive drafts myself after reading drafts and suggestions submitted by other people." He acknowledged the help he received in creating his speeches but wrote that those who claimed authorship of his speeches "are not accurate" — a conclusion with which every one of his major speechwriters agreed.[95]

The journalist Charles Michelson, who worked on some of FDR's early speeches, remembered an occasion when he, Hugh Johnson, and Raymond Moley each prepared a draft of a speech. Roosevelt went over the three drafts, "stretched himself on a couch and with his eyes on the ceiling dictated his own version, occasionally using one of our phrases but generally culling the best ideas that had been submitted and putting them in his own way." His experiences led Michelson to conclude that "Franklin Roosevelt is a better phrase maker than anybody he ever had around him."[96] Frances Perkins recalled what happened when FDR asked her to contribute to an address on social security: "I summed up one section by saying, 'We are trying to construct a more inclusive society.' I heard that speech over the radio some weeks later, and this is how he, with his instinct for simplicity, wound up that section: 'We are going to make a country in which no one is left out.' "[97] "The speeches were always Roosevelt's," Sam Rosenman testified. "He had gone over every point, every word, time and again. He had studied, reviewed, and read aloud each draft, and had changed it again and again, . . . by the time he delivered a speech he knew it almost by heart." Even when the draft was finished the President was not, and he altered it as he spoke, a habit that drove his speechwriters to form the "Society for Prevention of Ad-Libbing," but to no avail. "Poppa just thought of it at the last minute," he would explain when they complained about his departures from the text. "It was remarkable how little trouble he got into," Rosenman wrote, "considering how much ad-libbing he did."[98]

If studying the Fireside Chats and the responses to them teaches us about how FDR used the radio, it also helps us to learn about an equally important and even more neglected subject: how the American people used the radio. Radio was still new enough that people commented on the quality of the reception. E. D. Warren from Jackson, Michigan, wrote after the second Fireside Chat: "Both my sister and I heard it very clearly for the most part, altho there was a great deal of static."[99] "We heard your splendid speech over our radio last night," Harry Nelson of Ithaca, Nebraska, wrote, "it came in as clear as if you were right in the room with us."[100] Calling radio "a modern miracle," Frank Mercato reported from San Francisco that he had his radio "adjusted so finely, I could hear your Excellency, every time you took a breath. I really had a very front seat in your audience."[101] We know that FDR had a large and constant audience. Almost two-thirds of those questioned by a 1939 *Fortune* Survey responded that they "usually" or "sometimes" listened to the Fireside Chats, and as we've seen, his audience frequently rose far above that percentage.[102] Aside from its size, we know little concerning the ways in which that audience approached the Chats and what effects — immediate and long-term — the Chats had on listeners. Answers to these questions are contained in the letters themselves. Americans filled their letters to FDR with details describing how they listened to his Fireside Chats: where and with whom they listened, what they were doing and saying as they listened, and what they did after they listened.

Radio listening "was by no means antithetical to a sense of folk or community . . . before, during, and after the Great Depression, people enjoyed popular culture not as atomized beings vulnerable to an overpowering external force but as part of social groups in which they experienced the performance or with which they shared it after the fact."[103] The Fireside Chats bear this out: the majority of their listeners heard the Fireside Chats not in isolation but as part of groups, large and small. They listened with families and friends at home; in churches and synagogues; in offices, hotel lobbies, and movie theaters; in barracks and camps; in the streets and in parks; at celebrations, conventions, and business meetings. It was not uncommon for FDR to receive telegrams informing him: "TWENTY BUSINESS AND PROFESSIONAL MEN ASSEMBLED IN MY HOME TO HEAR YOUR MESSAGE."[104] "THE COLORADO CHIROPRACTORS . . . LISTENED TO YOUR ADDRESS TONIGHT EN MASSE."[105] "NEGRO FRATERNAL COUNCIL OF CHURCHES IN SESSION AT CLEVELAND . . . STOPPED OUR PROGRAM LAST NIGHT TO HEAR YOUR MESSAGE TO THE NATION."[106] "OVER THREE THOUSAND PEOPLE LISTENED TONIGHT IN RAPT ATTENTION TO YOUR BRILLIANT AND INSPIRING SPEECH WHICH WAS REBROADCAST TO THE BALLROOM OF THE PENN ATHLETIC CLUB RITTENHOUSE SQUARE PHILADELPHIA."[107]

The Reverend James W. Henley of the Centenary Methodist Episcopal Church, South, in Chattanooga, assured the President that even church services were not allowed to interfere: "A loud speaker was placed in the church auditorium and the service was arranged so as to make way for your radio address at the scheduled moment."[108] In Chicago a synagogue brought in a radio and made FDR "our principal speaker and guest of honor (in voice and spirit — although not in person.)"[109] Members of the Portuguese Workers Music Club in New York City "met in this club to hear your radio talk tonight."[110] Sidney Rothschild wrote following the Chat of April 14, 1938, that his daughter was in downtown Manhattan, "and she said that people were clustered around Taxi Cabs with Radios listening to your talk, and she went into a Childs resturant, There the waitress and customers were all listening."[111] Six years later, in another place called Manhattan — this one in Kansas — the room clerk at the Wareham Hotel wrote: "Tonight when you came on the air the lobby filled with people of all walks of life, they all listened to every word you said."[112]

Even when people listened alone, their experience could be a communal one. The novelist Saul Bellow, then a college student, recalled walking along Chicago's Midway past a row of parked cars whose drivers had pulled over "and turned on their radios to hear Roosevelt. They had rolled down the windows and opened the car doors. Everywhere the same voice, its odd Eastern accent, which in anyone else would have irritated Midwesterners. You could follow without missing a single word as you strolled by. You felt joined to these unknown drivers, men and women smoking their cigarettes in silence, not so much considering the President's words as affirming the rightness of his tone and taking assurance from it. You had some sense of the weight of troubles that made them so attentive, and of the ponderable fact, the one common element (Roosevelt), on which so many unknowns could agree."[113]

People not only listened, but reacted, together. Patrick H. O'Dea of Washington, D.C., wrote FDR that after listening to his Fireside Chat on banking, "the Banquet Committee of the Ancient Order of Hibernians and Ladies' Auxiliary, then in session, by a sort of spontaneous intuition began to sing 'Happy Days are Here Again.' "[114] The director of publicity for a movie chain wrote that his "fifteen (15) theatres in Philadelphia carried the entire Presidents address of Sunday Evening to their audiences thru a special hook-up from the radio to the regular theatre loud speakers." He reported that "the majority of the audiences kept their seats and only a few of the younger people left during the address. . . . After the address the majority of all the audiences applauded most generously."[115] Generally, after broadcasting his Chat, FDR repeated portions of it before newsreel cameras. "I was at a movie last night where there was a packed house, at least 4,000 people," Samuel Traum wrote in 1941. "When the reading of your speech was shown on the screen, there was a loud and vigorous applause."[116]

Other gatherings were smaller but no less revealing: In Brooklyn Ruth Lieberman gathered with her parents to hear FDR's first Chat: "My father, who is a determined pessimist, was airing his views on the banking situation. He was sure that the banks would never open — — that he would never regain his savings. Then you spoke. For fifteen minutes Dad was silent, his brow wrinkled in thought. Then, when you had concluded your talk, he grinned sheepishly and said, 'Oh well, I wasn't really afraid of losing my money anyhow."[117]

Listening to FDR on the radio was often a prelude to action. Following his Fireside Chats, many listeners functioned as FDR's eyes and ears and his self-appointed pollsters. A New Yorker named Hutchinson wrote on New York Athletic Club stationery: "I made it my business to circulate among clubs and hotel lobbies, after your last night's speech, for several hours. I do wish you could have been present and could have heard what I heard said about you. Men were slapping each other on their backs and enthusiastically shaking hands in self congratulation that, at last, the public has a BUDDY in the White House."[118] Roosevelt's 1937 Chat on his controversial plan to add Justices to the Supreme Court prompted a number of impromptu polls. F. P. McMahon strolled through his Omaha, Nebraska, neighborhood and reported: "I have checked carefully the people who live on my street of average 5 room homes, and find that at least 7 out of 10 voters are in favor of your plan."[119] A. J. Hamilton, "a travling man working on trains between Atlanta and New Orleans," wrote: "I have interviewed 3812 passengers relative to your Court reform proposal and here is the result — 2759 for and 1052 against." While he made no record of "non committals," he was sensitive to the nuances of class: "To my supprise a greater percent of Pullman passengers was for your proposal."[120] A resident of Galesburg, Illinois, also checking the reactions on railroads, telegraphed: "TEN PASSENGERS ON TRAIN HAVE JUST HEARD YOUR FIRESIDE CHAT. EIGHT OF US ARE STILL AGAINST YOUR PLAN. ONE IS FOR YOU. ONE SLEPT THRU YOUR TALK AND IS UNDECIDED."[121]

To judge from the letters FDR received, the radio was not an instrument inducing intellectual and political passivity in its audiences. On the contrary, the Fireside Chats — and we know this was also true of the radio addresses of Father Coughlin and Huey Long and of many other genres of radio as well — tended to *counter* passivity, to stimulate audiences to thought and action, and to give them a sense of participation and inclusion — often for the first time in their political lives. Throughout the Great Depression and World War Two, the radio presented the American people with an alternative and increasingly necessary means of learning about and understanding what was happening to them and others like and unlike them. The radio quickly eclipsed the newspaper as the chief means of disseminating national and international news. Seventy-one percent of radio owners queried by the Office of Radio Research in 1939 regularly listened to news broadcasts. In the fall of 1938, the American Institute of Public Opinion found that in all economic classes in both urban and rural areas decisive majorities of those interviewed expressed greater interest in radio than in newspaper accounts of the European crisis. In November 1945, a poll asked which medium — magazines, newspapers, moving pictures, or radio — best served the public during the war: 67 percent listed radio first, with newspapers a distant second at 17 percent.[122]

Perhaps even more indicative of the growing ubiquity and popularity of radio were the results of a 1939 *Fortune* Survey that asked: "If you had to give up either going to the movies or listening to the radio, which one would you give up?" More than 79 percent were willing to give up movies, while less than 14 percent were willing to abandon the radio. The survey concluded "that not a single group of people by class or occupation, or age or sex, votes less than 70 per cent for giving up the movies rather than the radio." Six years later a national survey repeated the question and found that the number willing to give up movies rather than radio had grown to 84 percent, while only 11 percent expressed willingness to forgo their radios.[123]

The letters Roosevelt received reinforce the findings of these polls and clearly demonstrate that the American people understood the revolutionary changes radio inaugurated. They appreciated, just as early and as explicitly as the many commentators and theorists, the democratizing potential of radio, and they made it their most popular form of leisure activity with bewildering rapidity. By the end of World War Two, some 90 percent of the population owned radios, 36 percent owned more than one, and almost a quarter of those surveyed had a radio in their cars.[124] Because so much of what was broadcast on radio fell into what by the 1920s and 1930s was classified as "lowbrow" culture — vaudeville, melodrama, adventure stories, comedy, children's shows, breakfast chatter, country and dance music — intellectuals and scholars have tended to ignore a medium that has had an incalculable impact on American politics, culture, and society. Happily, there are a number of hopeful signs that we are at long last ready to give radio its due in comprehending and recounting our history. There are equally encouraging signs that we are prepared, finally, to listen to the voices of all the American people.

PART ONE

THE NADIR: 1933–1936

Never can there have been a closer, a more intense union of leader and led . . . his mastery of radio was something never before known. His stature increased. He glowed and gave out light. The people responded.

Rexford Guy Tugwell, *The Democratic Roosevelt*

You are the first President to come into our homes; to make us feel you are working for us; to let us know what you are doing. Until last night, to me, the President of the United States was merely a legend. A picture to look at. A newspaper item. But you are real. I know your voice; what you are trying to do. Give radio credit. But to you goes the greater credit for your courage to use it as you have.

Mildred I. Goldstein, Joliet, Illinois, to FDR, March 13, 1933

CLOSING THE BANKS:
MARCH 12, 1933

"MY FRIENDS, I WANT TO TALK for a few minutes with the people of the United States about banking. . . ."[1] With these unassuming words, Franklin D. Roosevelt began his first radio address to the American people following his decision on March 6, two days after his inauguration, to close the doors of all of the banks in the United States, an action euphemistically termed a "bank holiday." It was the first of those national radio addresses, broadcast directly from the White House at prime time and delivered slowly, in simple language devoid of rhetorical flourishes, that were soon to be called his "Fireside Chats."

But if Roosevelt's approach was relatively low-key, the moment was one of the most dangerous and disheartening in American history. Although Roosevelt's Inaugural Address eight days earlier was widely noted — both then and since — for his assertion that "the only thing we have to fear is fear itself," the new President used the occasion of his inauguration to give voice to the monumental problems that beset the nation and gave rise to what were, in fact, very legitimate fears:

> Values have shrunk to fantastic levels; taxes have risen; our ability to pay has fallen; government of all kinds is faced by serious curtailment of income; the means of exchange are frozen in the currents of trade; the withered leaves of industrial enterprise lie on every side; farmers find no markets for their produce; the savings of many years in thousands of families are gone.
>
> More important, a host of unemployed citizens face the grim problem of existence, and an equally great number toil with little return. Only a foolish optimist can deny the dark realities of the moment.[2]

It is customary and convenient to depict the nation's plight statistically: a gross national product that had fallen by 1933 to somewhere between half and two-thirds of what it had been in 1929; corporate net profits and farm income figures that were well under half of what they had been only four years earlier; construction expenditures that had dropped by more than 70 percent; investment rates that were 98 percent below 1929 rates; unemployment figures that, according to Roosevelt's Secretary of Labor, Frances Perkins, ranged from 13.3 million to 17.9 million in 1933 and embraced at least one out of every four American workers, only about one quarter of whom were getting any sort of relief, most of it grossly inadequate. No one could estimate how many *under*employed Americans there were by 1933, as hard-pressed employers converted their employees into part-time workers. United States Steel, which employed 224,980 full-time workers in 1929, had not a single full-time worker on April 1, 1933. The Governor of Pennsylvania reported in early 1933 that only two out of five employable persons in his state had full-time jobs with full pay.[3]

Figures like these are crucial to our understanding of the Great Depression but give us only a partial picture of the American people during the nadir of their great crisis. If ever a people were unprepared for prolonged economic disaster Americans in 1929 were that people. Their culture had not only taught them to believe in continuing progress but had equated that progress with material growth and expansion. Thus, in one cruel blow, events from 1929 to 1933 stripped away a substantial part of their expectations and certainties. Their country had been transformed from a golden land of promise and opportunity to a place characterized by cruel incongruities: Everywhere there was want and everywhere there was plenty. People were undernourished while crops rotted in the fields. Children went without adequate clothes and shoes while clothing and shoe factories closed down for want of markets. As FDR frequently observed, the American people displayed remarkable patience as the calamities multiplied, but it was a patience accompanied by a pervasive bewilderment and a sense of impotent anger as they were beset by malevolent forces they could neither identify nor comprehend. Rational purpose had given way to confusion and inaction well symbolized by the more than one million men and women drifting through the country on foot and in freight cars in a massive display of movement without direction.[4]

Franklin Roosevelt understood the spiritual and psychic costs of the Depression far more clearly than his predecessor had. Shortly before taking his oath of office, he had written to Felix Frankfurter, a law professor at Harvard whom he would later appoint to the Supreme Court, of "the mood of depression, of dire and weary depression" when "the hand of discouragement has fallen upon us, when it seems that things are in a rut, fixed, settled, that the world has grown old and tired and very much out of joint."[5] During his campaign for a fourth term in 1944, FDR would look back on the early years of the Great Depression as "a time in which the spiritual strength of our people was put to the test."

> Our people in those days, might have turned to alien ideologies
> — like communism or fascism.
> But — our democratic faith was too sturdy. What the American people demanded in 1933 was not less democracy but more democracy, and that's what they got.[6]

FDR's Fireside Chats proved to be an important element in this democratic thrust. One of the most salient of the "dark realities" facing the nation — and the one that became a symbol of the entire crisis — was the destruction of the banking system marked by the failing of thousands of banks in the years after the onset of the Depression in 1929. Without a system of federal deposit insurance — which was not to be implemented until late in FDR's first hundred days — the closing of banks imperiled and often wiped out the savings of millions of Americans. Roosevelt well understood that this blow to the hopes of middle- and working-class Americans endangered not only the country's finances but the political and social fabric of the nation. Thus banking became the focus of his first informal radio address to the American people. In replying to an inquiry from one of his Hyde Park neighbors in the autumn of 1933, he revealed that he had aimed his first Chat at "the type of individual whom I thought of as the 'average depositor.' " He described how he had sat at his desk and tried "to visualize the types representative of the overwhelming majority. I tried to picture a mason, at work on a new building, a girl behind a counter and a farmer in his field. Perhaps my thoughts went back to this kind of individual citizen whom I have known so well in Dutchess County all my life."[7]

FDR had three goals in that initial Fireside Chat. The most immediate was to explain the banking system in extremely basic terms to those who used it primarily for modest savings and checking accounts.

> First of all, let me state the simple fact that when you deposit money in a bank the bank does not put the money into a safe deposit vault. It invests your money in many different forms of credit. . . . In other words, the bank puts your money to work

to keep the wheels of industry and of agriculture turning round. A comparatively small part of the money that you put into the bank is kept in currency — an amount which in normal times is wholly sufficient to cover the cash needs of the average citizen.

Since these were not "normal times," his second goal was to illuminate the present crisis — to try to put a face on the forces behind the emergency — and to explain why "it became the government's job to straighten out this situation and to do it as quickly as possible." "We have had a bad banking situation," he told the American people, but at no point did he blame the system itself; the culprits were those who had misused it. "Some of our bankers had shown themselves either incompetent or dishonest" by using the funds entrusted to them "in speculations and unwise loans." This, he assured his listeners, was "not true in the vast majority of our banks, but it was true in enough of them to shock the people of the United States for a time into a sense of insecurity" so that they no longer could differentiate between sound and unsound banks.

What, then, happened during the last few days of February and the first few days of March? Because of undermined confidence on the part of the public, there was a general rush by a large portion of our population to turn bank deposits into currency or gold — a rush so great that the soundest banks couldn't get enough currency to meet the demand. . . .

By the afternoon of March 3, a week ago last Friday, scarcely a bank in the country was open to do business. Proclamations closing them in whole or in part had been issued by the governors in almost all of the states.

It was then that I issued the proclamation providing for the national bank holiday, and this was the first step in the government's reconstruction of our financial and economic fabric.

His third goal was to subordinate platitude to detail and to take the American people into his confidence regarding the staggered system of bank reopenings so that they could comprehend what was about to happen:

We start tomorrow, Monday, with the opening of banks in the twelve federal reserve bank cities — those banks which on first examination by the Treasury have already been found to be all right. That will be followed on Tuesday by the resumption of all other functions by banks already found to be sound in cities where there are recognized clearing houses. That means about 250 cities of the United States. . . .

On Wednesday and succeeding days banks in smaller places all through the country will resume business. . . . It is necessary that the reopening of banks be extended over a period in order to permit the banks to . . . obtain currency needed to meet their requirements, and to enable the government to make commonsense checkups.

Please let me make it clear to you that if your bank does not open the first day, you are by no means justified in believing that it will not open. A bank that opens on one of the subsequent days is in exactly the same status as the bank that opens tomorrow.

The point of this involved plan was to ensure that the history of the past few years would not be repeated. "We do not want and will not have another epidemic of bank failures." The banks that reopened, he pledged, "will be able to meet every legitimate call."

I do not promise you that every bank will be reopened or that individual losses will not be suffered, but there will be no losses that possibly could be avoided; and there would have been more and greater losses had we continued to drift. I can even promise you salvation for some at least of the sorely pressed banks. We shall be engaged not merely in reopening sound banks but in the creation of more sound banks through reorganization.

Inevitably, he predicted, some "who have not recovered from their fear" would resume their panicky withdrawals once the banks reopened, but he was convinced they constituted a distinct minority.

It needs no prophet to tell you that when the people find that they can get their money — that they can get it when they want it for all legitimate purposes — the phantom of fear will soon be laid. People will again be glad to have their money where it will be safely taken care of and where they can use it conveniently at any time. I can assure you, my friends, that it is safer to keep your money in a reopened bank than it is to keep it under the mattress.

FDR's overarching purpose in this and in most of his subsequent Fireside Chats was to engage the American people, give them a sense of direction, and fortify their morale, or as he explained some years later, "to banish, so far as possible, the fear of the present and of the future which held the American people and the American spirit in its grasp."[8] If the President placed part of the blame for the banking crisis upon an insecure people who flooded banks with demands for their savings, he also placed the means of deliverance in their hands. It was on this note that he brought his first Fireside Chat to a close:

> There is an element in the readjustment of our financial system more important than currency, more important than gold, and that is the confidence of the people themselves. Confidence and courage are the essentials of success in carrying out our plan. . . . We have provided the machinery to restore our financial system; and it is up to you to support and make it work.
>
> It is your problem, my friends, your problem no less than it is mine. Together we cannot fail.

"Our President took such a dry subject as banking," the comedian Will Rogers commented the next day, "and made everybody understand it, even the bankers."[9] Raymond Moley, at the time one of Roosevelt's principal advisers, viewed the Chat of March 12 as the capstone of the events that began with Roosevelt's inaugural on March 4. "Capitalism," Moley proclaimed in his account of these events, "was saved in eight days."[10] It is certainly true that there were a number of courses FDR could have followed concerning the moribund banking system he inherited when he took office, particularly nationalization advocated by several Congressmen. Senator Bronson Cutting of New Mexico argued that the government could have taken over the bankrupt banks "without a word of protest."[11] The path FDR chose was the conservative one of reviving rather than drastically altering the banking system, and his first Fireside Chat proved to be a crucial step toward that end.

"My bank opened today," Will Rogers noted on March 15. "Instead of being there to draw my little dab out, I didn't even go to town. Shows you I heard Roosevelt on the radio."[12] Rogers had a lot of company; the American people seemed to have taken Roosevelt at his word. As the nation's banks reopened, deposits so far exceeded withdrawals that the hundreds of millions of dollars worth of new federal reserve banknotes on hand to ensure that the reopened banks had sufficient funds for the expected demand were scarcely used. As Roosevelt promised, no new run on the banks ensued. By the end of March, more than $1.2 billion had been restored to the banks by their depositors, and by April 12, roughly five weeks after FDR closed the banks, 12,817 of them had fully reopened.[13]

The *New York Times* marveled at the "wonderful power of appeal to the people" that radio had given the President. When, during the fight over the League of Nations in 1919, Woodrow Wilson decided to appeal to the people directly, "it meant wearisome travel and many speeches to different audiences. Now President Roosevelt can sit at ease in his own study and be sure of a multitude of hearers beyond the dreams of the old-style campaigner."[14] That Roosevelt's first Fireside Chat, to an audience one newspaper correspondent estimated — probably too conservatively — at some forty million people, helped to stem the panic and to restore confidence in the banking system is amply demonstrated by the remarkable flood of letters and telegrams that began to pour in upon FDR almost as soon as he left the microphone.[15] It was the beginning of a conversation that was to characterize FDR's presidency through all the days of depression and war.

MARCH 13, 1933

The President of the greatest Nation on earth honored every home with a personal visit last night. He came into our living-room in a kindly neighborly way and in simple words explained the great things he had done so that all of us unfamiliar with the technicalities might understand. When his voice died away we realized our "friend" had gone home again but left us his courage, his faith and absolute confidence.

As long as you talk to your people there is not one thing you cannot accomplish. From the lips of neighbors, acquaintances and strangers we hear this sentiment. Congress and other law-makers will find themselves puny interference when you have but to turn to the Radio and enter our home a welcome and revered guest. If you could only hear our response — but, I'm sure you sense the great hope and reliance of your people, We believe in you!

Of all precedents you have shattered is the theory that a man must come from the lowly to understand the needs of the common people. We love you for that perception that could only come from a great unselfish heart.

We are just a modest middle-class people having lost what little we had, but, since March 4th, . . . we knew we were not fighting alone. We have a LEADER at last.

If this should ever reach your eyes — don't take anyone's valuable time for acknowledgement when there is so much to be done. I hope that when the major things have been disposed of you will not forget a national old-age bill such as you fostered in New York. It will alleviate so much suffering and humiliation.

Since you addressed us as "friends" we have written our letter in this spirit and to express our faith.

Respectfully,

F. B. Graham
Mrs. F. B. Graham
Dubuque, Iowa

MARCH 14, 1933

My dear Mr. President:

Several neighbors (Republican and Democrat) happened to be spending Sunday evening with Mrs. Cregg and myself when it was announced over the radio that you were to talk on the banking situation in the United States at ten o'clock.

There was silence for a moment and then the discussion began. There seemed to be a wide divergence of opinion as to whether or not you were going to make good and whether or not you had the confidence of the people. They were unanimous, however, in agreeing that your Inaugural Address was a masterpiece, and that your message to Congress shot straight from the shoulder. Yet some were frantic and expressed the hope that your message would be such as to allow them to withdraw their life savings from some of the local banks.

When your radio talk began everyone seemed to become hypnotized, because there wasn't a word spoken by anyone until you had finished and then as if one voice were speaking all spoke in unison "We are saved." The frantic individuals of a few moments before declared that they would leave their money in the banks and that they were not afraid of the future. This little episode convinces me more than ever that you have the confidence of the people, that you are the man of the hour, and that with the united support of all its people, you are going to rehabilitate this great nation.

May God bless you.

Sincerely,

Frank J. Cregg
(Justice of the New York Supreme Court)
Syracuse, N.Y.

MARCH 13, 1933

Dear Sir.

While listening to your broadcast Sunday night, our little home seemed a church, our radio the pulpit — and you the preacher.

Thank you for the courage and faith you have given us.

May God bless and keep you to carry on the fight and we, the American people, will help you win.

Respectfully yours,

(Mrs.) Louise Hill
Chicago, Illinois

MARCH 15, 1933

Dear Mr. President:

You cannot hear yourself talk over the radio, so you must accept the testimony of others. You have a marvelous radio voice, distinct and clear. It almost seemed the other night, sitting in my easy chair in the library, that you were across the room from me. A great many of my friends have said the same thing. I suppose hundreds have told you this, but I thought you would like to know how perfectly your message reached us. As for the message itself, it was clear, forcible and direct — a wonderful thing for the President of the United States to talk to the people as you talked to them.

With regards, I am,

Respectfully,

James A. Green
Cincinnati, Ohio

MARCH 13, 1933

Dear Mr. President:

Your talk, last night, over the air, on our Banking Problems, was most inspiring. . . .

Most people, have very little money, and saving, a little for that "Rainy Day," is continual pinching, planning, scraping, and self-denial. And then it does not amount to very much. But at least, one has the feeling that in case of sickness, or unemployment, there is something in the Bank, to help out during a bad time. Then, out of a clear sky, one awakes to find oneself, out of work, and the bank holding the small savings, closed. And though worry does not help at all, one cannot do anything else but worry.

But you, Mr. President have instilled a new Courage, into the hearts of the American People. Even though, I have not worked for almost a year, and my savings are tied up, in a closed bank, I, and millions of others like me, feel, that at last, we can hope for the lifting of that terrible depression, that had almost broken the spirit of a good many of us.

To tell you that we are thankful to you, for the new lease on life that you have given us, would not describe how we feel. So instead we'll pray that God speed you in your good work.

With all Good Wishes for your success, I am,

Gratefully yours

Jane Covant
Fair Haven, N.J.

SUNDAY, MARCH 12

My dear Mr. President:

I thought it would interest you — and perhaps enhearten you —to know just how your radio address on the re-opening of the banks was received in one place tonight. Although the entire contents of your message was known to all of us many minutes before you began to talk (the A.P. sent it out about 9:30), the loudspeaker's audience consisted of the following:

. . . The Herald's editor . . . managing editor . . . financial editor, the night city-editor, five desk men, six reporters, four sports writers, two office-boys, and a couple of bums who had wandered in off the streets. Not one person spoke during your talk, hardly a word was said after you had finished, and everybody (except the two bums) went quietly back to work.

Our office radio is a pretty good barometer of public interest, and never before has it had such a large audience, except on broadcasts of big fights and Al Smith's speeches! Never, I can truthfully say, has it had a more serious and appreciative audience. Somehow you have captured the confidence and devotion of the people in a way that no public man has in our generation. Please, Mr. President, don't be careless with it.

Sincerely yours,

Leonard Ware, Jr.
Boston, Massachusetts

MARCH 14, 1933

AT A MEETING TODAY OF THE DIRECTORS OF OUR COMPANY I WAS RE-
QUESTED TO EXPRESS TO YOU OUR ADMIRATION OF THE MANNER IN
WHICH YOU HAVE HANDLED THE BANKING SITUATION AND PARTICULARLY
YOUR ABLE AND CONVINCING ADDRESS OVER THE RADIO LAST EVENING
WHICH HAS HAD A FAR REACHING EFFECT IN ALLAYING FEAR. ALSO TO EX-
PRESS OUR CONFIDENCE THAT THROUGH YOUR CONTINUED FIRM LEADER-
SHIP THIS COUNTRY WILL BE RETURNED TO PROSPERITY.

STANDARD OIL COMPANY OF CALIFORNIA
BY K. R. KINGSBURY, PRESIDENT
SAN FRANCISCO, CALIF.

MARCH 14, 1933

Dear Mr. President:

I have never yet written a "mail-fan" letter, but I cannot let your radio talk of last Sunday go by, without writing how I feel about your splendid talk of that evening.

Like all other business men, I have been going about in a daze for the past several months. Your talk, as well as your executive actions since you have taken office, has been a tonic to me as it probably has been to millions of others. I am glad that at last we have a man in the White house instead of a commission. If you could talk to the people every week for just fifteen minutes as you did last Sunday, I think that confidence would again be the order of the day.

I pray, that you retain your phenomenal vitality, so that under your leadership, we will emerge triumphant from this depression. I beg to remain,

Most humbly and sincerely,

Mark L. Rothman
Philadelphia, Pa.

MARCH 12, 1933

Dear President;

I would like to tell you that I enjoyed the speech which you have just finished giving. I have regained faith in the banks due to your earnest beliefs. I had decided that, as soon as the banks in Minneapolis reopened, I would withdraw my money. When you said that people's money would be safer in the banks than under their mattresses I decided I'd leave my money just where it is.

Although I'm only a high school student I take a great interest in the country's problems. I firmly believe that the country is on the upward grade and I believe that if people will remain calm and composed that the government will pull the United States out of this terrible depression.

. . . "God be with you and bless you," dear President.

Very respectfully Yours,

Viola Hazelberger
Minneapolis, Minnesota

MARCH 12, 1933

My dear Mr. President —

It is 9:30 pm. Central Standard Time and we have just had the great pleasure of listening to your talk over the air. Its effect on our little group was just short of being miraculous. Our group was a son & wife entertaining father and mother, who are of foreign descent with little education, not accustomed to listening to radio talks and all Staunch, hard shelled Republicans. No sooner had your voice died on the air when Mother, 70 years of age, jumped from her chair saying, "Isn't he a fine man" and father with tears in his eyes said "I feel 100% better already." He had been worrying about his small savings of a lifetime.

This, I am certain is the effect your talk must have had on all who heard you tonight. Couched in such simple language that all could understand, it could only serve to instill the deepest affection for and confidence in you and your undertakings.

Prayers and good wishes are going out to you for your continued success. We are strongly behind you and believe in you —

Sincerely yours

(Mrs H. C.) Bertha M. Lindquist
Minneapolis, Minn.

MARCH 13, 1933

Dear Mr. Roosevelt: —

The loop is packed with people, business is being transacted and their is a happy and cheerful feeling.

The high spot in your radio talk was its directness and also the 100% American language you used. Please keep it up.

I think our country is again united — all except a few people who would still ride in horse cars.

I talked to lawyers, brokers elevator men doctors janitors and the comment is the same in all quarters concerning your talk on the banks. All say — fine, just fine.

One old janitor said "I know everything he talks about, even my boy could understand, no foolish words but all good plain talk, and our president is already helping the people."

We are all catching the spirit of your courage and optomism — as we cannot have one quality without the other.

Very truly yours

Chester E. Bruns — One of the average citizens.
Chicago, Ill.

MARCH 20, 1933

My dear President Roosevelt,

I just want to tell you personally how much your recent radio speech impressed me — particularly our Jewish people, who are all with you. Every word you uttered came straight from the heart and struck a responsive cord in our hearts as well.

The next morning early, at the nearby synagogues our people offered up fervent prayers to God to guard and keep you in good health and happiness for many, many years to come. . . .
WITH SINCERE AND FRIENDLY WISHES FOR YOUR GOOD-HEALTH AND WELL-BEING
I am

(Mrs.) Betty Seigel
Roxbury, Mass.

* * *

Dear Mr. President,

Never having written to a President before even though I am a public school teacher, I am a little bit shaky as to correct address, etc. but after listening to your simple, concise address tonight, I just felt I had to write to you.

I am forty-three years old and during the past week is really the first time that I have felt that I am an active part of the U.S.A. — Your humane leadership has brought out all my latent patriotism and, Mr. President, I'm for you one hundred percent. . . .

One of your grateful people,

Mabel L. Morrissey
Brooklyn, N.Y.

MARCH 15, 1933

Dear Mr. President:

On Sunday evening . . . I went to my home and had as my guests about sixteen young people . . . from Harvard, Radcliffe, Technology, and Simmons College. At ten o'clock they requested that we turn on the radio and listen to the new president. As we stood together, or sat, some on the couch, some on the floor, we heard your voice.

May I assure you it was an inspiration to those youngsters. Washington has seemed a long way off to them and to many of us of the older generation, too. Some how, last night, we were made too feel that we are a part of the government and that we have some responsibility. That sense has been lacking on part of many of us who would have it otherwise. There was an intimacy and a summons about those fifteen minutes that had a tremendously wholesome effect on us all. . . .

Very respectfully,

Newton C. Fetter
(Minister to Students for the Baptists of Greater Boston)
Cambridge, Mass.

MARCH 14, 1933

Honorable Sir:

Believing that a humble citizen of the United States now has entry to the President, I beg leave to congratulate you upon the course you are following, but in particular to tell you how myself and other millions of your countrymen accepted your speech of March 12th.

To Washington it was given to insure the freedom of this country but at the cost of a bloody war with the country which was still "Home" to a large percentage of his countrymen.

To Lincoln it was given to preserve the Union of the States, but again at the cost of a bloody war — in many cases friend against friend, relative against relative.

But to you, Franklin D. Roosevelt, it has been given to preserve the existence of the United States, as a nation of happy contented workers, of healthy happy children, the land of opportunity. And this by the simple means of convincing the people of your sincerity, your capability, and your humanness by a speech which will go down in history as the greatest ever made.

Not sufficient is it to merely reopen the banks of this country, you have assured the only thing which can keep them open, the confidence of the people.

God Bless you Franklin Roosevelt. The need has again brought forth the man.

Ferris D. Gaskill
Chicago, Ill.

* * *

Dear Presedent — our Presedent

after listening to your wonderful talk Sunday a week ago — we all felt the magnetism, of the tone of your Voice — that you were sent for our delivery. When in times of deep distress God took pity on His people. He sent Moses to deliver the oppressed. Then He sent Jesus Christ — to show His people how to live — to redeem them — Then you a Comforter to put confidence in this so great a people. And you will do it — for God is at the helm. Our City needed help, so many idle, my son making every effort for a support after lost business. This is from no office seeker. I need my son here — for daily needs. I know that when the country at large is helped, we will be helped. An ardent, admirer and supporter

> Mrs. J. R. Adams
> Birmingham, Ala.

I am a widow, still clinging to my husband's name.

MARCH 13, 1933

Dear Mr. President: —

I want to thank you from the bottom of my heart for your splendid explanation of the Bank situation on last evening's broadcast over the National hookup. Out here on the Coast, we doubly appreciated this extra effort on your part to enlighten us, when our hearts are heavy and saddened by Friday's Quake, and our nerves still "on edge" by the continual tremors which we are still having; quite a severe one this morning at 5:00.

The broadcast brought you so close to us, and you spoke in such clear concise terms, our confidence in the Bank Holiday was greatly strengthened. . . .

May I suggest that whenever it is possible, you speak from 1 to 5 minutes on any outstanding Governmental move at the beginning of a week day Coast to Coast program such as the Tuesday's Lucky Strike, Rudy Vallee or the Chicago Mert & Marge program, when the whole country is tuned in for their program. . . .

Mr. President, you have an unusually fine radio voice, and undoubtedly your campaign radio speeches is what piled up your tremendous majority of votes. Your voice radiates so much human sympathy and tenderness, and Oh, how the public does love that, on the radio especially. I realize it takes time to prepare radio talks; that is why I suggest short ones, but it is surely the best way to get things over to the public the way you want it done, and not the way the Press decides on. . . .

Please pardon my presumption, but I see by this mornings Los Angeles Times, that you have been eating most of your meals on a tray in your office the past week. In the name of "All that Holy", please, Oh please give your body the rest and care it needs. As you well know, there's a limit to human indurance. We all need you so very much, and no one can take your place at this time. It would be a terrible calamity if you should break under the heavy strain, so do TAKE the required rest you should have, even if you have to keep Kings or Queens waiting outside your door.

Why not have an easy reclining chair with a head rest in your office and receive your interviewers in an easy resting position? Your strength will hold out much better. I know — have tried it and it works. One can think quicker and better when the head is resting on a pillow and the spine is relieved of all strain and weight. . . .

Gratefully yours, for your supreme efforts and quick action in our Country's behalf,

Virginia Miller
Sierra Madre, California

* * *

Dear Presedent

It gave me pleasure to hear your over the radio a Sunday night for what you have accomplished since you have taken office was never done by no other man that was ever in the white house for it was a God send for the way the people suffered this winter when you have to sit in your house and cannot get coal I am for one I could not buy a bit of coal in two months and I am not the only one there are thousands of others but thank God the time has come at last when we have got a man like you to save us from any more suffering for as God had sent Moses to deliver his chosen people out of the land of bondage so also I think he send you to free us from the hands of a lot of robbers like wall st. . . . I do also admire the courage of your wife for the part she is taking to relieve this present distress the day that you had the bank bill passed around nine OClock we had an extra paper and when my wife heard the boys with it she worried she thought that they shot you I had to get one to make sure of it for every night when she says her prayers she says a prayer that nothing will happen to you I am wishing you a long and prosperous life to yourself and family from a friend

Thomas Kennedy
Troy, N.Y.

P.S. Please excuse this letter for I am not a very good hand at writing letters also please excuse mistakes

MARCH 15, 1933

His Excellency;
The President,

Don't cut any fire for a long, long, time.

Think of having the President talk to us in our parlor. Thats great!!! good voice too.

If you have the responsibility, Congress must positively give you the authority. This Dictator talk gives me the wearies. Anyhow, I'd rather have an honest man tell me what to do, and what not to do, than be up in the air all the time. . . .

Yes, drive out the money changers, as our Dear Lord did of old. Approach the throne of grace, often, often, often. the supply of power from thence, is inexhaustible. Our Dear Lord keep you.

Sincerely Yours

John Watson
Reiffton, Pa.

MARCH 15, 1933

Dear President Roosevelt:

. . . In your ten minute radio talk Sunday Night you said more than Mr. Hoover did in four years, and although you have culture, aristocratic breeding and wealth you have one priceless gift, that of reaching out to the "common people" with a deep sympathy and understanding, that goes into their hearts and you can talk their language and when you talked banking you talked banking so all could understand.

Even hide bound Republicans are saying "Roosevelt will be one of the greatest presidents this nation has ever known". So you will be if you do not over work. We framed your picture that was used for the cover of a recent Literary Digest. It hangs on the wall in our very humble home and we are very proud of it. . . .

Some fault finders say "America has a King". Well if America has a King we must have needed one, and thank heaven we have a good one in our Franklin Roosevelt. You are too burdened with duties, do not think I expect you to answer this. I only wished to write you some things that are over flowing the heart and mind of one of the common people.

With sincere wishes for your success in your wonderful plans for the good of this whole nation and hoping you will keep quite well and fit for all the strenous duties you are facing I am

Sincerely yours,

Mrs. Paul H. Russell
Haskell, Okla.

MARCH 13, 1933

Dear Mr. Roosevelt:

In all fairness, I must tell you that politically I was on the opposite side of the fence, but even in this rock-ribbed Republican community, we are back of you to the last ditch.

I listened to your inaugural address, and I never heard a public utterance to equal it. Your talk over the radio last night was a good follow-up. Won't you please keep on talking to us in one-syllable words, and take us into your confidence? That is what the garden variety of us need so much.

I have written to our Senator Reed, and told him how we feel, and have asked him to please stand by you. Suppose you do make mistakes — isn't it all trial and error, anyway? And you have wrought miracles this week —you put some backbone in the people. Aren't you proud of your friends? (I love that "My friends — " it warms my heart.) . . .

Faithfully,

(Mrs. A. L.) Mary L. Woodruff
Glenolden, Pennsylvania

MARCH 13, 1933

My dear Sir:

After hearing your radio address last evening, March 12th, in regard to banking, in which address you used words of one and two syllables and showed such a tremendous underlying sincerity in what you were saying that I felt heartily ashamed that I did not vote for you last November and I sincerely hope that your acts will be successful in relieving our country of at least some of it's present depressing influences so that I will feel even more ashamed of myself.

With my best possible wishes for success in your various undertakings in your not to be envied position, I am

Yours very truly,

G. J. Hansen
Milwaukee, Wis.

MARCH 18, 1933

Dear Friend;

And I address you thus in all sincerity, as I feel you are the peoples friend.

I am a dentist and am coming in contact with people all day long, and because of the nature of my work have quite an exceptionally good opportunity to talk to my patients on various subjects. I have been talking to them for two weeks now principaly about you, and I want to tell you Mr President, that you have Mr Average Citizen behind you almost 100%. They are all hoping that you will keep up just as you have started.

I a good Republican, am delighted with you, and sort of feel like one of my patients did, who said he felt like kicking himself because he did not vote for you. I am absolutely in favor of everything that you have done so far, including the beer bill, and I am a Dry. . . .

Mr President, go right to it, for the vast majority of us are right behind you, in fact the Republicans that I come in contact with are behind you just as much as the Democrats are.

Sincerely yours

W. H. Daniels
Paterson, N.J.
A good Republican or used to be.

MARCH 13, 1933

My dear Mr. Roosevelt:

The fact that I voted for the Socialist candidate in the last election should make this note all the more of a tribute. Your speech on the radio, Sunday night, March 12 made me feel, first, that the main reason you wanted the job of our chief executive in this most trying period of the world's history was because you wished the opportunity to help; second, that one should be thankful to be an American; third, that at the end of four years, in the same breath with the name of Abraham Lincoln, we shall mention that of Franklin D. Roosevelt.

Sincerely,

Carolyn Harrow
New York, N.Y.

MARCH 14, 1933

Dear Sir: —

I want to thank you for that splendid talk you gave us last Sunday night. We do appreciate the way in which you have literally taken "time by the forelocks" in this big banking problem of our's, and we know much will be accomplished — when confidence is restored.

We are not soon forgetting the folly of the last Congress, how those leaders spent time and money, when such vital issues were at stake, parleying over legalized beer.

To we, who were on the outer circles trying to inspire confidence and faith in our government — Well this was nauseating. Many poor souls threadbare in heart and soul, bowed down with want and debts — They do not want beer, to add to their misery and degradation, they want a chance to live, once more, honestly, and soberly; that is the desire of your American citizens. And we the christian citizens of U.S.A. will stand right back of you with our prayers, and this battle will be gloriously won; but please remember, Christ and beer will not mix, confidence will never be restored by legalized alcohol in any form, Do not make a "Pontious Pilate" of your self, for those clamoring for greed and money. Please do not seek to balance the budget by sacrificing the lives of our youth.

Humbly Submitted

(Mrs) Harvey K. Garrison
Bridgeton, N.J.

MARCH 22, 1933

Esteemed Mr. President: —

. . . On all sides, Mr. President, there are assurances that the nation supports you. These assurances may be gathered from the remarks of public speakers, from the pages of newspapers and magazines, and, above all, from the conversations of the great, common people assembled in groups and knots at every fireside and street corner. . . .

The final victory reserved for you, Mr. President, is to secure legislation

compelling industry to divide profits equitably. Both capital and labor produce finished goods: both must share equitably in the fruits of production.
A just profit to the factory or plant owner, a just "living wage" to the workingman! . . .

Your grateful fellow-citizen,

B. A. Bonte
Bellevue, Kentucky

MARCH 16, 1933

Dear Mr. President:

. . . Mr. President, so many people that I know, including many dyed-in-
the-wool Republicans have become your enthusiastic supporters since listening to your radio talks, that I think it lies within your power to "turn the
tide", as regards public spending. As you are aware, many persons well able
to afford purchases have with held them due to the fear instilled in them
during the last few years. The time has come to dispel this fear, and you,
probably you alone, can end it.

Now this, Mr. President is my plan. If you, in your next radio talk, would
tell the public, that you, having done, and continuing to do, together with
your administration, everything possible to bring conditions to normal,
now put it up to the American people to do their share, and request those
among us who are able, every man, woman and child, to cast aside our
fears, and spend for those things that we would legitimately spend if conditions had never deviated from normal. And, very important, to spend, not
on "bargains", but wisely and well, not on the products of "coolie" or
sweatshop labor, ground out by unscrupulous employers. Such "cheap"
purchasing, for the consideration of price alone, is not consistent with the
American tradition and should be condemned.

Mr. President, if you would do the above, I believe American business
would receive the stimulus it so badly needs at the present time. Verily you
will become a second Moses, leading your people out of the wilderness.

Most respectfully,

Theodore Abrams
New York, New York

MARCH 15, 1933

MY DEAR MR. PRESIDENT. AS AN INDIANA BUSINESS MAN I WANT TO EX-
PRESS MY PERSONAL APPRECIATION OF THE SUCCESS OF YOUR STAND IN
THE RECENT BANK SITUATION AND THE CONSTRUCTIVE POLICIES YOU ARE
CARRYING THROUGH. I FEEL POSITIVE YOUR RADIO MESSAGE TO THE
AMERICAN PUBLIC LAST SUNDAY NIGHT DID MORE TO BUILD CONFIDENCE
AND ELIMINATE FEAR WHICH HAS BEEN THE PRIMARY CAUSE OF OUR DIFFI-
CULTIES THAN ANY OTHER EXECUTIVE ACTION IN YEARS. IN MY HUMBLE
WAY PERMIT ME TO SUGGEST THAT YOU BROADCAST TO YOUR CITIZENS
NEXT SUNDAY EVENING THE THOUGHT THAT THE WEEK OF MARCH TWENTY
FIRST BE DEDICATED BY EVERY PATRIOTIC CITIZEN TO THE PAYMENT OF
EVERY JUST DEBT THAT IT IS POSSIBLE FOR HIM TO PERFORM. YOU COULD
EASILY CONVINCE THE PUBLIC AND EVERY BUSINESS MAN THAT THE END-
LESS CHAIN OF BENEFIT ACCRUING FROM THIS PROGRAM WOULD RESULT
IN A WONDERFULLY IMPROVED BUSINESS SITUATION THAT WOULD REACT
TO THE BENEFIT OF EVERY AMERICAN CITIZEN.

J. E. FEHSENFELD

INDIANAPOLIS, IND.

MARCH 12, 1933

Dear Sir,

Your wonderfully clear exposition (on the radio, just finished) of the
bank and banking situation will do a great deal toward restoring confidence
in our banking institutions, and I am sure has done much toward giving
you the fullest support of the country. May I suggest an additional thought
to you, viz: — that you announce to the people that bankers who have betrayed trusts imposed in them shall be brought to trial and punished. That
easy escape shall be impossible and sentences not be light.

Your assurance to the public along these lines is all that is now needed
to restore their fullest confidence.

Very truly yours,

H. A. Plusch
Philadelphia

MARCH 22, 1933

Sir:

May I say that I feel your batting average to date is perfect? Also that your radio address on the banking situation, in its simplicity and clearness, in its sympathetic presentation, and in its potency could not be excelled? When you need to enlist the masses, for you the radio is a perfect organ.

My visits to our national parks, from McKinley in Alaska to the Grand Canyon, have shown me that they all need more and better roads, as well as guard rails and walls, for the comfort of the people. May I suggest that I believe from 5,000 to 10,000 men could well be employed in this way?

May I express the opinion, based on a visit to Russia last summer, that your recognition of the Soviet Republics would within a comparatively few months be completely approved by practically all Americans?

Very truly yours,

Thos. C. Blaisdell
Slippery Rock, Pennsylvania

MARCH 16, 1933

My dear President:

I wish to congratulate you sincerely on your militant leadership, and to tell you that I was particularly pleased with your radio talk of last Sunday evening.

May I suggest, not in a critical, but in a helpful, spirit, that "status" is pronounced with a long "a", not a short one. Men in high positions often are feared by others who dare not make suggestions such as I have made, but I know you are the type of person who wishes to do things right and will welcome this information. . . .

Sincerely yours,

Carl Wheaton
St. Louis, Mo.

MARCH 13, 1933

My President Roosevelt: —

While not a member of your party, I wish to congratulate you upon the splendid work that you have done since March 4th. . . .

May I, with all due respect, suggest that when concluding a radio address to the people, such as the one you gave last night, that you close by saying, "Good-night" or "Good-bye"?

When an address is concluded so abruptly as the one was last night, it leaves one with a peculiar feeling that something has been left out. . . .

Yours very respectfully,

J. J. Quinn
Rahway, N.J.

MARCH 13, 1933

Our dear President Roosevelt.

We live in eastern Colo. on our homestead of 18 yrs. ago. I've been wondering if a letter, written by an insignificant little farmers wife, would ever reach you. So curiosity has persuaded me to try it. After hearing of your wonderful address, last nite, we felt you must be, for the benefit of we poor, harding working people. We sincerely hope so. For we done all we could for you. We are having a struggle during these perilous times but feel confident you are going to get us out. We have two boys. We are trying to put the oldest one thru high school, he is 16, a senior, hardly see how we are going to graduate him, but we're hoping for better prices soon. We have a little grain & if we can raise $25. or $50. we will be Sitting on Top of the World. Hoping you are going to do all possible, I am Sincerely

Mrs Frank Owens
Lycan, Colo.

MARCH 12, 1933

Dear President.

I am writing you this letter from my little farm home, which I bought two years ago, and for which my Dad put up the dough. I am an American born citizen, and so are my parents. . . . I have been a steam engineer for 27 years. I lost my left hand at the wrist that long ago, and have followed up the steam work until about two years ago, and since that time find it impossible to get work in that line, or any other. I am on the unemployed list, work, get a food order, only the work is about one day in three weeks. I am not starving or anything like that, as I raised most of the eats, but others I know are in bad shape. We help them out as we can, with clothes etc. My Nephew gave us a Radio about a month ago, and we heard your March 4 Inaguration Speech, and tonight Your Speech on Banking Situation, on our Radio. I think you are the man for the job. I feel you have the courage to go ahead and do things, and I say to you that all people in my section have wonderful faith in you. I hope you get my letter. I would love to have you please send a line or two direct from you to my Dear old Democrat Dad, who is also crippled. . . .

Adolph F. Brior
Rohrsburg, Pa.

Please read my letter, and let me know you got it.

MARCH 13, 1933

Dear President Roosevelt: —

I am writing in the name of the Citizens of Chicago to express our joy in our new President, we have suffered for 4 years and now we hope everything will be alright.

I heard you on the radio and I started to cry, for 3 years I have no work and have 4 children for 2 years we pay no rent, we lived in very bad conditions. For 28 years I have been a citizen and have never remember suffering before like this, when I heard your wonderful speech on the radio my heart felt good, I know we are going to have better times now.

I hope you'll not only be President for 4 years but for many, many years

and the Best of Everything for Mrs. Roosevelt & Family. My name is Josie
D'Natale. . . .

Don't forget you're the "Father of the United States" and Mrs. Roosevelt
the "Mother" and we will look to you like a Child looks to its Mother and
Father, to lead us in the right way. . . .

Best regards to you and your family.

yours truly,

Josie D'Natale
Chicago, Ill.

MARCH 12, 1933

Dear Preisdent Roosevelt

Please except this letter of thanks for your very very fine speech over the
Raido this evening. it sure put the hearts back in the farmers around here
and we are putting the old Grays in the plows in the morning and turn over
the sod of prosperity again and feel like working, . . .

Yours very truly

Fred J. Mohrbacher and Family
New Brighton, Pa.

Please talk some more over the Raido when you get in shape and rested up.
But do not over due your self,

We are all glad to hear you speak anytime
Thanks
Good Luck & health
God Bless you

I do not know how to write a letter to a Preidesent. But we are trying to
tell you from our hearts.

MARCH 21, 1933

Dear Mr. President:

. . . I am only one of many thousands of citizens who have carried a burden that has been at the breaking point for some time. Our incomes, sav-

ings, homes, everything taken from us and we were helpless to defend ourselves against the forces that seemed bent on our destruction. But now our
heads are up again, and our backs will stiffen, too, because you have given
us a new hope — the hope that we can once again find ourselves and also
recover the pride in our country which we have been taught from the
cradle.

You will have plenty of opposition, Mr. President, and no doubt there
will be many bitter struggles for you, but one thing you may be sure of —
every honest man and woman in this great country is with you. If you have
any doubt of that you have only to talk to us as you did a week ago Sunday
night, telling us in the same simple, straightforward way what you want to
do, and we will see that Congress backs you up. Your greatest and surest
aid will be the radio.

May God bless you and keep you, Mr. President. We are a sorely tried
people and we need you very much, so please take care of yourself that you
may go on with the fine work you are doing. You will probably never fully
realize what you mean to so many of us.

> Very sincerely yours,
>
> Frances I. Hundley
> Brooklyn, New York

MARCH 12, 1933

Hon. Sir,

I listened gratifiedly to your radio address anent the banking situation
this evening. From this humble quarter is reflected your own confidence of
the future stability of the banking system. However, Mr. President, I beg to
ask, "Then what?" . . .

In a brief note, Mr. President, I can only write in generalities, but permit
me to express this much; having stabilized the banks, and established the
soundness of America's financial "structure," you have made an impression
in your Herculean tasks by comparison as the vacancy created in a huge
granary by the removal of one grain by the toiling ant.

You must be well aware of what yet lies before you. Let us be warned,
then, not to indulge in previous exultation, lest we relax our efforts ere we
have attained the ultimate consummation of our aims.

I have presumed to address you thus, Mr. President, because I am imbued with the idea that you would welcome expressions of this character from humble citizens.

Respectfully,

Eugene V. Krell
St. Louis, Mo.

A NEW DEAL:
MAY 7, 1933

EUGENE KRELL, the author of the last letter printed in the previous section, was correct: banking reform was not enough. Thus eight weeks after FDR's first Fireside Chat — just past the middle point of the special session of the Seventy-Third Congress, which lasted from March 9 to June 16 — he took to the air to inform the American people how well he was performing what Krell called "Herculean tasks." He reminded his listeners that when he assumed office "the country was dying by inches." The crisis that beset the nation in March of 1933 "did not call for any complicated consideration of economic panaceas or fancy plans. We were faced by a condition and not a theory."[16]

As these words indicate, FDR was at pains throughout his second Chat to demonstrate that he had not been seduced by the Sirens of radical ideology — as most American radicals would have readily agreed. There had been only two alternatives open to him when he took office, he insisted. The first was to allow the process of deflation to continue until the entire economy was recapitalized at a lower level. The result would have been "extraordinary hardships on all property owners and all bank depositors, and . . . all persons working for wages through an increase in unemployment and a further reduction of the wage scale." He had concluded even before becoming President that such a policy "was too much to ask the American people to bear. It involved not only a further loss of homes and farms and savings and wages, but also a loss of spiritual values — the loss of that sense of security for the present and the future that is so necessary to the peace and contentment of the individual and of his family." The second alternative was to adopt a "prompt program applied as quickly as possible." Accordingly, he turned to members of both parties in Congress who agreed with him that "the methods of normal times had to be replaced in the emergency by measures that were suited to the serious and pressing requirements of the moment." Congress had not surrendered power, he declared; it had merely designated the President "as the agency to carry out certain of the purposes of the Congress. This was constitutional and is constitutional, and it is in keeping with the past American tradition."

Doubtless many listeners to FDR's second Fireside Chat — and certainly most members of Congress — recalled the military metaphors the President had used in his Inaugural Address two months earlier when he called for "a unity of duty hitherto evoked only in time of armed strife" and for the need to "move as a trained and loyal army willing to sacrifice for the good of a common discipline." He hoped that the normal balance of executive and legislative authority would be "wholly adequate to meet the unprecedented task before us." Should it not be, he would ask for the "broad Executive power that would be given to me if we were in fact invaded by a foreign foe." The people of the United States, he concluded, "have asked for discipline and direction under leadership. They have made me the present instrument of their wishes. In the spirit of the gift I take it."[17]

Eleanor Roosevelt found it "a little terrifying" that when her husband warned those gathered at his inauguration that he would assume wartime powers if necessary, "he received his biggest demonstration."[18] She was likely discomfited as well by the blasé reaction of the nation's newspapers, which reported his address in a matter-of-fact manner under such headlines as "FOR DICTATORSHIP IF NECESSARY," and were filled with statements like that of Representative Loring Black of New York praising Roosevelt's courageous willingness "to assume the entire burden of the complex problem himself."[19] "The iron hand of a national dictator," Governor Alfred M. Landon of Kansas remarked, "is in preference to a paralytic stroke."[20] Several weeks before Roosevelt's inauguration, the business magazine *Barron's* confessed that "we have been longing to see the superman emerge," and suggested to the incoming President that "a genial and light-hearted dictator might be a relief from the pompous futility of such a congress as we have recently had. . . . Only, let our semi-dictator smile upon us as he semi-dictates."[21]

Comparisons between Roosevelt and Mussolini and between the New Deal and fascism were common, but as the Socialist Party leader Norman Thomas understood, and as FDR demonstrated over and over, the new President had neither the temperament nor the inclination to be a dictator, even a genial one.[22] Indeed, Rexford Guy Tugwell, who as an economic adviser to FDR observed the New Deal closely from within, concluded that if not for Roosevelt, "we might have succumbed to a dictatorship. For that was the alternative, much in the air, when he took charge."[23] In many ways, FDR was an ideological innocent who accepted the politics — as he accepted the religion — he had been brought up with. Secretary of Labor

Frances Perkins — the first female Cabinet member in American history — was present during the following colloquy between Roosevelt and a young reporter:

> "Mr. President, are you a Communist?"
> "No."
> "Are you a capitalist?"
> "No."
> "Are you a Socialist?"
> "No," he said, with a look of surprise as if he were wondering what he was being cross examined about.
> The young man said, "Well, what is your philosophy then?"
> "Philosophy?" asked the President, puzzled.
> "Philosophy? I am a Christian and a Democrat — that's all."[24]

"He never talked about his religion or his beliefs," Eleanor Roosevelt observed, "and never seemed to have any intellectual difficulties about what he believed."[25]

Roosevelt lacked the strain of strong ideology that had prevented Herbert Hoover from reacting more freely and decisively to the economic and social crises wreaking havoc around him, or that prompted others to believe that the Depression afforded the country the opportunity to set off on a new course entirely. But that is not to say that he lacked a set of beliefs that guided him and set very real constraints around what he was able and willing to do. If there was a consistency in the many complex and often confusing turns the New Deal took, it was Roosevelt's threefold determination to end the suffering, to restore the confidence and spirit of the American people, and to save capitalism from itself through a program of reform. His characteristic openness allowed him to pursue these goals in an innovative manner. "The rules and remedies of the past probably do not form an answer to the restoration of the machine," he had declared as Governor of New York in 1930, "it is therefore only logical and not radical to insist that through experimentation . . . we must solve the social and economic difficulties of the present." A year later, Governor Roosevelt declared that it was the government's "definite obligation to prevent the starvation or the dire want of any of its fellow men or women who try to maintain themselves but cannot."[26]

FDR's willingness to search for and experiment with new remedies and his strong sense of the responsibility of the state to its people made him in his own words, "a little to the left of center," but he always carried with him a strongly traditional sense of the way things should be.[27] Roosevelt has often been treated as the complete political pragmatist — his adviser Raymond Moley grumbled about the President's "pragmatic oversoul"[28] — who could say along with Ralph Waldo Emerson: "no facts are to me sacred, none are profane. I simply experiment, an endless seeker, with no past at my back." To a much greater extent than he himself sometimes recognized, FDR did have a past at this back, a past that influenced him profoundly. He would open the presidential campaign of 1936 by declaring that liberalism was the best protection for farsighted conservatives: "Wise and prudent men — intelligent conservatives — have long known that in a changing world worthy institutions can be conserved only by adjusting them to the changing time. In the words of the great essayist, 'The voice of great events is proclaiming to us. Reform if you would preserve.' I am that kind of conservative because I am that kind of liberal."[29] The "so-called New Deal," Eleanor Roosevelt has written, "was, of course, nothing more than an effort to preserve our economic system."[30]

In his Fireside Chat of May 7, Roosevelt may have spoken of himself as the instrument designated to carry out the purposes of Congress, but his tone was that of a democratic leader trying to convince the American people that the "well-grounded, well-rounded plan" he proposed — much of which was still before Congress — was necessary if the nation was to be rescued from its calamity. Indeed, at the time of his second Chat, Congress had passed only three major pieces of reform or relief legislation: the Emergency Banking Act, which established the ground rules for the reopening of the banks; an act authorizing states to raise tax revenue and create jobs by allowing the sale of beer, which presaged the ratification of the Twenty-First Amendment ending Prohibition on December 5, 1933; and the act creating the Civilian Conservation Corps (CCC), which enlisted a quarter of a million unemployed young men — five hundred thousand at its peak in 1935 and more than three million overall by 1942 — to work in reforestation, flood prevention, and other conservation-oriented endeavors.

It was now necessary, FDR told his millions of listeners, for Congress to pass the rest of the legislation he had requested or was about to request. He mentioned specifically the Tennessee Valley Authority (TVA) to provide public coordination and development of the resources of a large and troubled area of the nation; the Farm Credit Administration (FCA) and the

Home Owners Loan Corporation (HOLC) to "ease the mortgage distress among the farmers and among the homeowners of the nation," and help them save their homes and farms; the Federal Emergency Relief Administration (FERA) to grant half a billion dollars to help states, counties, and municipalities "care for those who at this time need direct and immediate relief," and to create jobs through work relief for the employable needy; the Agricultural Adjustment Administration (AAA) to increase farm income and stem agricultural overproduction; the National Recovery Administration (NRA) "to give to the industrial workers of the country a more fair wage return, to prevent cutthroat competition, to prevent unduly long hours for labor, and at the same time to encourage each industry to prevent overproduction," by adopting codes governing their industry; the Public Works Administration (PWA) to provide more than three billion dollars to "enable the government to undertake public works, thus stimulating directly and indirectly the employment of many . . . in well-considered projects"; the Railroad Coordination Act to stimulate railroads, with government assistance, to create a more rational transportation system with less duplication and waste.

These measures of reform and relief, along with a number of acts not mentioned by FDR, made the first three months of his Administration — which newspaper reporters came to call the "Hundred Days" — one of the most productive and creative in the nation's history. It would be "wholly wrong" to call what he was proposing government control, Roosevelt insisted:

> It is rather a partnership — a partnership between Government and farming, a partnership between Government and industry, and a partnership between Government and transportation. Not a partnership in profits, because the profits will still go to the private citizen, but rather a partnership in planning, and a partnership to see that the plans are carried out.

Raymond Moley, who helped to write the second Fireside Chat, did not let this statement go without prolonged discussion. "You realize, then, that you're taking an enormous step away from the philosophy of equalitarianism and laissez-faire?" he asked the President as they worked on the Chat. "F.D.R. looked graver than he had been at any moment since the night before his inauguration," Moley recalled. After long moments of silence, Roosevelt replied: "If that philosophy hadn't proved to be bankrupt,

Herbert Hoover would be sitting here right now. I never felt surer of anything in my life than I do of the soundness of this passage."[31]

While he did not ignore completely the problem of the maldistribu-
tion of wealth that made it impossible for millions of Americans to buy the
goods being produced, Roosevelt's propensity to view the nation's problems as the result of aberrations rather than fundamental flaws in the system
made him more comfortable focusing on the problem of overproduction,
which, in a nation where there was so much want and outright hunger,
seemed to many to be no problem at all: "The people of this country have
been erroneously encouraged to believe that they could keep on increasing
the output of farm and of factory indefinitely and that some magician would
find ways and means for that increased output to be consumed with reasonable profit to the producer." "We cannot," he emphasized, "ballyhoo ourselves back to prosperity." Mere optimism was not enough: coordination
and planning were essential in industry, in agriculture, and in the world of
finance. He demonstrated his point with the cotton-goods industry. Ninety
percent of cotton manufacturers would agree tomorrow to eliminate starvation wages, child labor, long hours of employment, and overproduction,
he asserted.

> But, my friends, what good is such an agreement of the 90 per-
> cent if the other 10 percent of the cotton manufacturers pay star-
> vation wages and require long hours and employ children in
> their mills and turn out burdensome surpluses? The unfair 10
> percent could produce goods so cheaply that the fair 90 percent
> would be compelled to meet the unfair conditions. And that is
> where government comes in. Government ought to have the
> right and will have the right, after surveying and planning for
> an industry, to prevent, with the assistance of the overwhelm-
> ing majority of that industry, all unfair practices and to enforce
> that agreement by the authority of government. . . .
>
> And, my friends, the same principle that is illustrated by that
> example applies to farm products and to transportation and to
> every other field of organized private industry.

"Our policies are wholly within the purposes for which our American
constitutional government was established 150 years ago," he reiterated. "I
do not deny that we may make some mistakes of procedure as we carry out
this policy," he admitted, and then turned to familiar cultural metaphors, a

device he used frequently in his Fireside Chats: "I have no expectation of making a hit every time I come to bat. What I seek is the highest possible batting average, not only for myself but for the team."

He closed his second Fireside Chat by thanking the American people:

> Throughout the depression you have been patient. You have granted us wide powers; you have encouraged us with a widespread approval of our purposes. Every ounce of strength, every resource at our command, we have devoted and we are devoting to the end of justifying your confidence. We are encouraged to believe that a wise and sensible beginning has been made. In the present spirit of mutual confidence, in the present spirit of mutual encouragement we go forward.

MAY 8, 1933

My dear Mr. President: —

I have just listened to your broadcast over the radio and feel that I have to write to you. I must tell you what effect your address to the people has had on me.

I am a member of the graduating class of the Abraham Lincoln High School of Brooklyn, New York and am not eighteen yet. Things aren't as nice at home as they might be. Bills keep coming in and Dad has to scrape up every cent he can get hold of to pay up. I see the way the world is treating him. With this staring me in the face I was a bit gloomy about my future. However, after listening to your speech, I feel as if there is a silver lining to every cloud. I feel inspired. I feel that if I go to college for more education I will not lose any opportunity that I might find during the four years to go to work. . . .

I am now going to go to bed with a fervent prayer in my heart for you, our country and God.

May God bless you!

Yours sincerely,

Jack Hamovitz
Brooklyn, N.Y.

MAY 8, 1933

My Dear President: —

For 25 years, I have been an ardent Socialist. the soap box, the lecture platform, the class-room are the means that I have used to further the Cause. I have been in jail for it at times.

Since your inauguration, I have withheld judgement — for once in my life I have not used the expression "He is only a Henchman of the Capitlast classes" I have faith in you and the people I meet every day in the business world have faith in you. I hardly think that you realize the power that you really have over the American people. You don't half realize what faith they have in you and they are willing to follow you blindly. If I a Socialist trust you, I can see why they worship you.

Your speech to-night was magnificent — and remember when a soap-boxer admits the other fellow speech is good — thats something

Mr. President, this ecomic distress that we are suffering from is getting too much for us all to stand. If you will help alleviate some of the suffering I see every day well let the historians of the future draw the conclusion

Well its a pleasure to listen to you — and Mr. President — I have a suspicion that you know your Karl Marx pretty well.

Good Luck to you and my best wishes to your family — who knows I am liable to call up my friend & comrade Norman Thomas three years from now & tell him I am out working for Franklin D. and I am going to vote for him and the party can throw me out if they want to.

As a former officer of the U.S.A. I salute the Greatest President since Lincoln.

Sincerely yours,

Harry N. Perlmutter
Brooklyn, N.Y.

MAY 16, 1933

My dear Mr. President: —

It is with genuine pleasure that I refer to your radio talk of Sunday night of May 7th.

Dictators dictate, Mr. President, Democrats discuss. The important difference is not so much in what they do, as the spirit in which they do it.

The dictatorship myth, woven so industriously about your excellency, was knocked over the fence on Sunday night. And it was all so simple. You took advantage of the radio and the great American Sunday evening at home, and for the second time talked over the problems of the day as a family matter with the families of the nation. You talked as easily and as informally as a neighbor who had just dropped in to visit the folks.

There was no more authority, mystery or pose about your talk than in the old time political arguments around the stove and cracker barrel of a country store or in the old fashioned wooden Indian city cigar store. Truly Mr. Roosevelt you revived the modes and manners of the primitive forums of American democracy. The old town meeting is now a nation's meeting.

The simplicity of your language was matched by the clearness of the thought. The democracy of your good self was reflected in your use of a baseball term to make it plain to everybody. The value of the great American game in teaching men and women how to visualize social, economic and political set ups and conditions was forcefully demonstrated when you said "I have no expectations of making a hit every time I come to bat — what I seek is the highest possible batting average, not only for myself but for the team".

Every man, woman and child over six knows exactly what it means. How could you say it so well and so plainly, if there was no game like baseball that everybody from president to street sweeper understands. . . .

Finally the clear statement of what you and the people want in the way of control of business. The dictionaries are crammed with long words which describe all the variations and shadings of the possible relations of government and private business. You used none of them. But you told your whole story in one word "partnership" — a word that is almost primer English, and has meant more in America than anywhere else. . . .

Partnership and dictatorship are at the two opposite poles of political thought and feeling — and never the twain shall meet. The grumpy men who insist on looking for gloom and who do not realize that America is not chained in slavery to worn-out ideas can sit in the dark corner and mumble the word "dictator" to themselves as long as they please. This country, under your great leadership, is going ahead without them.

It is the writer's intention to visit Washington at some future date and it will be his pleasure to make the necessary arrangements to meet you.

Very respectfully yours,

James J. Dunn
Chicago, Ill.

MAY 10, 1933

Dear President Rosevelt

You will no dout think I am a good one to write this as I am a woman with very little Education as you can see by my letter. but we can know Jesus just the same. I listened to you talk on the Radio and enjoyed it so mutch. people did not need a high school Education to understand it eather. what

I want is to ask you if you would not like to set one hour for the whole United states to pray that the Lord would hold fast to you and our Congres guiding you in all that is said & done that his power will sweep our country as a christian nation making our government one led by him for the word says with out him we will fall. it seams to me one hour the 30 day of May would be a nice time as that day we shoe our respect to the old soldiers. In Jesus God the Father & our government means all in all to us. God bless & help you to trust all with him

Mrs. Nellie Spunaugler
Salina, Kans.

MAY 8, 1933

Dear President Roosevelt

What could have been more wonderful I cannot find words too high to praise you your speech, was not a speech, but, a heart to heart talk, like a Brother talking to Brothers and Sisters. . . .

Your voice was as clear as a Bell and as steady as a rock —

When you coughed a little, I wanted to run and get you some water, yes we all love you, and pray for your good health and also that of your whole family

Yours very Sincerely

Mrs Anna Koulevard
Pawtucket, R.I.

MAY 10, 1933

Dear Mr. Roosevelt: —

I listened to your speech over the radio Sunday and want to say that I surely enjoyed it very much.

I am sure every right thinking American would say that what you have done so far has been for the benefit of mankind and not for the profiteers alone.

If you can in some way start the factories running again I think that will be one of the greatest blessings that could come to the American people.

In this connection I wish to suggest or ask about the employment of women in industry. It is my understanding that millions of women who do not have to work for a living are now employed I have spent most of my life in Detroit, Mich and from my own experience in trying to secure a position as an accountant I find most all positions are held by girls and women and also in applying for any kind of factory work conditions are the same.

I have always beleived and think it is true that the home is the heart of the nation, if the home is destroyed the nation surely will be.

Could not something be done to prohibit employers from hiring any woman that does not of necessity have to work. If possible I am sure millions more heads of families would be put back to work at better wages than are paid women and many homes saved as well as many made happier.

Considering the Christian spirit of all your undertakings I do hope you may find some remedy for what I think is one of the greatest evils of the country.

Anticipating a favorable reply at your convenience I will close wishing Gods richest blessing on you. Very truly yours

Norman Best
Greenville, Ohio

MAY 8, 1933

Dear Sir:

I heard your radio address last night and regarded it as encouraging.

I classify myself as a conservative but realize that present conditions required measures that might not be justified under other circumstances. I sincerely hope that an effort will be made to keep the government out of business as much as possible and that we will not have such inflation as to make money and security values doubtful.

I have always been a Republican but desire to say that I am very pleased with your official acts and likewise am pleased to express to you that the general sentiment is ninety per cent in your favor. This is considerably more than the seventy-five per cent that you referred to in your address last night. . . .

You have the commendation of the people of this country and will continue to have it unless your measures become too extreme. At present you are "ace high".

With best wishes for your continued success, I am,

Sincerely,

George Livesey
Bellingham, Washington

MAY 9, 1933

Dear Mr. President —

I have listened with great interest to your two broadcasts over the radio and I sincerely hope that somehow this short letter may reach you. I am a proprietor of a drug store in an industrial neighborhood and am familiar in a small way with the condition and hardships of the workingman. Within the last two months, in our neighborhood I have heard on good authority that several aeroplane factories have been hiring technical school boys for sheet metal and other work at very meagre wages while former employees are still waiting for their jobs. A number of these places are working on contracts for the government — General Aviation Corp. and Glen Martin — aeroplane manufacturer.

It seems to me that such action is contrary to the principles brought out in your talks. . . .

We — small insignificant citizens are following as never before in history — the action of our president and we are all behind him in his fight for prosperity. The influential citizen, however too often preaches one thing and practices something entirely different.

Very Truly,

John Donnet
Baltimore, Md.

MAY 8, 1933

Dear Sir

I listened to your speech last night and read it again this morning. Thank you!

There is hope that the measures you are taking may be effective. When you took office we were rapidly drifting toward a bloody revolution. Thanks to you there is now some light ahead.

Sincerely yours

L. L. Brande
Chicago, Ill.

MAY 8, 1933

Dear President:

Listened to your Radio address last night telling about what the National Legislature had done for the "Forgotten Man" Nothing has been done to help him according to my way of thinking.

Everything that has been done is constitutional you said in your address maybe so, but I demand you read the Declaration of Independence as you seem to have Forgotten that there is anything like equality for all the people of this land as all men are created equal. . . .

The Democratic party has had a great opportunity to do something for the people but does not seem to care to take advantage of the chance to go down in history as fighting the battle of the Forgotten man.

The Forgotten man will have to fight his own battle alone and without any help from the National Government. . . .

It is ridiculous for the Mortgage holders of this Nation to demand payment of interest when there is not enough money in circulation to even carry on the exchange of commodities necessary for the welfare of the people. I would write more a lot more but I feel that it is useless as it does not seem to have any effect whatever.

Hawkin Anderson
Clayton, Wisconsin

MAY 10, 1933

The Honorable President Of This Great Country. Please Except my Sincere Congratulations on your Wonderful, Sincere from the Heart, Radio Speech, of the Past Sabbath Day. My Object in Writing is many fold. Having been out of Employment the Past Three years, I am unable to send A Telegram of Congratulations, Is One Reason, another Reason is because I want to Apologize for not Having Voted for you. I am Sure, Had I known, That you realy were with the forgotten Man, I would Have Voted More Intelligently, and lastly I want to make a Suggestion, which might meet with your Approval. It is your Desire, to put as Many Men as Possible to Work, to the best Interest of this Great Country. As you Drive along the Highways you Notice many Pedestrians walking along on the Auto Right of way, Endangering their Own lives, and the lives of the occupants of the cars. Why not put Thousands of men to work Building about 14 or 18 Inch cement walks along the Roadways and Prevent Many Serious Axidents, to School Children, and Pedestrians. In General, Thank you, I am with Greatest Trust and Respect, yours very truly,

H. H. Greenberg
Cleveland, Ohio

MAY 10, 1933

Dear Friend

I have to Congratulate you that address you give us over the air last Sunday night and I know you don the whole Country good I heard so many People talk about that Address you maid over the Radio last Sunday night . . . there is one thing that I will ask you if you could do something about them Banks that Closed in 1930 and 1931 where we Poor working People lost nearly all our little savings that we had I'm one of them Mr Roosevelt I had a few $100 in the United Security Trust Company Phila Pa they Close there Doors Oct 1931 and got a small amount of it in three different Payments But the remainder is still over $500 the 27th day of November 1932 was the last that I heard of them which I'm very much in need of now I'm about 19 months out of work now Carpenter by trade for 31 years and was Raised on a Farm Schwenksville Pa My age is 52 Healthy and able to do any kind of work when ask for a Job they ask me if I have a Family I say no I ask a Man here some time ago weather a man like me is suppose to starve he said No, My Wife died in 1919 and had two Babies to Raise which are 2 Boys yong gentelman now 16 and 18 years of age and I'm very Proud of them But all most ashamed to look in there face now because I was never before out of a Job and had Money to Pay for there good training But I hope there is a better day coming again it looks so. . . .

I remain
Sincere Yours

Benj B Tyson
Lansdale, Pa.

P.S. Hope to here From you Some time

MAY 8, 1933

Dear Sir

I have heard your wonderful speech over the Radio and it was wonderful.

I am comming to you for help in the line of labor as all my money is now in the Bldg & loan Assn of which was taken over by the State for Liquidation of which i can not get nothing to live on so i ask you to give me a job so i can support my family

Thanking you for your help and also see that i get my money out of this Bldg & loan assn. for if Ever i knead my money it now

You Trully

John Harmon
Toledo, Ohio

MAY 9, 1933

Dear Mr. Roosevelt,

I heard your message on the air last night, and think you are the most wonderful president we have ever had, you are a life saver to the whole world same as the States. But all your bills you have put before the Houses you have not given the widows that is left with children a thought. I have four small ones oldest 12 youngest 6, been a widow over 4 years, up to over a year ago had a job that paid where I saved some. But now I've used it all up so what is to become off the widows, and men, and women of to-morrow. if some way is not provided for the mothers to support them. I do not want help from the county, as they have more now than they can pay, as no one is able hardly to pay taxes and that is what the county depends on. All I ask for is a job that I can make an honest living with. Will close as every second of you time is very valuable to the whole U.S.A.

A Worried Widow
Leesburg, Fla.

P.S. My husband is dead.

MAY 15, 1933

Dear Friend,

I have heard your wonderfull talk over the Radio and I know you are sincere in your help for the farmer. I have my garden all planted we have had splendid rains here this spring but a drought for two years before could I ask you just where I could borrow $52 for baby chicks and the feed to start them out. the 50 for the chicks and two for chick mash. I have only 25 hens and they are Leghorns and of course they do not sit. I have been waiting for the New Deal. but it is getting late for baby chicks. I should get them by the 22th of May — so they will lay for us this winter. I would be glad too pay this back out of the chickens this fall. I want too can the garden surplus and raise chickens and help out my Husband in any way I can. our bank in Canby is just cashing cream checks. Could you find time to ans my letter I would be more than pleased.

Respectfully

Mrs. George Plack
Canby, Minn.

MAY 7, 1933

Dear Mr. Roosvelt:

I have just heard that splendid talk over the radio. It sure did come in good and clear. "We are for you."

My Father and Mother died some years ago leaving me to care for myself. I was reared on the farm I am now finishing School by my own efforts. It has been a tough battle.

What would you sugjest for me to do now? I am past twenty years old but like advice.

Very sincerely yours,

Walter C. Tabor
Oklahoma City, Okla.

* * *

Sir:

Please accept the enclosed poem as my means of congratulating you on your splendid work.

Your successful speech Sunday night gave me the inspiration. I hope it pleases you.

Sincerely,

Laura E. Park
Greenville, Illinois

OUR PRESIDENT

The Hero of our hopeless hour,
Alone to fight the foe —
Into the battle front he rides
To fight Depression's Woe . . .

We are saved from grave disaster,
We are free from selfish scorn.
Our President has faced the Night;
And a new day is born.

THE FIRST HUNDRED DAYS:
JULY 24 AND OCTOBER 22, 1933

FDR'S NEXT TWO FIRESIDE CHATS — the last ones he was to deliver during his first year in office — were devoted to explaining and defending the accomplishments of the first hundred days, which he insisted were "not just a collection of haphazard schemes but rather the orderly component parts of a connected and logical whole."[32]

In the first of these addresses, on July 24, Roosevelt took obvious pride in the success of his banking policy — "Today only about 5 per cent of the deposits in national banks are still tied up" — and the various acts designed to help Americans pay off their mortgages and save their homes and farms. He described how the Civilian Conservation Corps had not only given employment to three hundred thousand young men in "practical and useful work" but also used their wages to help support "the nearly one million people who constitute their families."* He explained how the more than three billion dollars in public works would provide jobs in "thousands of self-sustaining state and municipal improvements." These he described as "the foundation stones" — the measures necessary to reestablish credit and provide "as much work as possible through governmental agencies."

He then turned to what he called "the links which will build us a more lasting prosperity." Although overproduction remained high on Roosevelt's list of the prime evils crippling the nation, he finally focused on the problem of distribution of income as well. Paraphrasing Lincoln's famous pronouncement that a nation cannot exist half slave and half free, Roosevelt decreed that "lasting prosperity" cannot be attained "in a nation half boom and half broke."

> If all our people have work and fair wages and fair profits, they
> can buy the products of their neighbors and business is good.
> But if you take away the wages and the profits of half of them,

---

*The CCC provided room and board for its enrollees and paid them thirty dollars a month, twenty-five dollars of which was sent directly to their families.

business is only half as good. It doesn't help much if the fortunate half is very prosperous — the best way is for everybody to be reasonably prosperous.

FDR singled out the National Recovery Administration — to which he devoted the substantial portion of this Chat — as the instrument best designed to assure this "reasonable" national prosperity. What he termed the "economic hell of the past four years" had been created by the lack of coordination and cooperation in industry. The NRA was based upon the model of industrial self-government and cooperation experimented with during World War One and continued in the private trade associations of the 1920s. The New Deal added to this voluntary program the guiding hand of the government, which authorized industries, in consultation with representatives of labor and the general public, to establish codes regulating wages, competition, and labor practices. These would be submitted to the government and when approved would be binding on all members of the industry. Labor's right to organize and bargain collectively was guaranteed. This "democratic self-discipline in industry," carried out "in the big industries, in the little shops, in the great cities and in the small villages" would make possible "general increases in wages and shortening of hours sufficient to enable industry to pay its own workers enough to let those workers buy and use the things that their labor produces." It was an old principle, FDR insisted, "that people acting in a group can accomplish things which no individual acting alone could even hope to bring about."

As in his Inaugural Address, Roosevelt utilized the metaphors of war to rally the American people "in this great summer offensive against unemployment." He asked that all businesses that adopted NRA codes display on their premises as "a badge of honor" an emblem with the NRA's official blue eagle and the legend "We do our part." He asked the American people to favor those employers. While "the shirking employer may undersell his competitor," Roosevelt charged, "the saving he thus makes is made at the expense of his country's welfare." He requested all businesses — "the big fellows and the little fellows" — to "write or telegraph to me personally at the White House, expressing their intention of going through with the plan. And it is my purpose to keep posted in the post office of every town, a Roll of Honor of all those who join with me." As Roosevelt hoped, the NRA with its symbolic Blue Eagle, its parades, and its ebullient director,

General Hugh Johnson, whose bearing matched his title, became for a time the very symbol of national unity and recovery. The ubiquitous eagle became a familiar part of American popular and folk culture. It wasn't long before the Mississippi bluesman Walter Vinson was singing:

> Now, the Government said right from the start,
> Do as he say do: "We will do our part." . . .
>
> It's on windows and doors in the shape of a bird,
> You don't have to wonder or neither say you heard.
> Lord, the Government's before me, oh, and I can't go wrong,
> Oh, the reason I'm singing this old lonesome song.[33]

FDR ended his July Chat by turning to the deeply ingrained American notion of will. He related the question asked after Andrew Jackson's death: "Will he go to Heaven?" and the reply: "He will if he wants to."

> If I am asked whether the American people will pull themselves out of this depression, I answer, "They will if they want to." . . . I have no faith in "cure-alls" but I believe that we can greatly influence economic forces. I have no sympathy with the professional economists who insist that things must run their course and that human agencies can have no influence on economic ills . . . but I do have faith, and retain faith, in the strength of common purpose, and in the strength of unified action taken by the American people.

It was in the midst of this third Fireside Chat that FDR reminded his audience that they were not only listening to the President of the United States but to a fellow human being. He paused, asked for a glass of water, took an audible sip, and explained: "My friends, it's very hot here in Washington tonight."[34] He then assured the people that they had weathered the worst:

> We are not going through another Winter like the last. I doubt if ever any people so bravely and cheerfully endured a season half so bitter. We cannot ask America to continue to face such needless hardships.

Within the first hour after the Chat FDR received five thousand telegrams and enough phone calls to swamp the White House lines. "AF-

TER LISTENING TO THE PRESIDENT'S APPEAL," a woman telegraphed from Long Island, "I AM RAISING MY MAID'S WAGES 10 PER CENT." The following day, as the telegrams multiplied, the firm of Farrar & Rinehart followed suit, informing the President: "EMPLOY-EES' SALARIES INCREASED 10 PER CENT."[35] Hugh Johnson, the head of the NRA, called this "deluge of telegrams of approval and agreement . . . the most inspiring thing that has happened in this country since the war — the men and women of a great nation, who for more than four years have been stunned and helpless under one of the worst blights that ever plagued a people, suddenly stirring to one man's voice, and rising together like a vast army from a dismal bivouac at a clear bugle call at day-break."[36]

It was on a considerably cooler night in October that FDR delivered his fourth and final Fireside Chat of 1933. He took up where he had left off in July, examining the state of the nation. Although some economic indices — especially production — were lower than they had been when he last addressed his fellow citizens, Roosevelt remained upbeat in a Chat which Rexford Guy Tugwell characterized as "a masterpiece." Looking back on the address more than four decades later, Tugwell wrote: "As I read it through now, so many years afterward, and recall the troubled situation of that fall, I am still amazed at its confidence and its appeal. It did certainly put a better face on the situation than was warranted; but it had almost the same calming effect as the Inaugural."[37]

Roosevelt contrasted what his administration had inherited — "In the early spring of this year there were actually and proportionately more people out of work in this country than in any other nation in the world" — with "the edifice of recovery" the New Deal was endeavoring to construct: "the temple which, when completed, will no longer be a temple of money-changers or of beggars, but rather a temple dedicated to and maintained for a greater social justice, a greater welfare for America." Once more he spoke of the millions of jobs being created, of the humanitarian relief being extended, of the public works projects being constructed. Once more he made it clear how directly involved the New Deal was in the lives of the American people by asking all creditors to refrain from foreclosing on farms and homes "until every mortgagor in the country shall have had full opportunity to take advantage of Federal credit," and by urging "any family in the United States about to lose its home" to telegraph "at once either to the Farm Credit Administration or the Home Owners Loan Corporation in Washington requesting their help." In the face of often well founded criticisms that the billions of dollars of public works projects were being implemented too slowly and deliberately out of a determination not to create scandals by spending the funds too loosely, FDR appealed to states and municipalities to create "proper projects" and apply to Washington for public works money as quickly as they could. Once more he dwelt on the NRA: "It has abolished child labor. It has eliminated the sweat shop. It has ended sixty cents a week paid in some mills and eighty cents a week paid in some mines."

Finally, he revealed the newly adopted and, as it turned out, relatively short-lived policy of restoring prices from their deflated state by manipulating the currency through the government purchases of gold at prices above the world market. Though this policy may not have worked as he hoped it would, and though there were complaints that it was one of the few proposals he set forth that was unclear,[38] the purposes FDR articulated — "the permanent welfare and security of every class of our people" — registered with his audience:

> The object has been the attainment of such a [price] level as will enable agriculture and industry once more to give work to the unemployed. It has been to make possible the payment of public and private debts more nearly at the price level at which they were incurred. It has been gradually to restore a balance in the price structure so that farmers may exchange their products for the products of industry on a fairer exchange basis.

"I have told you tonight the story of our steady but sure work in building our common recovery," Roosevelt concluded:

> In my promises to you both before and after March 4th, I made two things plain: First, that I pledged no miracles and, second, that I would do my best.
> I thank you for your patience and your faith. Our troubles will not be over tomorrow, but we are on our way and we are headed in the right direction.

JULY 24, 1933

Dear Mr. Roosevelt: —

I just listened to your talk on the radio.

May I say that it gave me the thrill of a life time.

It made me feel as though you were really one of us — in other words, a man that you could say to, "Come on, here's a can of worms, let's go fishing." Trudge down a dusty road, arm in arm, your poles over the shoulders and be close to — well, a regular guy.

With every best wish for your success and health, I am,

Sincerely yours,

Frank W. Hadley
Oakland, Calif.

P.S. Of course I realize that the chances of Mr. Roosevelt ever seeing this letter is very remote but at least a good thought can hurt nobody.

JULY 26, 1933

[Addressed to Marvin H. McIntyre, Secretary to the President]

Dear Sir:

My reason for addressing this communication to you is that I realize full well the absurdity of my hoping to reach President Roosevelt himself by letter.

In this morning's Washington Post I read that shortly after his broadcast of monday evening the President asked Mr. Butcher of Columbia Broadcasting Company: "Was it all right for me to have said that about the glass of water?"

I want to tell you what my own reaction was to that spontaneous insertion: I was already inspired by the challenging manner in which the Chief was making his appeal to the country, but I was inspired by words coming from the height of a great man in a great office — down to me. When the speaker uttered the parenthesis about the glass of water, however, the human element of the speech was immeasurably reinforced. I was reminded that it was a man of flesh and blood who was talking to the country and to me, and my own attitude of comradeship and loyalty was correspondingly strengthened.

Among the group of my family and friends who listened to the speech there was a general laugh, a laugh of friendship and understanding, and from the later comments of others I am certain that the unpremeditated remark was received in the most favorable way.

If there is an opportunity, and you happen to think of it, would you be so kind as to mention this letter to the President? My identity is of no importance. I would just like for him to know what I know about his listeners' reaction to the remark which he is reported to have questioned.

Respectfully yours,

J. Harvey Edmonston
Washington, D.C.

P.S. TO MR. MCINTYRE's SECRETARY: Please show this letter to Mr. McIntyre.

JULY 25, 1933

Dear Mr. President;

Doubtless the men who necessarily supervise your mail, and who do not know what the "little man" is, will not let you ever see this letter, but you ought to see it. . . .

The forgotten man has been forgotten, if he was ever really remembered. I happen to be an approved attorney for the Federal Land Bank, and on publication of the information about the new loan legislation, the little man came to see me vainly hoping that at last he had been remembered. He is representative of thousands of farmers in North Carolina, owning maybe 50 acres of land and doing all of his own work, and about to lose his farm under a mortgage. But to get the loan he is obliged to pay $20 in advance for appraisals, and another $10 for a survey, and he no more has that much cash than he has the moon. I have written to everyone from Mr. Morgenthau on down about this, and no one is interested. The prevailing idea seems to be that if a man is that poor, he should stay poor.

Before any of this loan and public works legislation was enacted, I wrote you that you ought to put at least one human being in each supervising body, and by that I meant a man who actually knows there is a "little man" in this nation and that he never has had a fair chance, and that he deserves one. I hope yet that somehow you may remember this forgotten little man, who has no one in high places to befriend him.

Respectfully yours,

Bruce Craven
Trinity, North Carolina

JULY 25, 1933

Dear Mr. President:

As I telegraphed you, I went purposely last night to the New York Athletic Club to hear your magnificent speech, and also to get the reaction of men, none of whom I knew or knew me.

There were between three or four hundred men in the room listening to what you had to say. During your speech there were bursts of applause several times and when it was ending I wandered from group to group exchanging a few words here and there to get their reaction. There was not a man present who did not, in every way, back up everything you said and they were especially pleased at the way you handled the Child Labor situation throughout this nation. You told the truth when you said that we could not go through another winter like the last one. The situation is drastic, but I feel convinced, more than ever, that the outcome will be a great success, and that at least five or six million men will be back to work by Christmas through the moves you are making. As I see it it also comes to the front door, at this moment, of every good citizen in this country to back you up to the full, and I want you to know that as far as I am concerned, I will be only too delighted to drop all business and other things that I am doing and fulfill any small job, naturally without any compensation, from now until as long as you want me, to try and help this matter out, if you should desire my services. I also feel that I can, should you wish it, round up many other men who feel exactly the way I do. I have seen enough of the unemployed when I was connected with them on Long Island to know that we must find work for them at once. It is impossible, as you know to raise money any more from those who would be only too delighted to give, but are not in a position to do so.

Again wishing you all the success in the world in this undertaking, which you are so fearlessly going into, and in which I know the entire nation is behind.

Yours as ever,

Aymar Johnson
New York

JULY 25, 1933

My dear President:

Your radio talk last night was the brightest ray of hope for the future of the American Nation that I have seen in many a year. . . .

At present I have $.22 in my pocket but we have a home and other real estate free from encumbrance except $12,000.00 on a 200 acre farm in Logan Co. I was with my brother in the architect business until the slump nearly closed us up. He is still keeping the chair warm in the office in the hope that the New Deal will finally bring results although he has not been able to pay expenses for several years. I have been out since 1929 and have used up all my savings. Our bank has been closed since March 4th which has tied up my wife's and son's small savings. We are living on what my son gets working three days a week for $9.00. I am registered at the local labor bureau but being 62 years old there is little chance of results from there unless my technical training gives me a chance upon the Farm Relief or some other Federal project. I will starve before I will pauperize myself as required by the new Illinois relief law by applying for relief. There are thousands of others of the same mind.

. . . The Republican Party has been controlled by the exploiters and I hope now that the American people are convinced that it is not a good business proposition to turn all their savings over to private individuals to use as they see fit for private profit. The control of the money was given Congress by the Constitution and it should be taken from private control and returned to the Government. The time is again ripe for driving the money changers from the temple.

Like Frankenstine they have created an immortal monster in human form with all the human selfishness in concentrated form but without the redeeming features of a soul, conscience, love and the Divine human qualities that separate man from the beasts. If we do not wake up to the danger and realize what we have done this corporate monster is going to utterly destroy us and own and control all branches of profitable business and all humanity will be again abject slaves. . . .

You have already eliminated child slavery from industry are you going to be able to free us all from wage slavery and the domination of wealth and material possessions? . . .

Yours truly,

Ralph W. Braucher
Chicago, Ill.

JULY 24, 1933

My Dear Mr. President.

Have just heard your wonderful broadcast and it so filled me with new hope that I find it difficult to restrain from writing you to express my feelings toward you.

Your outstanding achievement is the abolition of child labor (of which I have been a victim) a blot on the American nation that was perpetuated till now. . . .

And your statement regards the workingman and his rights made me feel as if we the workers are about to enter a new world.

If I may, I have elevated you in my mind on an equal with Abraham Lincoln.

Abraham Lincoln freed the chattel slaves and now Mr. President you are about to free the child and wage slaves.

May you have strength and health to continue the great work in the emancipation of the workers.

Yours Respectfully,

Rocco Verri
Dania, Fla.

JULY 31, 1933

Dear Mr. President,

Your radio address of July 25th, dealing with business and industrial problems, was highly stimulating and inspiring to the entire nation. However, there is another group of activities in gripping need of the same kind of encouragement from the head of the nation — namely the cultural arts.

At this particular time orchestras, opera companies, civic theatres and other similar organizations are engaged in the difficult task of raising sufficient funds for their continued existence in the autumn. This means a desperate struggle, not only to save valuable and important art organizations, but also to prevent a large increase of unemployed among the already huge number of musicians, actors, etc. without means of subsistence or prospect of work.

If you, Mr. President, were willing to state that the arts should not be neglected in the general plan for industrial and commercial recovery, the uplifting and practical result would be incalculably great and far-reaching.

The successful maintenance of our musical and art institutions means the employment of many thousands, and an important contribution to the higher culture of our country.

A few words from you at this critical moment would inspire many to acts of courage and generosity.

Sincerely yours,

Ossip Gabrilowitsch
Detroit, Michigan

OCTOBER 23, 1933

Dear Mr. President:

A recent New York Times Magazine says you get several thousand letters a day, mostly encouraging and approving but some of a different tone. You could hardly expect the confidence and approval to be unanimous. But around here it is nearly so. Even most of the farmers are not yet afflicted with the heart sickness which is said to come from hope deferred. They believe in you and trust you and I am sure that trust and confidence will be greatly enhanced by your radio address of last night. I have listened with profound interest to all of your radio addresses. May I say that they are gems, — models of lucidity, simplicity, clarity, and vastly effective. They ring true, with no adulteration of demagogic sophistry. To illustrate:

A twelve-year-old boy was deeply immersed in a tale of stirring adventure last night when your address came on (8 P.M., M.S.T.). He was asked to lay aside his book and listen to the address of the President.

"Aw, Ma, what's the use? The president's talk is not for me. I won't understand it."

"Well, listen awhile, anyway. You may get something out of it that will help you in school."

So he did. After two minutes the interest and understanding were apparent in his face. He moved over close where no word would escape him in what seems to be the inevitable "fading" in all radios. At your conclusion his Mother asked him if he liked it.

"Sure I liked it. Anybody could understand that."

I have been making public addresses of a sort for a good many years and would welcome a compliment like that. But I doubt if I shall ever get or deserve it. You get it, and what is more, merit it. That opinion seems unanimous around here even among those few who are inclined to question the contour, strength and efficacy of some of the pillars of the economic structure you are earnestly trying to build for your country. You are listened to not only with the respect your office commands, but with interest and understanding because you have the gift of simple words well and effectively chosen and spoken. The people like you. Even though they may not agree with you in all things you have their faith and trust. Your voice sounds friendly and sincere. The money changers may squirm under your scourge, but they have no rightful place in your temple any more than they had in that at ancient Jerusalem. The "forgotten man" feels that you remember him and it warms his heart toward you.

With all good wishes.

Respectfully and sincerely, yours,

Walter Aitken
Bozeman, Montana

OCTOBER 23, 1933

Dear Mr. President:

Please accept my heartiest congratulations upon your splendid radio talk last night. Not only did your voice come through clearly, (and may I say you have a splendid radio voice), but what you had to say thrilled Mrs. Howell and myself as we haven't been thrilled since the time of your in-augeral address, which came over the radio perfectly. It would seem to me that no patriotic American could listen to that explanation of what your administration is doing, and be not only thrilled, but filled with a burning desire to co-operate in every way possible. . . .

I want to assure you also that I am wonderfully pleased with your decision to recognize Soviet Russia. I have been a follower of the Socialist philosophy for a long time, and have fought the battles of Soviet Russia in this part of the country when it was almost heretical to mention the names of Lenin and Trosky.

This letter is already too long for a busy man, but I want also to say that while I didn't vote for you, being a Socialist, I am convinced that what you are doing at Muscle Shoals, and with the NRA is giving us the substance of Socialism without the name, which is just as satisfactory to me.

I am a busy physician, and in writing this I want you to know I am not seeking any political appointment. However, if there is any non-remunerative work I can do in this part of the country, please feel at liberty to call on me at any time.

With sincerest wishes for the continued success of your administration, and kindest personal regards, I am

Very truly yours,

J. C. Howell
Orlando, Florida

OCTOBER 24, 1933

Dear Mr. President,

Last Sunday evening six of our friends came in for dinner and contract. The men were not so much depressed as thoroughly frightened — their wives were wonderful — pretending to make light of the situation with such remarks as "You know, John, always worries about the things that never happen," etc. but in my dressing room after dinner they spoke differently — i.e. "I wonder if the President means to make a Soviet Russia of this country," "Why the new tie-up?" "I don't pretend to follow politics, but I hope things ar'n't a tenth as bad as John imagines" —

At ten o'clock all playing ceased, while each and everyone strained forward to catch the least inflection of your magnetic, inspiring voice. As you finished, the effect was a combustion of gaiety — taut nerves let loose. The men fairly jumped up and down like happy children, the women were inwardly thanking God, and one dear soul let loose the flood gates of tears of relief —

Mr. President, I'm sure that scene was duplicated in thousands of homes the length and breadth of the land, and I can't help writing you to thank you. You said you couldn't preform miracles — but you have!

I haven't been in Washington since the time my father and I were guests of President and Mrs. Wilson, but if Fate or Chance bring me there during your administration I hope I may have the privilege of thanking you personally.

With the assurance of my highest regard,

(Mrs. H. Howard Harper) Marguerite Harper
New York

OCTOBER 24, 1933

Dear Mr. President:

. . . I am of Scottish birth and humble origin, coming to America nearly half a century ago, to follow my trade of granite cutting, and with pride let me say it, that my skill such as it was, entered in to the construction of a few of the finest of our public buildings in Washington, namely the Congressional Library Building, the old Washington Post Office, and the National Museum. I mention these things that you may get a mental picture of the writer.

I am prouder of my adopted country since you were inducted in-to the Presidency than ever I have been before, because of the courageous leadership you are giving to millions of your fellow citizens, in all walks of life, and especially to those that may be described as under priveleged.

When you made your speech at the Chicago Democratic convention, I was listening on the radio with my wife and we have been following you ever since, I and many others did not have any idea what kind of a deal you were going to give us, but you established your-self in the confidence of a great majority of your people that it would not only be a new deal, but a good deal. . . .

You are bringing to reality dreams that I have had nearly all my life about social reform, brought about in an orderly and lawful manner, such reformation as you are inaugurating would in some countries have only been possible of attainment after violent revolution and much blood shed. . . .
    I am,

Your loyal and obedient fellow citizen

Jas. H. Paterson
Charlotte, N.C.

OCTOBER 22, 1933

FROM EVERY PORTION OF THIS LAND
DELIGHTED PEOPLE GRASP YOUR HAND
RIGHT WELL WE KNOW YOU STILL COMMAND
NEW COURAGE GRIPS OUR HEARTS TONIGHT
RESPONSIVE TO YOUR SPEECH FORTHRIGHT
AND GIVES US STRENGTH TO PRESS THE FIGHT
AMERICA IS STRONG AGAIN
AROUSED OUR RED BLOODED MEN
AND ALL OUR CHILDREN SAY AMEN

FRANK M. PADDEN
CHICAGO, ILL.

"RELIEF, RECOVERY, REFORM
AND RECONSTRUCTION":
JUNE 28, 1934

DURING THE EIGHT MONTHS of his presidency in 1933, FDR delivered a Fireside Chat every two or three months. Always fearful of overdo-
ing this direct approach in spite of the many letters he received pleading
with him to go on the air even more frequently, Roosevelt allowed eight
months to elapse between his final Chat in 1933 and the first Chat of 1934.
"I am purposely avoiding the use of the air," he wrote Colonel House, who
had been one of Woodrow Wilson's principal advisers, in the beginning of
May, "because to use it at the controversial stage of a controversial legislative body spells more controversy!" He would speak to the people as soon
as Congress adjourned in June, he told House and assured him that his
radio silence indicated no slackening of reform: "there will be many new
manifestations of the New Deal, even though the orthodox protest and the
heathen roar! Do you not think I am right?"[39]

He asked the very same question of the American people when he finally
did take to the air on June 28, with Congress adjourned until 1935. He
thanked Congress for its cooperation and praised it for displaying "a
greater freedom from mere partisanship than any other peacetime Congress since the administration of President Washington himself."[40] He outlined three related steps his administration had taken "toward the saving
and safeguarding of our national life." The first was relief "because the
primary concern of any government dominated by the humane ideals of
democracy is the simple principle that in a land of vast resources no one
should be permitted to starve." Relief would be administered on two principles: "First, that direct giving shall, wherever possible, be supplemented
by provision for useful and remunerative work and, second, that where
families in their existing surroundings will in all human probability never
find an opportunity for full self-maintenance, happiness, and enjoyment,
we will try to give them a new chance in new surroundings."

The second step was recovery, which economic data confirmed was well
under way. FDR supplemented that data with a more immediate test of recovery that allowed him to reach out and make his audience participants:

Are you better off than you were last year? Are your debts less
burdensome? Is your bank account more secure? Are your
working conditions better? Is your faith in your own individual
future more firmly grounded?

Had the American people paid too high a price for these gains? Citing
those "plausible self-seekers and theoretical diehards" who lamented the
loss of individual liberty, the President again asked his listeners to judge
these claims by the realities of their own lives:

> Have you lost any of your rights or liberty or constitutional free-
> dom of action and choice? Turn to the Bill of Rights of the Con-
> stitution, which I have solemnly sworn to maintain and under
> which your freedom rests secure. Read each provision of that
> Bill of Rights and ask yourself whether you personally have
> suffered the impairment of a single jot of these great assurances.
> I have no question in my mind as to what your answer will be.

Those denying "the substantial gains of the past year" were not the
"overwhelming majority of the farmers or manufacturers or workers" but
rather the seekers after special political or financial privilege. In the imple-
mentation of "a great national program which seeks the primary good of
the greater number" the only toes stepped on were those of "the compara-
tive few who seek to retain or to gain position or riches or both by some
shortcut which is harmful to the greater good."

Intimately connected to these considerations was his third and final
step, reform and reconstruction: "reform because much of our trouble . . .
has been due to a lack of understanding of the elementary principles of justice and fairness by those in whom leadership in business and finance was
placed; reconstruction because new conditions in our economic life as well
as old but neglected conditions had to be corrected." The nation was in the
process of making gains in eliminating child labor, establishing fair minimum wages and shorter hours, and creating conditions that protected consumers from skyrocketing retail prices. The goal of all of this activity was
"the security of the men, women, and children of the nation."

> That security involves added means of providing better
> homes for the people of the nation. That is the first principle of
> our future program.

The second is to plan the use of land and water resources of this country to the end that the means of livelihood of our citizens may be more adequate to meet their daily needs.

And, finally, the third principle is to use the agencies of government to assist in the establishment of means to provide sound and adequate protection against the vicissitudes of modern life — in other words, social insurance.

Those who fear progress, Roosevelt warned, "will try to give you new and strange names for what we are doing. Sometimes they will call it 'Fascism,' sometimes 'Communism,' sometimes 'regimentation,' sometimes 'Socialism.' " In truth, he assured his listeners, "what we are doing today is a necessary fulfillment of . . . old and tested American ideals." Characteristically reaching for familiar, simple metaphors to drive his point home, FDR spoke of the renovation of the White House office building that would begin during that summer. The additions would include modern electrical wiring, plumbing, and air cooling, but the structural lines of the old building would remain.

The artistic lines of the White House buildings were the creation of master builders when our republic was young. The simplicity and the strength of the structure remain in the face of every modern test. But within this magnificent pattern, the necessities of modern government business require constant reorganization and rebuilding. . . . It is this combination of the old and the new that marks orderly peaceful progress — not only in building buildings but in building government itself.

Our new structure is a part of and a fulfillment of the old.

All that we do seeks to fulfill the historic traditions of the American people.

FDR concluded by speaking, as he frequently did, of his immediate plans and shared with his audience the excitement with which he was embarking on a ten-thousand-mile trip beginning on the first of July. He would board the USS *Houston* at Annapolis, sail to the Caribbean, Colombia, Panama, Hawaii; then to the Pacific Northwest, from which he would embark on an inspection of projects on the Colombia, Missouri, and Mississippi Rivers, visit several national parks, and "learn much of actual conditions during the trip across the continent back to Washington." He ended on a note of patriotism and destiny:

> While I was in France during the war our boys used to call the United States "God's country." Let us make and keep it "God's country."

* * *

Dear Mr. President,

For the first time in my life I am writing to a public official. For the first time in my life I feel that I have a President. I read what you write, I listen to what you say. I believe in you. I talk to you.

You asked us tonight to take stock of our own particular affairs. Yes, I am better off. My brother, who was out of work for over three years got a job last January and I no longer have to contribute to his support. I do not earn more money but have a feeling of greater security in my position. But better than the economic side is my feeling of pride and satisfaction in you as my President. I — together with millions of other Americans — have become 'President conscious'. For the first time I feel that the leader of my country has some interest in me — that those in my walk of life are not altogether forgotten.

I hope you have a pleasant vacation and that you will continue to enjoy the confidence of your followers. And you will because I am convinced that your program is grounded in sincerity and we Americans fundamentally recognize and 'lay up to' this rare trait. It's what we want. Not perfection, nor miracles but a square deal.

Sincerely,

Alice Timoney
New York, New York

JULY 1, 1934

Dear Sir,

You asked in your radio address of June 28, 'Are you better off than you were last year?' I believe that there are thousands who would answer in the negative. I know many that would. Professional men, teachers and others who have been provident and thrifty, who have lost their positions or have had salary cuts, and who have seen their savings and investments adversely affected by measures of your administration, which seems to assume that all debtors are good, all creditors, bad. But unfortunately for them, fortunately for you, they are not organized. They are 'those exceptions in professional pursuits whose economic improvement, of necessity (Why 'of necessity'?) will be delayed'.

And is it good sportsmanship or even good politics to admit no errors on the part of your administration and to brand all criticism or opposite views as due to partisanship, ignorance or some evil motive?

You were elected by a bipartisan vote; your sole aim should be to work for the welfare of all. It should not be divided between this and the welfare of your party and securing a second term for yourself.

Very truly yours,

George Ellas Wisewell
Rochester, New York

JUNE 28, 1934

Dear President,

Tonight is the first time I heard you speak. I was listening to your speech as a child does when he listens to grandmother tell a Mickey Mouse Story or The Three Bears. I sat close to the Radio so I would be sure, I would get every word you spoke. And I did too. . . .

My father is a farmer. He lives with his wife and us seven children in his ranch 8½ miles from the nearest town. He does not understand that the English very well, but he understood your speech just the same. You speak to the stand where every one understands you.

I am a graduate from La Joya High School . . . and wish to continue my education, so some day I will earn the sufficient money and go to visit the White House. . . .

Wishing you success in your summer trip.

Your friend,

Miss Micaela Chapa
Mission, Texas

JULY 14, 1934

Honorable Roosevelt;

. . . You seem to be anxious to help the people who are in debt. But you fail to remember that those debts were incurred with the intention of making a profit. If the debtor made a profit, I am sure he would not divide it with the rest of us. But because he failed to make a profit, you want to help him, and make the rest of us suffer thru devaluation of the dollar, experiments, and inflationary measures. I have a little life insurance, together with two hundred dollars in the bank, left. I hope you will not take it away from me thru further devaluation, purchases of gold, and silver. I am anxious concerning the security you are promising to us thru your radio address.

Another matter, I, together with you am anxious that nobody starve here in this abundant land of ours. The needy must be fed. But, I do not think that the savers and the thrifty should suffer, because of the errors of others who squandered their money. Further-more, I do not see why people who have farms, buildings, lands, and other capital goods, in fact more than they can handle, receive aid from our government in various forms.

I am sending you this letter in answer to your radio address, and for the common good of the people of the U.S. I hope you will accept this letter in that friendly spirit. I do not wish to compete with the Brain-Trusters of Washington, D.C., but if you should need further plans, ideas, reforms, and programs concerning recovery, I will be glad to furnish them upon request.

Yours respectfully,

Michael Cornwall
Garfield, N.J.

JUNE 29, 1934

Dear Sir:

I heard your message to the people last night over the radio and was very much empressed with it. You asked in your Message are you better off than you were last year? My answer I am sorry to say is, I am not. I have not had very much work in the past year. Another one of your questions was, Is your faith in your own individual future more firmly grounded? To that I am glad to say It most certainly is. If I did not have more faith in the future than I have had in the past three years I don't know what in the world I would do. Although I havent got a job and havent had one lately. I have eight (8) in family encluding my wife's father which is 81 years old. Her Mother having died some three months ago. But I am hoping and praying that through Gods help that you will pull us through this crisis. Which you are doing at a rapid rate. You are doing wonderful work just keep it up I think the N.R.A. is grand although I think I lost my job on account of talking for it. The Co. got turned in for working us mechanic from 60 to 70 hours per wk. and they suspect me of writing them up. I am an auto mechanic by trade and I have been working with Cooke Chev. Co. Wadesboro, N.C. This year up until the 19th of May the first work I have had in over a year. I hope you will pardon me for writing you, but I wanted to thank you for what you have done for us and to endorce your new deal whole heartedly. Well hears hoping you will have a grand time and the best of health on your vacation. Also hoping I will get a job soon or get me a little place on my own which I am trying to do. Hope to be of service to my country some time.

Remain as loyal as ever,

John W. Meeks
Wadesboro, N.C.

JUNE 29, 1934

My dear Mr. President:

In your radio address last night you asked a number of questions of the individual and I assume from this that I may answer individually and collectively for Leas & McVitty, Inc., because I am the head of this company that has been in operation since 1812. We are in the tanning business and employ 525 people.

You ask:

Question: Are you better off than you were last year?

This is answered by comparing this week with the week that you took office sixteen months ago.

We are securing only 4.7% more for our leather now.

We are paying 122% more for our hides.

We have had the dollar contracted to 59% of it's former value.

Question: Are your debts less burdensome?

Answer: Our debts are 150% increased.

Question: Is your bank account more secure?

Answer: We think it is, but what it is securing seems more doubtful.

Question: Are your working conditions better?

Answer: Judging from a committee representing our men, we would say "no." These men reported that they were entirely satisfied with the increase in hourly rate of wages, but they are dissatisfied with the limitation of hours and their liberty of choice.

Question: Is your faith in your own individual future more firmly grounded?

Answer: It is utterly shaken.

Question: Have you as an individual paid too high a price for these gains?

Answer: The above are not gains. Your policies have added to our confusion by taking away our former standards of stability and giving us no future guide.

Respectfully yours,

S. H. McVitty
Salem, Va.

JUNE 30, 1934

Dear President; I listened with profound interest to your Broadcast, the other night, and want to assure you, that your diagnosis was absolutely true.

I have since 1880, owned and operated a small department store at Ashville, Ohio. A comparison of the figures, as shown by my books, for the first six months of 1934, compared with the first six months of 1933, show a gain of 64⁄₁₀% am past 70 yrs. of age, Am confident by the end of the first 6 months of 1935, we'll be showing parallels of 1928 business.

Yours truly

G. A. Hook
Ashville, Ohio

JUNE 29, 1934

Dear President: —

I read in the Memphis Commercial Appeal your radio address of last night about the New Deal. I believe all that you have done is very profitable to all masses of the people and will result in great improvement of business conditions.

I am a Jewish merchant in a small town and during the years of the depression it was hard sailing for me and for all the people. Since you have been in office my business is better and all the business in my community is better. You have inspired faith and courage and helped the poor and oppressed. I think you are the best President since George Washington and greater than Moses for it took him 40 years to bring the Jewish people out of the wilderness and you have accomplished wonders in such a short time. I am a good Democrat and in my opinion it would be unnecessary to have an election for next term as it should be the unanimous consent of the people for you to remain in office for life. I am not fishing for a job but only good-will.

Your admirer,

Victor Zieff
Newbern, Tenn.

JUNE 29, 1934

Honorable President Roosevelt:

In answer to your radio address of last evening, I wish to state that I would answer NO to all of your questions. . . .

If Labor and Capitol do not go hand in hand, we will not get out of this depression, and as long as your General Johnson sees fit to antagonize Capitol, all the Public Work money that you can print and give away will not help because as soon as it is all used up we will be right where we started. It has to be perment and must come with the help of Capitol, and Capitol is not going to help as long as it is soaked upon every turn.

I respectfully ask you to forgive this frank message, but now that it is out of my system I feel better.

Yours sincerely,

Alvin Icke
San Antonio, Texas

JULY 3, 1934

My dear Mr. President: —

Thank you many times for your cheerful message over the Radio. My family and I answered each of your questions as they were asked, in the afirmative, some in the negative. "Are you better of than last year" Yes, decidedly. "Are your debts less burdensome" Yes, Yes, thanks to your H.O.L.C. [Home Owners Loan Corporation] — Heretofor only the wealthy could hope to receive favors from our Goverment, but now even the "forgotten man" is remembered. "Is your bank account more secure?" Absolutely! "Is your faith in your future more firmly grounded?" Yes.

And now the negatives.

"Have you lost any rights of freedom of action or choice" None whatever, but I have gained some sense of greater freedom under the New Deal — But let the Goverment continue to appoint and manage The [New] Dealers, and not listen to the clammering of the Old Crowd, the "Malfactors of great wealth."

Sincerely

John Pauer
Sacramento, Calif.

JULY 12, 1934

Dear Mr. Roosevelt:

Several weeks ago in a radio address, shortly before you sailed on your vacation, you asked the public to answer two questions. My answer, in both cases, is emphatically "yes", but if I am not too impertinent, I would like to ask you a few questions and shall earnestly hope for some explanation of the questions that have been troubling me.

First — why do you consider it necessary and wise to extend Government control and regulation to business through the actions and activities of the tremendous number of new bureaus that have been established in Washington?

Second — don't you think it was a horrible mistake to devalue the American Dollar and repudiate the promises of the United States Government to pay off it's obligations in Gold coin or money of a certain stated gold value?

Third — Isn't it a stupid thing to do, to kill so many pigs and to plow up so many crops when people are both hungry and unclothed, and isn't it still more stupid to pay a farmer more for failing to produce something, than he would receive for creating something that could be used?

Fourth — Isn't it silly to artificially raise the price of American Cotton, which is one of our largest export commodities, first, by reducing the acreage, and second, by debasing the dollar when such actions must, inevitably, act to stimulate production in foreign countries?

Fifth — Isn't it absurd to suppose that anyone, regardless of whether they are Government, industry or individual, can continue to consume more than they produce?

Sixth — Just what is the theory back of the thought, that people can work less, produce less and earn more? Is it true that the Government is prepared to accept full responsibility for each and every one of us, and that it is no longer necessary to teach our children self-denial, self-discipline, self-reliance, and some sort of a plan for saving for their old age?

These are some of the things that have been troubling me and your answers to these troubling problems will be very much appreciated.

Yours very truly,

H. W. Spencer
Louisville, Ky.

JUNE 29, 1934

Dear Sir,

I listened to your address last night with a great deal of interest. I would enjoy your radio talks even if you were not President.

I want to tell you how my family was situated a year ago as compared with today.

In 1932, we lost everything we had, even cashed in our insurances. My daughter could not get a job, my husband was selling furniture on commission for a store on the verge of bankruptcy. We were desperate, we felt the end of the world had come.

The store decided to join the N.R.A. In reorganizing, they decided to make my husband manager. The same week my daughter got a job secretary to an insurance executive. Today both my husband and daughter are making a fine salary and the store has paid off its obligations and is paying the same dividends it paid when prosperity was at its peak.

That is our story.

A year can make unbelievable changes, especially when the people have confidence in their President.

Yours very truly,

Mrs. L. H. Thompson
Atlanta, Ga.

JUNE 28, 1934

Dear Mr. President: —

Permit me the liberty of congratulating you, on the clear and lucid address delivered to-night to the people of the U.S.A. It was forceful and convincing beyond words to express; and the pleasing and captivating voice, was vibrant with utter sincerity.

You invited your listeners to test "Recovery" in the light of their own circumstances. May I offer mine?

My parish is in the great metropolitan area. Mostly industrial. My church membership is over a thousand. In addition I conduct a "Men's Bible Class" of about 300. A "Women's Bible Class" of 150. I have struggled through the "depression" and done many unusual things to help my needy folk. I have greatly alleviated their distresses and lack of employment.

To-day the complexion of the situation is completely changed.

Since your administration began, there is such improvement, that my humble efforts are really no longer necessary. My long list of unemployed men and women, is no longer in evidence. The N.R.A. did it.

This is the acid test, and I regard my own as no mean one.

May I be further permitted, to wish you the pleasure you so much deserve, in your approaching holiday, and that your wish to make America, "God's Country" may be fully realized, and may the Grace of Christ, support you.

Respectfully,
Your humble servant,

John M. Macmillan
Kearny, New Jersey

JUNE 28, 1934

Dear Sir: —

Your words of tonight have touched me, so that I appreciate, as never before, the gigantic efforts you are making in behalf of your fellow human beings.

I am an alien. For over ten years I have remained deliberately so, having felt all along that there could be no security in this country, with so much corruption and selfishness. Now, before the week is over, I shall apply for citizenship, determined to be amoung the millions of proud and priviliged people you address as "fellow citizens and friends;" determined to help, if only spiritually, to ease the gigantic burden you so gamely and ably struggle with in order to make America truly "God's Country." For, like millions of others, I now feel secure. There is no longer that fear for the immediate future, as looming up from behind the black clouds of doubt. . . .

Yours Humbly,

Robert E. Reid
Corona, New York

JUNE 29, 1934

My Dear beloved President.

I heard your talk on the radio last night and it was grate But in the same time when I heard you that you are going on your vacation for a few weeks, so I am very much afraid of about your safty my heart tells me same thing I don't know what so for good protection pleas dear beloved President be very carffuly whit your every step.

A good Cityzen.

Sam Zelmanowitz
New York, New York

ORDER OUT OF CHAOS:
SEPTEMBER 30, 1934

FDR REMARKED more than once that he found going out among the American people a tonic; he much preferred it to working in his White House office. "I regain strength by just meeting the American people," he enthused. His extensive trip West in the summer of 1934 was no exception. After his return, he told his Emergency Council that the faces of those who crowded around him wherever he went were different than they had been when he had traveled the country during the campaign of 1932. "You could tell what the difference was by standing on the end of the car and looking at the crowd. They were a hopeful people. They had courage written all over their faces. They looked cheerful. They knew they were 'up against it,' but they were going to see the thing through."[41]

While he praised the everyday folk for their courage and persistence, he had different emotions for those in his own party, including the former presidential candidates John W. Davis and Al Smith, who — along with such business magnates as the du Ponts, Alfred P. Sloan, Jr., of General Motors, J. Howard Pew of Sun Oil, Nathan Miller of U.S. Steel, and Sewell L. Avery of Montgomery Ward — formed the American Liberty League in August 1934 to oppose the New Deal and its leader with an unrelenting vehemence that led the journalist Marquis Childs to brand them "the Roosevelt Haters." The President's ultimate desire, the League charged over and over again in the coming months and years, was to destroy liberty: "Louis XIV never went so far. Neither Mussolini nor Hitler, nor Stalin of Russia, have gone so far."[42]

But Roosevelt's troubles were not confined to those he dubbed the "I CAN'T TAKE IT CLUB." He also found himself at odds with close advisers like his Budget Director Lewis Douglas, who in April of 1933 had called Roosevelt's abandonment of the gold standard "the end of Western civilization" and in August of 1934 resigned in disagreement with his chief's policies of public works and deficit spending, which he denounced as the road to socialism. During the summer of 1934, FDR also resisted the counsel of another principal adviser, Raymond Moley, who urged him to declare that with the addition of a social security program, the New Deal's legislative program was complete. FDR believed, as he confided to Colonel House in May, "We must keep the sheer momentum from slacking up too much and I have no intention of relinquishing the offensive in favor of defensive tactics. I think we can keep the tide on the flood for a good long time to come."[43]

During these months, the Book of the Month Club offered as a selection Herbert Hoover's *The Challenge to Liberty,* in which the former President characterized the New Deal as a system of national regimentation bordering on fascism and called it "the most stupendous invasion of the whole spirit of Liberty that the nation has witnessed since the days of Colonial America."[44] The nature of the conservative attacks on FDR throughout most of his tenure bring to mind the remark of Rexford Guy Tugwell that Roosevelt's reputation as a "political wonder-worker" was in part due to his political genius and in part "due to the extremely bad judgment and to the incredible ineptness of the conservative opposition." At one point, after committing what he considered to be an egregious political blunder, FDR himself commented: "Oh well, I always have one comfort. The opposition will come up with a worse boner tomorrow or next day — soon enough to blanket mine."[45]

In this heated atmosphere, FDR delivered his second and final Fireside Chat of 1934 just a little more than a month before the November midterm elections.[46] In the face of his myriad attackers, he reminded the nation of the New Deal's accomplishments thus far: "after years of uncertainty, . . . we are bringing order out of the old chaos." He adroitly quoted the words of Elihu Root, the elderly Republican corporate lawyer who had served as Theodore Roosevelt's Secretary of State, in order to let a respected member of the Republican establishment articulate the realities of the context in which the New Deal was operating: "Instead of the give and take of free individual contract," Root had written,

> the tremendous power of organization has combined great aggregations of capital in enormous industrial establishments . . . so great in the mass that each individual concerned in them is quite helpless by himself. The relations between the employer and the employed, . . . between the small producer, the small trader, the consumer, and the great transporting and manufacturing and distributing agencies, all present new questions for the solution of which the old reliance upon the free action of in-

dividual wills appears quite inadequate. And in many directions, the intervention of that organized control which we call government seems necessary to produce the same result of just and right conduct which obtained through the attrition of individuals before the new conditions arose.

FDR dwelled on his Administration's successful efforts to heal the sickness prevailing in banking and investment and then turned to the National Recovery Administration's efforts to halt child labor, raise wages, create jobs, and produce standards of fair competition. He admitted that much remained to be done: "There is no magic formula, no economic panacea, which could simply revive over-night for example the heavy industries and the trades that are dependent upon them. Nevertheless, my friends, the gains of trade and industry, as a whole, have been substantial and everybody knows it."

FDR then launched into a surprisingly detailed technical assessment of the NRA, which had been under intense criticism for favoring those business groups that were already entrenched and powerful and thus in the best position to utilize the powers of setting prices and allocating production quotas. Some have interpreted Roosevelt's remarks as a warning to businessmen that if they didn't acknowledge the benefits bestowed on them by the New Deal and continued to carp and criticize, those benefits could be reviewed and withdrawn, while others have seen in them evidence that FDR was hardening his attitudes toward big business and moving to the left. The President's statements doubtless manifested a bit of both. He admitted that some of the codes adopted for various businesses and industries might be too complicated or too prone to price fixing and limitation of production but stressed that this is what businessmen had wanted since "the representatives of trade and industry were permitted to write their own ideas into the codes."

> It is now time to review these actions as a whole to determine
> . . . the wisdom of many of those devices to control production,
> or to prevent destructive price cutting which many business organizations have insisted were necessary, or whether their effect
> may have been to prevent . . . lower prices and increased employment. Another question arises as to whether in fixing minimum wages on the basis of an hourly or a weekly wage we have
> reached into the heart of the problem which is to provide such

annual earnings, earnings throughout the year, for the lowest paid worker — such earnings as will meet his minimum needs. And we question also the wisdom of extending code requirements suited to the great industrial centers and suited to large employers, to . . . the great number of small employers in the smaller communities.

While reiterating his support for Section 7(a) of the National Industrial Recovery Act (NIRA) guaranteeing labor's right to organize and bargain collectively, Roosevelt noted that during the past twelve months "our industrial recovery has been to some extent retarded by strikes" and asked both labor and industry to "lay aside the weapons common to industrial war" at least for the duration of the economic crisis and "civilize our industrial civilization" by availing themselves of the vehicles of mediation and arbitration established just a few months earlier by the National Labor Relations Board (NLRB). He then turned to the public works provisions of the NIRA, which were "designed to put more men back to work, both directly on the public works themselves, and indirectly in the industries supplying the materials for these public works." He answered those critics who maintained that public works were a wasteful and unaffordable indulgence by declaring that "no country, however rich, can afford the waste of its human resources. Demoralization caused by vast unemployment is our greatest extravagance. Morally, it is the greatest menace to our social order."

> Some people try to tell me that we must make up our minds that for the future we shall permanently have millions of unemployed . . . I stand or fall by my refusal to accept as a necessary condition of our future a permanent army of unemployed. On the contrary, we must make it a national principle that we will not tolerate a large army of the unemployed, that we will arrange our national economy to end our present unemployment as soon as we can and then to take wise measures against its return. I do not want to think that it is the destiny of any American to remain permanently on relief rolls.

The President turned with scorn to those "who are frightened by boldness, who are cowed by the necessity for making decisions, [who] complain that all we have done is unnecessary and that all we have done is subject to great risks." He was especially irate at those in the business community who had urgently sought his aid in the deeply troubled early months of 1933 and then with the onset of recovery began to oppose the very measures that had saved them. "Now that these people are coming out of their storm cellars, they forget that there ever was a storm." But FDR affirmed his faith in the "sensible and calm" American people. "We do not get greatly excited nor is our peace of mind disturbed, whether we be business men or workers or farmers, by awesome pronouncements concerning the unconstitutionality of some of our measures of recovery and relief and reform. We are not frightened by reactionary lawyers or by political editors. All of these cries have been heard before." He joined with former Chief Justice Edward Douglas White who in the days of Theodore Roosevelt and Woodrow Wilson decried those "creating the general impression that the Constitution is but a barrier to progress instead of being the broad highway through which alone true progress may be enjoyed."

In his program of reform, FDR argued, "we have avoided . . . the theory that business should and must be taken over into an all-embracing Government . . . [and] the equally untenable theory that it is an interference with Liberty to offer reasonable help when private enterprise is in need of help." The course the New Deal was taking "fits the American practice of Government — a practice of taking action step by step, of regulating only to meet concrete needs — a practice of courageous recognition of change." There was no more potent political icon during the Depression than Abraham Lincoln, and FDR eagerly aligned himself with Lincoln's definition of the legitimate object of government: "to do for a community of people whatever they need to have done but cannot do at all or cannot do so well for themselves in their separate and in their individual capacities." "My friends," Roosevelt concluded:

> I still believe in ideals. I am not for a return to that definition of Liberty under which for many years a free people were being gradually regimented into the service of the privileged few. I prefer and I am sure you prefer that broader definition of Liberty under which we are moving forward to greater freedom, to greater security for the average man than he has ever known before in the history of America.

OCTOBER 3, 1934

Dear Mr. President:

One hundred and twenty millions of Americans ought to go down on their knees daily to thank the Almighty God that a man of your caliber is at the head of this Nation.

Of the remaining few, some are to be pitied, while others deserve the hospitality of Alcatraz Island —

Your stirring address to the Nation last Sunday night was a master piece of statemanship, honesty, frankness and knowledge.

Mr. President I have a wife and a child —, I love them but I do worship you —

Someday I hope to have the pleasure to see you — this is one of my ambition in life.

With best wishes for your health and success, I am

Devoted yours

Joe Frigo
Keystone, W.Va.

OCTOBER 1, 1934

Dear Mr. President:

Everybody who has any sense and was able to get to a radio heard your speech last night. I desire to add my firm approval to every utterance which came from your lips.

Surely under the guidance of your great constructive genius the country is gaining. It is well that you take us into your confidence and tell us Mr. President; your address reveals what we had not heard. There is such a welter of publicity about the alphabetized programmes that much wisdom is lost in confusion, but when you speak everybody understands.

You know what your government is doing. You know how to explain it. You know where you are heading and you are on your way.

God bless and keep you strong for the battle Mr. President is the sincere wish of a red-hot, jet-black Democrat.

Melvin J. Chisum
(Field Secretary of the National Negro Press Association)
Philadelphia, Pa.

⊰ 113 ⊱

SEPTEMBER 30, 1934

My dear Mr. Roosevelt:

In my little apartment here about as far away from you as I could be I have listened with great interest to your talk tonight and when you were through, I wished that you were here or I were there because there were many things that I wanted to hear more about. I detected a bit more of the fighting spirit than in previous speeches and I heartily endorse your unwillingness to believe in the necessity of continued unemployment and its subsequent human waste: also regimentation of free people to work for the privileged few.

From childhood one of my greatest anxieties has been concerning the material inequalities of our 'land of the free', the mental and moral inequalities can never be regulated so satisfactorily as can the material, but they too will be lessened when, under the guidance of men with ideals similar to yours, the material needs of every human being are permantly and irrevocably provided for. I'm confident it can be done and I wish, impatiently, that I could do something tangible toward advancing the day. Isn't there anything I could do to help?

Congratulations on your success so far and best wishes for satisfactory future developments.

Sincerely your friend,

Beth Fisher
Long Beach, Calif.

OCTOBER 1, 1934

Sir:

I wish to express my appreciation of your very reassuring message over the radio last evening. As the wife of one of the many millions of men still unemployed, I believe I was especially grateful for your statement to the effect that it was not the destiny of any American to be continuously unemployed. Such a statement must do much towards restoring the confidence and self-respect of those worthy men who are forced to be supported by either the relief agencies or relatives.

During this trying period, we have been very fortunate in that I have been able to maintain the home for the past three years, but such a condition, grateful as we are, does not engender a spirit of happiness in a man, and it is difficult for him to maintain his self-respect. We have a boy of six and I certainly would hate to see him grow up to join the army of unemployed that we have been told lately would have to be supported in the United States.

Our prayers are with you, Mr. President, and we know that with right motives you can and must succeed in your efforts to lift the country out of its present state.

Yours very respectfully,

(Mrs. George S. Hardy) Madge B. Hardy
Chicago, Illinois

OCTOBER 2, 1934

Dear President of the United States of America

Listened to your talk Sunday evening. All things considered, needed no adding to, and could not have been rendered in a more friendly or determined spirit. . . .

I am at present working as a laborer on one of the many FERA [Federal Emergency Relief Administration] projects. Commencing only last week, and although I am 54 years of age, these few days, mark the greatest days of my life. Picture me with a pick and a shovel, right out on the end of Point Loma near the old Spanish light house, helping make things ready for a little park, working under overseers, who seem able and considerate, for all concerned. . . .

Now as I work on the project mentioned, the days I labor, hark me back twenty years or more, when as individuals and in bodies we were trying for the programs of today. And at that time we said, there is a class who cannot or will not see, and because of selfishness and lust, the life blood of labor is dripping from their house tops. . . .

These are great days, because the dreams we dispared of in our life, surely are closing in on us, through the timely efforts of a Great President and his able assistants. . . .

George W. Ball
San Diego, Calif.

OCTOBER 1, 1934

Honored Sir:

With thousands of other citizens of the United States I listened to your talk over the radio last night. I am wondering if there are not many others who have the same questions to ask which came to me as you finished your talk.

Your concern seems to be over two classes of people or possibly I may say three groups, the employer, the wage earner or employee and the farmer.

What percentage of our people form the employer, the union wage earner and the farmer? Is there not a large class who are not included in either of the above groups, such as the salesman, agent, professional man or woman, clerk, etc who have no connection with any union, chamber of commerce, society etc. These people of whom I am one are struggling to keep going with rising prices and dropping off of business.

Uncomplainingly we have paid the mounting taxes which have been increased from time to time to care for the unemployed, the cotton grower and the western farmer. Now we are militantly demanding something should be done indirectly to step up prosperity for us.

Your administration has never mentioned that there are thousands of law abiding citizens who have reached the age where their services are not wanted by an employer. No union cares whether these people exist or not.

As one of this group I with the members of my family are too proud to beg, too proud to look to relief agencies who would probably refuse any assistance, no matter how urgent the need because we have in the days gone by accumulated some property, life insurance, a car and by frugal effort built up what looks like a well to do existence.

As a member of this group I ask that you use your good office to institute some new course of action which will bring to us some hope of something better than being the underlings, forever ground between the millstones of excessive wealth and poverty.

Sincerely yours,

F. W. Allen
Erie, Penna.

OCTOBER 3, 1934

My dear President Roosevelt:

Your fireside talk was very fine, and I am one of your admirers. Next time I hope you will include some conclusion on the thoughtless increase in population of those dependent on relief, or with very small earning capacity.

It is unfair to children to bring them into the world doomed to misery, nor should the more far sighted be taxed to support them. . . .

Sterilization of the unfit should follow, and our crime record would not be so shocking. There are 40,000 persons in New Jersey who should be segregated. 10,000 only can be accommodated in our excellent institutions.

These people cannot help being a burden to the normal, but should never have come into the world.

With best wishes for continued success,

Sincerely,

Florence K. Amos
Princeton, New Jersey

SEPTEMBER 30, 1934

Dear Sir: —

Recently I read an article by Stuart Chase (econimist) which said you must soon take a leftward (liberal) course or a rightward (reactionary) one. Your speech with its emphasis on protection of the billions in American industry seemed to be pandering to the money of the country and not the people. Till now I have had the utmost faith in you. I feel a little sick now. Hope I have misunderstood or am wrong.

Very truly,

Richard Martin
San Francisco, Calif.

OCTOBER 1, 1934

My dear Mr. President:

I listened to your radio talk last night. It occurs to me that you would be interested in knowing the reaction of the average man.

In order that you may get the proper background, I will tell you something of my past history — as a boy, I had nothing. I worked hard, was economical, sacrificed many of the pleasures that the average young man indulged in, married a girl who was no better off than I was, and together we suffered many sacrifices. We finally managed to save enough money to get into business, our business grew and flourished. . . .

I have a program of expansion that has been in the balance for many months because of the uncertainty of the political situation. This expansion program would give employment to quite a number of people, but because of uncertainties, we do not want to go ahead.

I was in hopes in your talk last night you would say something that would encourage the average businessman, but from what I can gather, you propose to go thru with the New Deal as is.

The thing that worries me is the class of people that you have surrounded yourself with — I refer to . . . the bunch of college professors that are nothing more than theorists, and very impractical to say the least, in addition to having Socialistic and Communistic tendencies that scare the average good citizen. . . .

What we need in the White House, is a man who is courageous enough to put into effect a program to balance the budget, reduce our taxes and quit spending the peoples' money wrecklessly.

I have gone along with you up to the present time, but if matters do not get better and if business does not have a fair shake, then I will take my little 30 cents, put it away in a tin can and live off of it for my few remaining years — that is what many people are doing and being driven to by these Brain Truster ideas.

This letter is not intended in any way to be disrespectful, and I hope that you will agree that my contentions have some merit.

Yours very truly,

R. R. Englehart
Davenport, Iowa

* * *

My dear President:

Your speech last night should go down in history, along with many of your previous acts, as a display of mental incompetancy. A small time politician could really have done better. However, the poor people of our glorious country are governed by their emotions and prejudices and you know it, so we can expect you to continue the way you have been going. But as "Eddie" Leonard used to say "You can fool some of the people some of the time, but you can't fool all of the people all of the time."

Hugh F. Colliton Jr.
Wayland, Mass.

OCTOBER 1, 1934

YOU STUTTER TERRIBLY IN YOUR SPEECHES I DONT THINK YOU HAVE THE CONFIDENCE I DONT REALLY BELIEVE YOU ARE SOLD ON YOUR OWN IDEAS ANSWER ME WHO WROTE YOUR SPEECH AGAINST PUBLIC SENTIMENT I NEED AN ANSWER.

E. B. SCARSDALE
DAYTON, OHIO

OCTOBER 1, 1934

RESPECTFULLY ALWAYS MY DEAR FRANK . . . DONT LET THEM KID YOU TONIGHTS TALK WAS AS UNCONVINCING AS A CREAM PUFF ASSAULT ON THE GREAT WALL OF CHINA. DO STOP THIS SHADOW BOXING WITH REALITIES. DONT LET ANYONE TELL YOU THAT INDUSTRY WONT COOPERATE. THE TRAGEDY IS THAT INDUSTRYS ATTITUDE HAS BEEN DISTORTED THERE IS MORE GUT AND ROMANCE IN INDUSTRY THAN THERE EVER HAS BEEN IN POLITICS. LET US CUT OUT THIS SLIDE RULE AND STRATOSPHERE THEORIZING AND IF I CAN BE OF ANY SERVICE IN THIS EMERGENCY YOU HAVE ONLY TO COMMAND ME. DO TAKE THIS COMMUNICATION IN THE SPIRIT IN WHICH IT IS SENT FOR I HAVE NO AXE TO GRIND BUT I DO BELIEVE IN IN-

DUSTRY AND THE MEN WHO ARE STILL ON A SIXTEEN HOUR DAY TRYING TO KEEP THEIR MEN EMPLOYED.

FRANK C. REILLY
DETROIT, MICHIGAN

SEPTEMBER 30, 1934

DEAR MR PRESIDENT ALTHOUGH I AM A REPUBLICAN AND A FRIEND OF THOSE OTHER GREAT PRESIDENTS THEODORE ROOSEVELT THE LATE PRESIDENT TAFT AND FORMER PRESIDENT HOOVER I DESIRE TO AVAIL MYSELF OF THIS OPPORTUNITY TO CONGRATULATE YOU ON YOUR SOUND SPEECH OF TONIGHT WHICH HAS JUST COME OVER THE RADIO IN MAGNIFICENT MANNER. YOU ARE DOING A GRAND JOB UNDER THE MOST DIFFICULT CIR-CUMSTANCES AND JUSTLY DESERVE THE INDIVIDUAL AND COLLECTIVE SUPPORT AND SYMPATHY OF EVERY TRUE AMERICAN WHO PUTS HIS COUN-TRYS NEEDS ABOVE PARTY POLITICS OR PERSONAL INTERESTS. I CONGRAT-ULATE YOU AND WISH YOU SUCCESS.

ELMER R. JONES
(PRESIDENT WELLS FARGO & CO.)
NEW YORK, N.Y.

OCTOBER 1, 1934

BUSINESS MEN OF THIS TOWN ENDORSE YOUR PROGRAM AS OUTLINED IN YOUR RADIO ADDRESS OF SUNDAY NIGHT. THE NEW DEAL HAS BROUGHT PROSPERITY TO THE FARMERS OF THIS SECTION AND THAT MEANS PROS-PERITY FOR OUR TOWN OF KENBRIDGE. IT WOULD DO YOUR HEART GOOD TO SEE THE HAPPY FLUE CURED TOBACCO GROWERS OF THIS GOLDEN TO-BACCO BELT UNDER THE AAA WHO WERE POVERTY STRIKEN UNDER THE OLD RAW DEAL OF OTHER DAYS.

CHARLES M. ALLEN
(PRESIDENT KENBRIGE CHAMBER OF COMMERCE)
KENBRIDGE, VIR.

OCTOBER 1, 1934

Dear Mr. President: —

Please, not that it matters, but as an encouragement, please, keep it up. Your speech last night was one of your BEST. Now you talking turkey thats the language they will understand and will right back they go, in the storm cellar with the rats.

Please, fear NOTHING the people are WITH YOU!

Get that full dictatorship, you will never get them to do things otherwise. Get them with the coming Congress, they will be yours you MUST ACT NOW or later it will be too late, people will be out of bounds, even you will not be able to control them.

God bless you and more power to you!

HAIL ROOSEVELT!

Very respectfully yours.

Oliver Kovacs
Perth Amboy, N.J.

OCTOBER 2, 1934

Dear Sir,

Heard your radio talk on Sunday . . . big business is not playing cricket. The small wage earner, the farmer and small business are for you. Big business has legal and financial aid to try and thwart your efforts. If you abolish the Federal Reserve and establish National Bank I don't think you would have the trouble with the bankers that you spoke of Sunday. I think any profits to be made from the distribution of money should go to the government.

If labor gets out of hand troops are called out to put them in order. With the government bank in effect if big business got out of hand, call in their money to put them in order. In either case after a settlement is reached the cancellation of privelages is lifted. I think this would shorten strikes considerably. In any event it would put labor and big business on an even footing if they were not willing to arbitrate. Hope you dont think I am a crank or nit-wit.

Here's hoping for your continued Success.

W. S. Wilson
Philadelphia, Pa.

occupation — auto-mechanic
age 31
color white
Employed at $.50 an hr.
13 years experience

OCTOBER 3, 1934

Dear Mr. President,

Following your radio address of Sunday evening I felt much as one would who, having been invited to a dinner, goes away hungry — Or as a child, having asked for milk — is given water. Not one word about balancing our Government budget. Not a bit of assurance about this monetary policy. No help promised investors in large corporations or small business men. . . .

The Administration has invited strikes when it assured strikers that it would care for them with relief when unemployed. Better have announced that any one receiving fair wage & in decent working condition — who enticed a strike would be ineligible to Federal Relief & considered an obstructionist to Recovery. Labor has become insolent and violent. . . .

HOLC [Home Owners Loan Corporation] in Philadelphia is in many instances inefficient and most unbusiness like — to put it mildly.

House wives in Pennsylvania know full well how much more it costs to fill the market basket — and what few incomes have increased. In fact, some of us wonder how we can keep our homes and carry on the education of our children with securities, even Government bonds — below what we paid for them. . . .

We've tried to follow our leader, Mr. President, but the past six months — we wonder where we may be led. Too many experiments — too much corn-hog money just before elections — too much radical thought — too little good common sense on cost-balance and private initiative.

Respectfully — but earnestly,

Mrs H. H. Smith
Ardmore, Penna.

OCTOBER 1, 1934

Mr. President:

Thank you for your profoundly impressive radio address of last evening. I was particularly pleased with its leftward leanings. The rebukes which you gave your reactionary adversaries struck me as being polite, forceful, and unbeatable in their logic.

I am convinced that more and more Maine people are coming to believe that the interests of those called "middle class" are more closely tied up with the interests of the workers than with the interests of the owners. This trend accounts to some extent for the outcome of the Maine elections. . . .

Respectfully yours,

Robert F. Skillings
Portland, Maine

SEPTEMBER 27, 1934

My dear President:

Your radio address this evening was as usual very pleasing to hear, I never miss your friendly talks when it is possible for me to listen.

. . . We judge the new deal by the opposition it receives from the bankers, if they are against it surely it must be all right for the majority.

Many of us think this administration is headed in the right direction, but is to easy, has made to many threats and no action. I have heard even Republicans say that the NRA is O.K. if it was enforced.

Why delay action any longer? If this new deal is for the little fellow as most of us think, then lets fight the big fellow now and not allow him to hinder progress or to tear down that which has been rebuilt. They are fighting us, lets fight back. If the money changers refuse to loosen up, take it away from them, confiscate their property, declare their money null & void. Step all over them, show them who is boss.

The constitution. Who started all this talk about preserving the constitution? It seems as though the opposing side has taken quite a liking to that document all of a sudden, if they want it let them have it, it is only a scrap of paper, and so far out of date that it has become useless. When G. Washington and his companions drew up that document little did they ever dream that this great land of ours was some day to have three nation wreckers in a row as Presidents. Harding, Coolidge and Hoover. If it is constitutional for a few to gobble up all the money, then it is constitutional to take it away from them. Who thought about the constitution when millions of us were out of work, and still are. I tasted unemployment for 3 long years and yet never mentioned the constitution. . . .

A 30 hour week and 75 cents per hour as a minimum wage will do more than all the NRA's to bring a return of prosperity providing the manufacturers are prevented from reducing their payrolls by the use of labor saving devices. Companys should be compelled to add more men instead of laying them off. In the plant I work 4 men could be added nicely if the employers were not so set on making one man do two mens work.

Your success is my daily prayer and I hope God will bless you in every way.

Faithfully Yours

O. D. Armstrong
Dishman, Wash.

P.S. I hope this letter gets past the examiners, If the President does'nt personally receive one of my letters soon I shall quit writing.

SEPTEMBER 30, 1934

Dear Mr. President:

I am writing at the close of your Sunday night address before I see or hear comments by other persons. . . .

The policy you uphold is the best under the circumstances. The outcome will be very largely a success.

But — permanent security and prosperity can rest only on a much more extensive socialization of the larger enterprises in production and distribution. I hope this Larger Deal will come in your lifetime so that you may see the fruitage of the New Deal which has in it the promise of an ultimate economic revolution on the basis of human brotherhood.

Very respectfully yours,

H. L. Latham
Chicago, Illinois

OCTOBER 6, 1934

Dear Sir: —

I want to congratulate you upon your recent radio address, during which you outlined so courageously the stand of the New Deal in it's relation to human liberty. . . .

I have been following your efforts, since you took office, with the keenest interest and I am fully aware of the appalling problems, which confront you. Of these problems, I think, none is harder than to convince our big business leaders of their responsibility towards the citizens of this country and towards the common good. While life and nature seem to point to an everlasting struggle among the forces of the cosmos, there is no reason, why human beings endowed with reasoning power should not be taught, by force if necessary, to hold a helpful attitude towards each other. That attitude can be brought about through the education of the young or it must, as in our present case, be brought about through government regulation. . . .

All this means reforms of a most drastic manner, but reforms, which in their final effect will free us from the fear of an old age in poverty or from the humiliating spectacle of the soup kitchen or other forms of a hit and miss existence, which had been the order of the day until you became President. If all this be loss of Liberty to the money changers, but freedom from serfdom to the average wholesome American family, then I feel that the gain outweighs the loss and my wish is, that I shall be able in some way to contribute my own efforts towards the building of that better life for all of us, which you are trying so hard to give to this generation and it's future descendants. . . .

Sincerely yours,

H. W. Arth
San Fransisco, Cal.

OCTOBER 2, 1934

Dear Mr. President:

Sunday evening I spent with a friend in the country, a man who runs a small chicken ranch. About six thirty oclock, as we sat there talking, neighbors who had no radios began to drop in to listen to your talk which came to us at seven oclock.

As your voice began to come to us, the room became very quiet. If you could have seen the faces of those folks, hanging on your every word; their expressions when your talk was finished, you would have new strength to go ahead. During the following Monday, friends called at the studio to pass the time of day. All sorts of people; a newspaper representative, a writer of action stories, a house-to-house solicitor, the postman, express man, and grocery man. The first word of all was, "Did you hear Roosevelt's talk?"

In the evening, the Ritchfield Newsflashes told us the bankers were not satisfied, you had not made the promises they had hoped for; that business was dissatisfied; that the Socialists were distrustful.

Looks like nobody was satisfied but old John Public.

But the ordinary people with whom I came in contact showed new faith and courage after listening to your words. To them, your talk promised one thing, you would not turn back, and they were satisfied with that. That, in fact, was all they wished to know. They are willing to follow as long as you face forward.

Sincerely

C. H. Van Scoy
Seattle, Washington

OCTOBER 2, 1934

Dear Mr. Presidents;

We want you to know that we appreciate your Broadcasts over the Radio. In the past 3 years that I have searched for work and so far have not had to go on relief rolls. Your radio talks have did a great deal to give me encourgement to keep on trying. A great many more of my friends feel the same way and we are looking forward to more of your interesting chats soon. Being a

Boilermaker and Ship Yard worker, I like your efforts in trying new things. Many thanks Mr. President.

Very Truly Yours,

M. J. Lane
Chicago, Illinois

OCTOBER 1, 1934

Mr. Secretary to the President,

Dear Sir: Do you happen to have in your files a picture of President Roosevelt taken a short time ago when at West Point reviewing the Cadets? I saw him in the "Movie" at that time and as he opened his mouth to speak I noticed the absence of a lower tooth and immediately felt a "bond of sympathy" as I too have lost a lower tooth at the same point and at once said "I wish I had a picture of him in that pose — something unusual.* I listened eagerly last night to see if I could detect a lisp as mine has caused me, but I could not and imagine he has had his replaced and not deferring from the same reason I have — he is young — I am seventy this month — so it is hardly worth while. . . .

Very Truly Yours,

(Mrs) Florence D. Price
Dania, Florida

---

*FDR did in fact have a false tooth that he kept in a small silver box when he was not using it. More than once, just before he began a Fireside Chat, he discovered he had left the box on a table near his bed and a Secret Service man had to be sent to retrieve it. It was, then, quite possible he had left the tooth behind when he made his trip to West Point. See Grace Tully, *F.D.R. My Boss* (New York: Charles Scribner's Sons, 1949), 100.

PROTECTING THE WEAK:
APRIL 28, 1935

LESS THAN FIVE WEEKS after the September 30 Fireside Chat, the American people went to the polls for the midterm elections of 1934. Rather than reducing the congressional margins of the party in power — which they normally did in midterm elections — voters strengthened the Democratic hold on the national government, increasing their numbers in the House from 313 to 322 and in the Senate from 59 to 69, more than two-thirds majorities in both houses. The Republicans had only 103 seats in the House and 25 in the Senate — their slimmest representation in Congress since before the Civil War.

The historian Charles Beard viewed the victory as "thunder on the left." Many members of the Seventy-fifth Congress were now clearly to the left of the President, while as the *New York Times* observed, the election had "literally destroyed the right wing of the Republican Party." It was, the *Times* proclaimed, "the most overwhelming victory in the history of American politics." FDR could not have been completely surprised. After his August trip across the country, he had remarked: "The reception was grand and I am more than ever convinced that, so far as having the people with us goes, we are just as strong — perhaps stronger — than ever before."[47]

But even Roosevelt could not have predicted how broad his mandate would be. Now, as in the early months of his presidency, FDR may have had a potential opportunity to alter the system in directions many of his opponents ceaselessly claimed he desired to. He could have attempted a permanent realignment of parties, endeavored to inject the government more powerfully and permanently into the fundamental matrix of the economy, experimented with alternate and more vigorous forms of central planning and collective action. Though he did speak from time to time of reshuffling the parties so that by the end of the eight years he hoped to serve there might or might not be a Democratic party but would be a Progressive one — a goal he never implemented — he had neither the plans nor the intentions to initiate radical change. Secretary of Labor Frances Perkins surely was correct when she observed that FDR had no central unified plan: "he had, I am sure, no thought or desire to impose any overall economic or political change on the United States."[48]

It was this lack of planning that led to Rexford Guy Tugwell's famous complaint that 1933 had been "a lost year of opportunities passed over." Instead of leading a weary nation down new and better paths, Roosevelt fell back on restoring confidence and bolstering faith in the very institutions that had created the disaster. On March 4, 1933, "Americans would have followed him anywhere," Tugwell asserted, but FDR "had no place much to take them." It is certainly true that Roosevelt had no new ideas or destination that would have structurally reconstituted the American system. His goal was to make that system work more efficiently and justly by creating greater balance between its parts and extending greater security and equity to its people. Tugwell, a Columbia University economics professor who was serving as Assistant Secretary of Agriculture, was a loyal New Dealer who supported and worked for these ends until he resigned after the election of 1936, but from the beginning he feared that the New Deal's patchwork of reforms would ultimately leave the old economic establishment "more solidly planted than ever," its functions not nationalized, its elite not disciplined. FDR, Tugwell concluded in retrospect, had erred "on the minimal side. He could have emerged from the orthodox progressive chrysalis and led us into a new world. He chose rather rickety repairs for an old one."[49]

Tugwell's was a distinctly minority voice among New Dealers, most of whom found themselves enthused by the "repairs" being implemented. After the elections of 1934, FDR's relief administrator, Harry Hopkins, turned to his staff and proclaimed: "Boys — this is our hour. We've got to get everything we want — a works program, social security, wages and hours, everything — now or never. Get your minds to work on developing a complete ticket to provide security for all the folks of this country up and down and across the board."[50]

Though a substantial number of those responding to the Fireside Chats continued to urge the President to deliver them as often as possible, FDR created his own deliberate pace. He tended to give the Chats more frequently in periods of crisis and reduce the number when events seemed under control, as they certainly did following the November elections. In the face of FDR's long radio silence after his September 1934 Chat, the old Wilsonian Democrat Ray Stannard Baker wrote in March 1935 pleading with him to keep before the country a vision of high moral purpose. FDR respectfully reminded Baker that "the public psychology and, for that matter, individual psychology, cannot, because of human weakness, be attuned for long periods of time to a constant repetition of the highest note in the scale. . . . People tire of seeing the same name day after day in the important headlines of the papers, and the same voice night after night over the radio." Nevertheless, he did agree that "the time is soon at hand for a new stimulation of united American action. I am proposing that very thing before the year is out."[51]

Whatever FDR's own inclination might have been — and there were those like *Time* magazine who predicted that he would reconcile with business and end reform — the nation itself seemed to be moving to the left. Not only the midterm elections attested to that, but the rise of voices demanding more intensified reform appeared to be everywhere. In Wisconsin, Senator Robert La Follette and his brother, Governor Philip La Follette, created the Wisconsin Progressive Party to work for the more equal distribution of wealth. In Minnesota, the Farmer-Labor Party under Governor Floyd Olson called not for a New Deal but for a New Deck. In California, the novelist Upton Sinclair established the End Poverty in California movement (EPIC) to create a production-for-use economy in which the state would take over idle farms and factories and allow the unemployed to use them to produce for their own needs. Sinclair won the Democratic gubernatorial primary and almost won the election in spite of FDR's refusal to support him. Demands for radical change were hardly confined to these states. Father Charles E. Coughlin's immensely popular radio programs, along with his National Union for Social Justice, demanded an end to an exploitative economic system ruled by the greedy few; Huey Long's Share Our Wealth movement advocated redistributing wealth by limiting personal fortunes and providing a five thousand dollars estate for every American family; Dr. Francis Townsend articulated a widely acclaimed plan to give two hundred dollars a month to every American over the age of sixty if they pledged to spend it within thirty days. Such movements enlisted millions of supporters and spread the ferment of left-leaning "thunder" throughout the nation.

It was in the midst of this agitation that Roosevelt finally returned to the airwaves on April 28, 1935, almost seven months after his last Fireside

Chat.[52] He began with still another defense against those — on the left and the right — who accused him of having no definite course of action. He assured the nation that the New Deal's programs were not haphazard: "Each of our steps has a definite relationship to every other step." He documented his assertion not with details but with a homey metaphor comparing the creation of a program for the nation's welfare to the building of a great seagoing ship. When such a ship was under construction it was difficult to tell what it would finally look like when sailing the high seas. "It may seem confused to some, but out of the multitude of detailed parts that go into the making of the structure, the creation of a useful instrument for man ultimately comes. It is that way with the making of a national policy."

The objective of the nation had changed greatly in the past three years, he assured his audience. Where "individual self-interest and group selfishness" had been paramount, where the "general good was at a discount," now people "are considering the whole rather than a mere part, a part relating to one section, or to one crop, or to one industry, or to one individual private occupation. That is a tremendous gain for the principles of democracy." He defended himself also against the charge that he was moving too slowly. The overwhelming majority of the people, he asserted, "know that the process of the constructive rebuilding of America cannot be done in a day or a year, but that it is being done in spite of the few who seek to confuse them and to profit by their confusion. Americans as a whole are feeling a lot better — a lot more cheerful than for many, many years."

To maintain and further this mood, it was crucial to make plans to eliminate unemployment in the future and to deal with the immediate necessities of the unemployed in the present. The first objective would be aided by the Social Security Act pending before Congress (it would be passed by the House on August 8, by the Senate a day later, and signed into law on August 14):

> It proposes, by means of old age pensions, to help those who have reached the age of retirement to give up their jobs and thus give to the younger generation greater opportunities for work and to give to all, old and young alike, a feeling of security as they look toward old age.
>
> The unemployment insurance part of the legislation will not only help to guard the individual in future periods of lay-

off against dependence upon relief, but it will, by sustaining the purchasing power of the nation, cushion the shock of economic distress.

The second objective — to meet the current needs of those still unemployed — would be met by the Emergency Relief Appropriation Act, which Congress had passed earlier that month, under which FDR established the Works Progress Administration (WPA) a week later. More than 80 percent of the WPA's funds went directly as wages to its workers, some 90 percent of whom were classified as needy. The WPA would employ as many as 3.3 million jobless Americans at one time, and before it was phased out in 1943, its workers had repaired 85,000 public buildings and 572,000 miles of roads, built 78,000 new bridges and viaducts, laid 67,000 miles of city streets and 24,000 miles of sidewalks, created 8,000 parks, built 350 airports and 40,000 buildings, improved flood control on rivers and water and sewage systems in cities and towns, produced books in braille for the blind, decorated uncounted public buildings with the works of unemployed artists in the Federal Arts Project, sent out unemployed actors in the Federal Theatre Project to bring theater to Americans throughout the nation, hired unemployed photographers to save the nation's images for posterity and unemployed writers in the Federal Writers' Project to record the oral histories of its people, including two thousand former slaves. It was, in short, enormously creative and useful in the ways in which it injected more than ten billion dollars into a stagnating economy, although it never had the funds necessary to employ more than one-third of the people in need of jobs.[53]

His Fireside Chat reflects the fact that FDR understood that the opponents of a project of this magnitude would distort it by claims of corruption and by painting images of indolent men leaning on shovels, and thus he patiently explained the fundamental principles for his work relief program: projects should be useful; most of the money spent should go directly into wages; funds should be spent promptly; employment should be given first to those on the relief rolls; projects would be allocated to localities in relation to the number of workers on the relief rolls in those areas. Through the WPA, Roosevelt converted the dole into work relief on a scale the United States has never known before or since. It was in some ways his most radical act, and politicians after him, for all their excoriation of the dole — giving relief payments without demanding work in return — have never exhibited

FDR's courage or determination in creating programs of work relief that conservatives envision as competing with capitalism but that Roosevelt saw as saving his people body and soul from the failures of capitalism. "This is a great national crusade," he told his listeners, "a crusade to destroy enforced idleness which is an enemy of the human spirit generated by this depression." Once again he endeavored to turn his constituents into participants:

> I call upon my fellow citizens everywhere to cooperate with me in making this the most efficient and the cleanest example of public enterprise the world has ever seen. It is time to provide a smashing answer for those cynical men who say that a democracy cannot be honest, cannot be efficient. If you will help, this can be done. I therefore hope that you will watch the work in every corner of the nation. Feel free to criticize. Tell me of instances where work can be done better, or where improper practices prevail. Neither you nor I want criticism conceived in a purely fault-finding or partisan spirit, but I am jealous of the right of every citizen to call to the attention of his or her government examples of how the public money can be more effectively spent for the benefit of the American people.

He devoted the remainder of his Chat to legislation pending before Congress. He called for the renewal of the NRA (the Supreme Court would declare it unconstitutional on May 27); passage of the Public Utility Holding Company Act, which provided for "the elimination of unnecessary holding companies in the public utility field" (a weaker law than he requested was signed into law on August 28); the strengthening of the Interstate Commerce Commission (signed into law on August 3); and most important, passage of the Banking Act of 1935, which made central banking more feasible by concentrating power in the Federal Reserve Board (signed into law on August 23).

All of these measures, he insisted, were "wise provisions for the protection of the weak against the strong."

> Never since my inauguration in March, 1933, have I felt so unmistakably the atmosphere of American recovery. But it is more than the recovery of the material basis of our individual lives. It is the recovery of confidence in our democratic processes, our republican institutions. We have survived all of the

arduous burdens and the threatening dangers of a great economic calamity. We have in the darkest moments of our national trials retained our faith in our own ability to master our own destiny. Fear is vanishing. Confidence is growing on every side, renewed faith in the vast possibilities of human beings to improve their material and spiritual status through the instrumentality of the democratic form of government. That faith is receiving its just reward. For that we can be thankful to the God who watches over America.

APRIL 29, 1935

My Dear Mr. President: —

Your inspiring talk to the Nation over the Radio of last evening prompts me to set an example in patriotism by offering my service gratis to you in whatever capacity I can be the most helpful.

I have the honor to remain

Your most obedient servant,

Walter R. Dodson
Richmond, Va.

The following poem suggested itself to me while listening to your Radio talk:

What builds a Nation great and strong,
What makes it mighty to defy,
The foes that 'round it throng?
Not gold, but only men can make
A Nation great and strong;
Men, who for truth and honor's sake,
Hold fast and suffer long;
Men who work while others sleep,
Who dare when others sigh —
They make a Nation great and strong,
And lift it to the sky.

APRIL 28, 1935

PLEASE STOP TALKING WE WANT TO HEAR SOME MUSIC.

[UNSIGNED]
LYNCHBURG, VIR.

APRIL 28, 1935

Honorable and Respected Sir: —

I have just heard what I consider a speech from you which will stand out in bold relief as one, if not the most note-worthy, of the many speeches which you have made since you assumed your present exalted office.

As a humble textile weaver, unemployed for the greater part of the past four years, at the present time in temporary employment, I beg to tender to you my thanks as a rank and file worker and citizen for the greater consideration you have given, and evident from your speech of this evening, is continuing to give, to alleviating the burden carried by those willing to work but can get no job.

A firm believer that an Almighty Creator has in the past given leaders of this nation inspiration and strength to grapple with the critical times and crises, so I believe that "thou art the man" chosen to lead us out of this slough of despondency through which we have been wallowing these many years past.

May God grant to you health, inspiration and wisdom in continuance of your good work for the welfare of the people of our country.

Yours very humbly and respectfully

William G. Ingham
Philadelphia, Penna.

APRIL 30, 1935

Dear Mr. President:

. . . The socialization of this Government worries no right thinking man and I personally feel that the only criticism which I can make is that it is not rapid enough. Drastic times demand drastic measures and in a free Government like this often drastic measures cannot be taken on account of the many ramifications of the Government in its initial set up and that created by the construction of the Courts. I do wish that the Courts were more ready to see the handwriting on the wall and join whole-heartedly with you in these efforts. . . .

Believe me to be,

Sincerely and respectfully yours,

C. T. Graydon
Columbia, S.C.

APRIL 30, 1935

Sir:

Your latest piece of glorified propaganda — miscalled fireside chats — was disheartening and sickening. I must confess, I am ashamed that I once had some faith in you and your New Deal.

Prosperity? How you mock us. There can never be any true prosperity under your administration. Nothing but a vast destruction of wealth and hope, — a degrading and demoralizing of our national character.

Why not be perfectly frank with your people just once, and admit that you are engaged in a subtle and gigantic effort to ruin the investing classes, big and little. Why not come out in the open, and declare your unalterable and all too evident purpose to usher in government ownership of all important businesses and a Socialist state.

For the hypocricy of the New Deal is revolting.

Raymond E. Click
Prospect, Ohio

* * *

Dear Sir

I listened to your speech tonight and heard all your fine words about justice.

As a Utility stockholder your sense of justice sounded rather flat. You evidently dont care one single dam about justice to the Utility stockholders as long as you can gratify your inbred hatred to the industry. It is as evident that stubborn dutch streak in your being wont be satisfied until you ruin hundreds of thousand of us. . . .

I voted for you in 1932. Ordinary I take little interest in polotics but I have a hatred for you now that exceeds any you have for the heads of the Utility industry. I swear by every fiber of my being to preach and do every thing in my power to influence people against you and there will be a million others like me.

If I cant influence 50 people I will be ashamed of myself.

Fred S. Willard
Rockville Centre, New York

MAY 3, 1935

Dear Mr. President:

Your talk last Sunday night, in my opinion, was wonderful and inspirational. It created a further feeling of confidence and I don't know what more you could have said.

This letter is prompted by the resolutions of criticism that are being adopted at Washington at the present time by the National Chamber of Commerce. When one reads them and knows the selfishness and the small caliber minds that are behind some of them, they lose weight. In reading them, I could not help but think where these giant intellectualists and captains of industry were during March and April of 1933 when the banks were popping all over the country. They were willing enough then to pass the buck to the new President. Where were they when the public utility holding companies stock dropped in some cases from $250.00 to less than $5.00 per share?

The wonderful banking fraternity did not have any solution for preventing the captains of finance from using the mails for exploiting stocks and bonds and unloading them on the public at high prices, an enormous percentage of which were absolutely worthless. And then they have the audacity to criticise an administration that is interfering with business. My dear

Mr. President, you are not interfering with business, you are interfering with road agents and bandits and every thinking man in this country knows it. . . .

Yours truly,

Thos. J. Vernia
Chicago, Illinois

P.S. Don't you think Mr. President that it would be a good idea to have your heart to heart talk to the people oftener? I attended four or five conventions of the Chamber — and know.

APRIL 29, 1935

Dear Mr. President:

In your radio address Sunday night you invited comment and criticism. Therefore I would first like to make the statement that I was not particularly impressed, nor did I find any word of encouragement to the average American citizen.

You likened the present Administration to the building of a ship, wherein no one but the builders know what the ship would look like until it was completed. This is not true. Anyone who would be sufficiently interested in the construction of an ordinary vessel, would have no difficulty in being shown the draftsman's completed work. Take the new French liner the "Normandie" as an example. Long before she was launched, the papers published photographs of the artist's conception.

Why, therefore, is it not possible for the American citizen to have your conception of the ultimate finished work in which you ask us now to place so much confidence?

Yours very truly,

F. C. Elkins
Philadelphia, Pa.

APRIL 29, 1935

My dear Mr. President:

I had great pleasure in listening to your radio talk last night and, at your suggestion, I am taking this opportunity of writing.

In the discussion of this great public works' appropriation, no one, so far as I know, has stressed the very important point that the people of the United States will be wealthier by the tangible increases in the real wealth of the Federal government, as a result of the proposed expenditures.

This great fund will not be used simply to give men work. It will give to us, the people, more highways, more Boulder Dams, more civic improvements, more bridges, more tunnels, better harbors, etc., etc.

The balance sheet of the United States of America, if such a thing could be prepared, would reflect a tremendous increase on the asset side, and the proprietary interest of each citizen (for that, after all, is what the bonds represent), will increase enormously. . . .

So few people see this. Our New England reactionaries, particularly, can not realize that as long as men are willing to work, we should put them to work. We should have brains enough to arrange our affairs so that we, the people, can have and enjoy the countless things that these very people are anxious and willing to produce.

I consider it a great privilege to be able to write to you, and I can assure you of my small but wholehearted cooperation in this great endeavor of yours. I am

Very respectfully yours,

F. W. Beinecke
Boston

APRIL 28, 1935

President Roosevelt;

I was very much disappointed in your talk over the Radio Sunday night and I believe so were thousands of other people. To begin with you said there was not much graft or red tape in the U.S. Government. If you think that I'm pretty sure you're the only educated person in the U.S. who believes that. Everyone knows there is more dirty work carried on in the government today then in any other business or profession. Men who are not statesmen but politicians that get huge salaries, do nothing but argue and call each other names, and who pays, the poor American citizen. Things may be picking up in the East but as far as the Middle West is concerned things are worse than ever and there is no use kidding ourselfves that things are improving when they're not.

Millions of dollars being spent now for temporary work for men. The minute the work is completed they are as bad off as they were before they started. It looks as if those politicians, who are being paid such immense salaries (for doing nothing) and are suppose to be such intelligent, educated men could think up something that would be permanent, without taxing the citizen to the limit and doing nothing else.

If something isn't soon done this country will reach its end and there is no use in kidding ourselves about that either.

Just an Unemployed College Girl,

Hope Adams
Tulsa, Okla.

APRIL 28, 1935

Dear Mr. President,

. . . several weeks ago I had an opportunity to visit at Washington on a week-end excursion. I spent all of Sunday, April 28th, just browsing about the federal buildings there. When I passed through several of the buildings, I became impressed with the magnitude of our government. . . .

Of course, the government is of people not buildings but anyway the structures seem to cast some kind of awe upon the average citizen. We often wonder whether all of the work that goes on in these buildings really means much or what it should to the individual American. It seems so aloof and one cannot imagine himself as a part of the government. When I looked at the physical structure of our government, I thought of the poor and downtrodden coal miners and workers back home. I recalled their plight and squalor and their loss of hope and I thought of their attitude toward their government. I couldn't help but think of what dependence they place upon their government to bolster their lives — to help them to have new hope and to gain decent livings. The hopelessness of the people during the past years is, no doubt, gradually being allayed but everything seems to be so slow.

Mr. President, I am a student at West Virginia University and my main purpose in writing to convey to you the appreciation of the many students here, who like myself have only been able to remain in school by working their way through. I refer to the F.E.R.A. work that has been carried on in our University and in other schools of the nation. Many of the students are really deserving and to many of them this work has been a godsend. True it has only been enough to pay our tuition and a little extra but it has meant very much to us. . . .

Very truly yours

William Nels
Pursglove, West Virginia

APRIL 29, 1935

Dear President: —

We listened to your chat with all of us over the air last evening and enjoyed it, you are very sincere and as you say there are many chiselers and grafters.

Just a word or two of comment.

The government has been more than generous in taking care of the unemployed and there are many of the lower class of people also some of the colored ones, who think they should have more. Dear Sir they have more than any working man who works every day but does not get enough only to pay his bills and nothing left to buy things we need so badly.

My husband is in a place to see these things they are paid so much a month, given clothes bedding food, coal etc and then they take the money for entertainment and I used to worry about it but those out of work are cared for better than we. Until the wages of the common man is raised so he can purchase the many things we need business will never be any better, we dont have it to buy with, and I'll go with out sooner than have collectors hounding the door all the time. One house dress in 3 yrs, mend, patch, and fix it sure gets tiresome. We need new mattresses clothes floor coverings bedding. . . .

Employers just want to pocket the money and make one work for a pittance.

Excuse my long letter but you are so sincere in your talk I just wanted to tell you where one trouble is. Best wishes and much good health be yours and I hope you can live to fulfill all your hopes —

Yours truly,

Mrs. H. A. Thompson
Cedar Rapids, Iowa

APRIL 27, 1935

Sir

Your talk over the radio Sunday night, plainly shows your complete ignorance as to present conditions, in other words, you say that you are dealing out that enormous sum of money, borrowed to finance the Work Relief Bill, to the most irresponsible, lazy, dishonest and shiftless group of people in the U.S.A.

The people who have the decency and pride to get along without relief, even though they have had to go far in debt and even loose the roof over their head, will get no help or consideration. I refer to the taxpayers, principly, and to the old people, who will never be able to regain their great loss, while the lowest, possibly the least deserving element among our people get help.

For God's sake, I beg of you, consider what you do.

Very Truly Yours,

(Mrs.) Laura Manning
Pleasantville, N.J.

APRIL 29, 1935

Dear Sir,

After I had listened to you talk over the Raido, I had to just relax and rejoice in how wounderful you have brought the present conditions about, at the beginning of your work I did not think it was possible, but thank God and our President we have learned that all things are possible. . . . I have ben living on Relief my self for nearly a year now, and do not know what I would have done if it had not ben for the Relief. I was a merchant here for years, But went down to the Bottom in the depression just finishing up a year ago. I am not to good to work and am very grateful to think I am going to have a chance to earn my living in an honist way and by the swet of my Brow, in my last days, I was just about at the point to become discouraged as living on Relief and too old to get a job in Factorys or other industries any more, I had begun to think I was doomed. But God will Bless you Mr. Roosevelt for what you are trying to do, and that all things will work out for the best, and myself a small mind, doing things in a small way, you have my support heart and sole as one American citizen.

from

Mr. Archie Tickner
Waukegan, Ill.

APRIL 30, 1935

My dear Mr. President:

. . . Your Social Security program seems a most important step for a great betterment and spiritual advancement of our citizens. In this connection, may I mention for your consideration that, whatever old age pensions are given it be done in the spirit and on conditions that the recipients are ENTITLED to it and not given to them as mendicants. Why entitled, you may ask. Because, at the age reached, the average person has contributed a life work to the sum total of labor and wealth of the country. . . . Age gathers wisdom that the country needs disseminated among its people, tho it could not be if smothered under the belief of being a beggar in order to get a limited sustenance. Whether entitled or not, if given at all and it will be in some way, citizens receiving that benefit may as well be blessed with an uplift as to be made to feel degraded.

Very respectfully yours,

John M. Russ
Jacksonville, Florida

APRIL 30, 1935

Our Beloved President that God has placed over our own United States,

In your address over the Radio Sun. night you said anyone that had in mind any plan that might be of a benefit in their estimation in the management of the problems of today, you wanted them to feel free to write in, therefore I take advantage of the opertunity.

A year ago the Lord Layed it upon my heart to write you but I let the Devil talk me out of sending it. But this time I am sending it through. . . .

If you could bring about a three day fasting and prayer Service and get the Faith of the people as you do in other affairs, you would save more Souls for the Glory of God in three day than all the preachers in the United states in three years and, by that much food supply would be gained and all would be stronger at the end of the three day than they were the first, you try it and see.

From a Friend who believes in Prayer and the Power of God.

Mrs. Nellie Loch
Enid, Oklahoma

APRIL 30, 1935

I listened to you Sunday and believe you want to do the right thang. I relize you are the head & ruler of our cuntry you can govern for the good, or the eavle you can make thangs better or worse. By the help of our creator you can get help & knowledge to make thangs better. . . . I am a farmer live 23 miles back from town have famly of 10 children. I want to see you rule for the good. your friend & suporter

S. A. Allsup
Wilson, Texas

1. Crop & Seed Loan
Loan a man enough to by seed, and run him, and give him 4 years to pay same.

2. All Foods
Dont destroy any food at all. Lay up in store.

3. Relief

Let the relief run same There is as well qualified men & women on relief as run same That will do away with creads [?].

4. Cotton

Pass a law to restrect any from planting but one half of crop in cotton. If it take a vote we will vote it on. We are not babes, have to be paid to do right.

5. Law

Pass a law that USA dont protect no mans welth out of our cuntry.

6. Insurance

Let a man pay one cent on every dollar paid to any insurance company. Let company pay same. This will pay the ex soldiers.

7. Tax

Put a special tax on all new cars $5 motersckle $2 yats $20 Privet Plaines $10

Let suport relief

8. Special Tax

Silks Face lotions & Powders One cent on the dollar Silk Hose $100. be $101 yard goods To suport old people relief.

"AN ORDERLY ECONOMIC DEMOCRACY": SEPTEMBER 6, 1936

FDR WAITED UNTIL EIGHT WEEKS before the presidential election of 1936 to deliver his next Fireside Chat. More than sixteen months had elapsed since his last Chat, the longest he was ever to go without directly addressing the American people over the radio. In the interim, the century's worst drought, which had begun in the Great Plains in 1934, returned in 1936 to hold much of agrarian America from Texas to the Dakotas in its grip. At its worst, the drought displaced more than one million Southwestern tenant farmers — who came to be known collectively as Okies, though they came not only from Oklahoma but such states as Arkansas, Missouri, and Texas. The sense of bewilderment and frustration with which many of these tenants greeted their plight mirrored the spirit that had pervaded much of America when Roosevelt first took office. In *The Grapes of Wrath* (1939), John Steinbeck captured the sense of confusion and impotent anger that characterized so much of Depression America, as in the following dialogue between an outraged Oklahoma tenant farmer dispossessed from the land he and his father and grandfather had farmed and the tractor driver sent to knock down his house and fences:

> "[This house] is mine. I built it. You bump it down — I'll be in the window with a rifle. You even come too close and I'll pot you like a rabbit."
>
> "It's not me. There's nothing I can do. I'll lose my job if I don't do it. And look — suppose you kill me? They'll just hang you, but long before you're hung there'll be another guy on the tractor, and he'll bump the house down. You're not killing the right guy."
>
> "That's so," the tenant said. "Who gave you orders? I'll go after him. He's the one to kill."
>
> "You're wrong. He got his orders from the bank. The bank told him, 'Clear those people out or it's your job.'"
>
> "Well, there's a president of the bank. There's a board of di-

rectors. I'll fill up the magazine of the rifle and go into the
bank."

The driver said, "Fellow was telling me the bank gets orders
from the East. The orders were, 'Make the land show profit or
we'll close you up.' "

"But where does it stop? Who can we shoot? I don't aim to
starve to death before I kill the man that's starving me."

"I don't know. Maybe there's nobody to shoot. Maybe the
thing isn't men at all . . ."[54]

FDR was more upbeat, less prone to explore questions of ultimate exis-
tential responsibility, and more inclined to use his political power to find
solutions for those farmers who owned the land they were suffering on than
for tenants and sharecroppers who did not own their own land. He began
his eighth Fireside Chat by recounting his recent trip through nine agricultural states to inspect the results of the drought.[55]

> I talked with families who had lost their wheat crop, lost
> their corn crop, lost their livestock, lost the water in their well,
> lost their garden and come through to the end of the summer
> without one dollar of cash resources, facing a winter without
> feed or food — facing a planting season without seed to put in
> the ground.

He spoke also of those farm families who had not lost everything but who
needed help to supplement their partial crops if they were to be able to continue farming in the spring. But he seemed haunted by the extreme scenes
of want he had witnessed:

> I shall never forget the fields of wheat so blasted by heat that
> they cannot be harvested. I shall never forget field after field of
> corn stunted, earless, stripped of leaves, for what the sun left
> the grasshoppers took. I saw brown pastures that would not
> keep a cow on fifty acres.

He took care not to let this litany of disaster become a litany of despair:

> No cracked earth, no blistering sun, no burning wind, no grass-
> hoppers, are a permanent match for the indomitable American
> farmers and stockmen and their wives and children who have

carried on through desperate days, and inspire us with their self-reliance, their tenacity and their courage. It was their fathers' task to make homes; it is their task to keep these homes; and it is our task to help them win their fight.

The choice for farm families "who need actual subsistence" was to put them on the dole or to put them to work. "They do not want to go on the dole and they are one thousand percent right. We agree, therefore, that we must put them to work, work for a decent wage." This would allow farmers to buy food for their stock and seed for next year's planting and thus to remain farmers in the future. The work supplied to those farmers needing help would be "directly aimed at the alleviation of future drought conditions" — projects that would mitigate future water shortages and soil erosion, projects that would build roads to markets. "Spending like this is not waste. It would spell future waste if we did not spend for such things now."

Underlying his Chat was a didactic message that FDR had stressed since the establishment of the Tennessee Valley Authority in 1933: the interdependence of every group of people and every geographical area in the nation:

Every state in the drought area is now doing and always will do business with every state outside it. The very existence of the men and women working in the clothing factories of New York, making clothes worn by farmers and their families; of the workers in the steel mills in Pittsburgh and Gary, in the automobile factories of Detroit, and in the harvester factories of Illinois, depend upon the farmers' ability to purchase the commodities that they produce. In the same way it is the purchasing power of the workers in these factories in the cities that enables them and their wives and children to eat more beef, more pork, more wheat, more corn, more fruit and more dairy products, and to buy more clothing made from cotton and wool and leather. In a physical and in a property sense, as well as in a spiritual sense, we are members one of another.

This interdependence did not mean dependence. "The people in the drought area do not want to be dependent on Federal or state or any other kind of charity. They want for themselves and their families an opportunity to share fairly by their own efforts in the progress of America." Nevertheless, there was need for a sound national agricultural policy — implemented by the federal, state, and local governments — which would create a permanent land use program, would maintain farm prices in times of drought and times of bumper crops, would maintain a fair equilibrium between farm prices and the prices of industrial products, and would devise a means of guaranteeing sufficient food supplies in good years and lean years.

He admitted that when the drought began in 1934 "none of us had preparation; we worked without blue prints and we made the mistakes of inexperience. . . . But as time has gone on we have been making fewer and fewer mistakes." For FDR, responses to the drought illustrated what he considered to be two of the pillars of his Administration. First, to prevent the growth of a Leviathan state, the administration of New Deal policies should be kept as local as possible. "Remember that the Federal and state governments have done only broad planning. Actual work on a given project originates in the local community. Local needs are listed from local information. Local projects are decided on only after obtaining the recommendations and the help of those in the local community who are best able to give it." Second, he stressed experimentation and pragmatic responsiveness to the specific needs of a given situation:

> In the drought area people are not afraid to use new methods to meet changes in Nature, and to correct mistakes of the past. If over-grazing has injured range lands, they are willing to reduce the grazing. If certain wheat lands should be returned to pasture, they are willing to cooperate. If trees should be planted as windbreaks or to stop erosion, they will work with us. If terracing or summer fallowing or crop rotation is called for, they will carry them out. They stand ready to fit, not to fight, the ways of Nature.*

Turning to the problem of industrial employment, FDR praised "the brave spirit with which so many millions of working people are winning their way out of depression." Dependable employment at fair wages was the city and town equivalent to good farm income. He announced that "re-

---

*Although the drought was one of FDR's two major themes in this address, we have been able to find only two letters responding to this Fireside Chat that refer to the drought.

employment in industry is proceeding fairly rapidly" and pointed to government spending as the reason. "Government orders were the backlog of heavy industry; government wages turned over and over again to make consumer purchasing power and to sustain every merchant in the community. Businessmen with their businesses, small and large, had to be saved." Private enterprise was necessary to maintain democracy, and by saving business the government had saved private enterprise no less than it had saved drought-stricken farmers. It was now the "deep responsibility" of businessmen "to take men off the relief rolls and give them jobs in private enterprise." The United States Employment Service, established in 1933, was available to enable business to find workers with the skills they needed and workers to find jobs they were qualified for. Government relief programs like the Works Progress Administration (WPA) and the Public Works Administration (PWA) would continue "until all workers have decent jobs in private employment at decent wages. We do not surrender our responsibility to the unemployed." Still, it was the New Deal's intention "to use every resource to get private work for those now employed on government work, and thus to curtail to a minimum the government expenditures for direct employment."

"Tomorrow is Labor Day," he reminded his listeners:

> Labor Day in this country has never been a class holiday. It has always been a national holiday. . . . In this country we insist, as an essential of the American way of life, that the employer-employee relationship should be one between free men and equals. We refuse to regard those who work with hand or brain as different from or inferior to those who live from their own property. We insist that labor is entitled to as much respect as property. But our workers with hand and brain deserve more than respect for their labor. They deserve practical protection in the opportunity to use their labor at a return adequate to support them at a decent and constantly rising standard of living, and to accumulate a margin of security against the inevitable vicissitudes of life.

It was those who "would try to refuse the worker any effective power to bargain collectively, to earn a decent livelihood and to acquire security . . . who threaten this country with that class dissension which in other countries has led to dictatorship."

He concluded by emphasizing the need to build "an orderly economic democracy in which all can profit and in which all can be secure from the kind of faulty economic direction which brought us to the brink of common ruin seven years ago."

The Fourth of July commemorates our political freedom — a freedom which without economic freedom is meaningless indeed. Labor Day symbolizes our determination to achieve an economic freedom for the average man which will give his political freedom reality.

SEPTEMBER 7, 1936

Dear President Roosevelt,

We listened with great interest to your "fireside chat" last evening, and are in accord with your plans and ambitions for the Farmer and the less fortunate of our people in this United States.

The fact that you go about and observe personally and take the keen interest and have the intelligence to know how to correct the evils which exist, make you the outstanding President of all History. It is such a relief to hear about human beings and natural resources, and not "gold" & "statistics" by the yard.

I am one former Republican who has voted for you, and been your most devout follower. Your indomitable courage; your never finding any problem insurmountable is a guiding spirit to this nation;

We must win next November — and you will!

Most Sincerely yours

Gertrude Irene Falk
Waltham, Massachusetts

SEPTEMBER 6, 1936

Your Excellency: —

Just heard your wonderful speech in which you made yourself another 1,000,000 Votes. One of the very best you ever made. Also it came over fine all was perfect including the local weather. Thot you would like to know of this. Kindly excuse pencil.

Sincerely Yours,

Leo Weiler
El Paso, Tex.

SEPTEMBER 6, 1936

SPEECH TOUCHED WITH THE THRILL OF GREATNESS. NO LEADER IN EU-
ROPE WOULD HAVE MADE IT; NONE IN AMERICA COULD HAVE MADE IT. UT-

TERLY UNMARKED BY PARTISANSHIP IT MADE ALL WHO HEARD IT YOUR
PARTISANS.·. . . AFFECTIONATELY.

HERBERT BAYARD SWOPE
PORT WASHINGTON, N.Y.

SEPTEMBER 7, 1936

My Dear President —

My President I together with an elderly friend of Yours and Mine — listened to Your Radio speech over Radio Station W.B.B.M. and We thoroughly approve Your program of spending federal money in Your effort to
bring about better times but Industry is not doing Their part therefore I put
the blame on Industry for prolonging recovery but I believe You will succeed regardless of their policy on hinderance they blamed the N.R.A. for
retarding recovery but soon as the Supreme Court declared the N.R.A. Ille-
gal They cut wages & lengthened working hours so I predict you will be
elected President again I voted for You in 1932 and do not regret it and am
going to vote for You again in November and hope You can find some way
to induce or force industry to do their part

I lost My Job at Stewart-Warner factory after 6 years of continous work
in 1929 and was idle untill you gave Me a Chance Oct - 29 - 35 on the
W.P.A. And am still working and thanks to You but the wages of $55.00 per
month do not seam to be hardly enough for prices of food and clothing are
mounting in price right along and it is pretty hard for a family of 5 or 6 or
more get along without going into debt but even as it is it is better than direct relief count on Me in November

Respectively,

E. L. Emerson
Chicago, Ill.

SEPTEMBER 7, 1936

Dear Friend:

We listen in to your fire side address yesterday and it was wonderful. I
am sure that you made friends amongst the thousands of listener. you deliv-

ered a constructive address and you didn't abuse republican. I think the public appreciate listening to good constructive addresses.

I attended a movie theatre patronized by the poorest people. They showed new reel of one of Coughlin meeting. The audience remained silence during the Coughlin address. One person tried to get the people to applause but he couldn't get a response.

I listen to the Richfield new commentator and he claimed there were 46000 straw ballots voted in Washington, Oregon and California. He gave you 10,000 more votes than the combine candidates. The labor day parade here was the largest in the history of L.A. The marcher yell your name throughout the parade.

Wishing you and your family the best of health.

Yours very truly

Homer C. Allison
Los Angeles, California

SEPTEMBER 6, 1936

Dear Sir:

Just a few minutes ago, you finished your Fireside Chat. From the time I learned that it was scheduled, I have been looking forward to what you would have to say. After your recent trip over this part of the country, I felt you would talk on subjects which are very close to me and mine: the wonderful things you said leaves me without adequate words to express my opinion of your tonight's talk.

May I introduce myself. Indiana is my home state. I spent my entire life here up to the time that I came out of college and went to Washington, D.C. to seek — and find — employment in January 1935. From that time until just last Friday, I have lived in Washington. I am employed in the Resettlement Administration, and effective 9-8-36 I have been transferred from the Administrator's Office in Washington to the Audit Division here in Indianapolis. I am just 22 years old — I cast my first vote this year. . . .

I daily gain inspiration in my work in the Resettlement Administration from the thought that I am playing a small part in your effort to establish a fuller life for the citizens of our great Country. I sincerely believe that in years to come, I shall point to the pages in a history book covering this period and your work and proudly say: "I was a part of that — he was MY BOSS!"

May God bless and strengthen you for the work you are doing and will continue to do for the benefit of us all.

Respectfully yours,

J. Murray Parker
Indianapolis, Ind.

SEPTEMBER 9, 1936

My Dear Mr. President,

Listened to your talk Sunday night. It was an address quite worthy of you and should create new courage in the down-hearted and remind them that they have at least one friend in this rather selfish-laden world of ours. Having never taken up your time before, as I know 24 hours aren't enough to perform your many duties, am prompted to do so because of a personal collision with what I think is a very short-sighted attitude of corporate business.

Am 39 year of age, and therein lies the tragedy. Was just old enough to be in the army six months. Have a college degree in Civil Engineering, and some 18 years experience in the oil business, in geological and land department work. Entered oil company work with Senator Guffy's company in Oklahoma in 1918. Later was in the oil business for myself till that "mild Hoover boom" wiped me out. Worked in the topographic division of the U.S.G.S. [United States Geological Survey] from Nov. 1933 to June 1935, being paid out of PWA funds, for which employment, I'll always be most grateful to you. In July 1935 started to work for a large oil company at a low-paying job considering my experience. On Jan. 1, 1936 changed companies to get a little better paying job. Now, after 8 months of work, of which they were quite lavish in their praise, and only offered minor criticisms, they "resign" me despite the fact, that the corporation is showing a profit for the first time in several years, and tell me that there is no hope of any further work there, as when that position is re-filled, it will be with a younger man. The man firing me intimated that insurance rates and pension rules influence this tendency toward younger help. Friends of mine say 40 is almost a deadline, which prevents entrance into company employment.

It appears that I will have to create my own job, or become an "odd-job" man. With so many people unemployed, the employers have a tremendous advantage and do not hesitate to use it. The golden rule has been suspended for some time. If there were no labor unions, I'd hesitate to predict the wage levels.

It is rather difficult to enter on a business venture of your own today due to the tremendous competition from corporations, that can operate at a loss more than half the time and still stay in business. There is no lack of confidence among people today, as I see it, but a fear of competition from entrenched corporate wealth, which has never hesitated to be just as ruthless as necessary to hold their ground.

These same corporations also showed this same short-sightedness in using so much machinery and eliminating man-power faster than new uses of labor could absorb it. Reminds me of a man trying to eat three beefsteaks a meal, when one is all he can digest.

The management of this corporation as well as others, constitute your chief opposition to-day, as to both recovery and you re-election, showing absolutely no gratitude for your efforts in their behalf. Rich men aren't always smart. Their selfishness often consumes them.

I appreciate your efforts in behalf of humanity and you have my wholehearted support.

Sincerely,

Tell T. White
Tulsa, Oklahoma

SEPTEMBER 6, 1936

Dear President Roosevelt: I listened with great interest to your address from the White House, to-night (E.S.T. 9:45 p.m.) and agree with every word of your plan with reference to employment of drought stricken farmers, and the employment of persons living in town and cities — and the general welfare.

One trouble confronting many is the age limit placed upon workers, no matter what their ability may be, no matter how needy they may be, by industry, and the government, may I say as well — and I feel that you would correct that situation, if possible, and I am writing in the spirit of Constructive Criticism, no person with any ambition, possessing at least, some pride wants to go on Charity or government Relief.

The idea of refusing employment to capable persons who are more than 40 years of age is all wrong, as you know, and will bring its own just reward, in just what way I do not know. Women over 25 or 30 not wanted — I refer to stores factories, etc. I hope every one in this country heard your remarks, and will profit by them.

You have my thanks, and appreciation — and congratulations.

Certainly my support and sincere Congratulations,

Very Respectfully,

Ralph E. Race
[illegible], O.

SEPTEMBER 6, 1936

My Dear Mr. President. —

I have long wanted to write you a note of thanks and appreciation. —

I so enjoyed your talk tonight, the sound of your voice gives one so much courage I hope and pray you are our President for the next-term. When I look back & allow my thought to dwell on the condition that this country was in when you first took office, I think every Americian should thank God that we had a man like you to bring us out of these terrible times. All during your term of office as our President I have felt you were the right man in the right place. A man who loved his Maker & loved his fellow creatures.

Moses was choosen by God to lead the children of Isarel out of bondage. —

I also know that God the God of love was working in the Americian people when they choose you in 1932 to lead them out of these terrible times. —

To day we need more love in our hearts towards God & our fellow man, more gratitude towards those who are trying to make this a better world to live in. —

"If a man is not thinking about himself he is himself," no great man ever yet lived for himself alone.

Yours gratefully,

Mrs Wm. Semple
Cleveland, Ohio

SEPTEMBER 6-7-8, 1936

My Dear President Roosevelt:

After your talk tonight this thought came to me, "Let your light so shine that men may see your good works and glorify our father which is in heaven." In this world of ours we can not ignore the great problems that confront us each day and so we pledge our selves anew to the task of demonstrating the brotherhood of man.

You remember how Jesus went about teaching the people; He didn't do much preaching He walked among them and spoke as one having authority. when you go among the people, they have the joy of seeing you and hearing you say just what the Federal Government can and will do.

That harmony and peace for which I have been praying and working is coming here and now and I know your burden is much lighter for "where there is peace there is God."

I am wearing three out-ward signs for you. First a little gold cross that my father wore from birth, he was born an Episcopalian. A stirling silver ring on the third finger of my right hand made by my daughter of Hyde Park High School in Chicago and a handpainted medallion broach, which I painted in 1931 after the snap shot was taken; there are two roses with folage painted on the pin. Each article plays its part in your re-election. I have worn them all constantly.

Faithfully,

Margaret H. Moore
Normal, Illinois

PART TWO

THE CONTINUING CRISIS: 1937–1938

. . . constantly I seek to look beyond the doors of the White House, beyond the officialdom of the national capital, into the hopes and fears of men and women in their homes. . . . My friends, my enemies, my daily mail, bring to me reports of what you are thinking and hoping. I want to be sure that neither battles nor burdens of office shall ever blind me to an intimate knowledge of the way the American people want to live and the simple purposes for which they put me here.

FDR, Fireside Chat, April 14, 1938

Our only means of expression is a ballot and a three cent stamp.

Anthony N. Rodrigues, Springfield, Massachusetts, to FDR, March 9, 1937

"PACKING"
THE SUPREME COURT:
MARCH 9, 1937

"ROOSEVELT IS THE ONLY PRESIDENT we ever had that thought the Constitution belonged to the pore man too," George Dobbin, a recently unemployed sixty-eight-year-old Southern millworker, proclaimed during FDR's second term of office. "The way they've been areadin' it it seemed like they thought it said, 'Him that's got money shall have the rights to life, freedom and happiness.' . . . Yessir, it took Roosevelt to read in the Constitution and find out them folks way back yonder that made it was talkin' about the pore man right along with the rich one. I am a Roosevelt man."[1]

There were, as the elections of 1936 demonstrated, a great many Roosevelt men and women — enough to give Roosevelt one of the most lopsided victories in the history of the American presidency. He received almost five million more votes than he had in 1932, winning 60.8 percent of the popular vote and 523 of the 531 electoral votes — only Maine and Vermont went to his opponent, Governor Alfred M. Landon of Kansas. The already swollen Democratic majorities in Congress increased, with Democrats winning 331 House seats to the Republicans' 89 and controlling 76 of the Senate seats to the Republicans' 16. When Alf Landon was asked how his defeat felt he told the story of the Kansas farmer who watches a tornado engulf first his barn, then his out buildings, then his home, reducing them to splinters, and begins to laugh. "What are you laughing at, you darned old fool?" his wife asks him. "The completeness of it," her husband replies.[2]

If FDR had been similarly tempted to mirth at the completeness of his own political tornado in 1936, he would have laughed too soon. As it turned out, his victory was not quite as complete as it appeared. In the light of George Dobbin's praise for Roosevelt's constitutional acumen, it is ironic that FDR's most stunning electoral victory preceded by only several months what was undoubtedly his most striking political blunder: he gave the appearance, to millions of foes and supporters alike, of placing himself above the Constitution. The problem was that FDR's successes at the polls and in Congress were not duplicated in the federal courts. From the beginning of his presidency, FDR worried that the conservative Republican composition of the Supreme Court was a potential threat to the reform legislation that he deemed necessary to bring the nation out of the crisis. He himself believed, as he had proclaimed pointedly in his First Inaugural Address, that the Constitution was "so simple and practical" that it was entirely feasible "to meet the extraordinary needs" imposed by the Depression "under the form of government which we have inherited from our ancestors."[3]

On what came to be called "Black Monday," May 27, 1935, FDR's worst fears were realized: the Court in three unanimous decisions found against the New Deal, most importantly invalidating the National Recovery Administration. During his press conference four days later, Roosevelt, reading from a pile of telegrams sent by panicked businessmen pleading with him to take some action to revive the NRA, referred to the Court's "horse-and-buggy definition of interstate commerce" and spoke about what he called "the very great national non-partisan issue . . . whether we are going to relegate to the forty-eight States practically all control over economic conditions — not only State economic conditions but national economic conditions; and . . . social and working conditions throughout the country," or restore to the United States government "the powers which exist in the national governments of every other Nation in the world to enact and administer laws that have a bearing on, and general control over, national economic problems and national social problems." It was, he insisted, "the biggest question that has come before this country outside of time of war, and it has to be decided." "We are the only Nation in the world that has not solved that problem," he told the assembled reporters. "We thought we were solving it, and now it has been thrown right straight in our faces."[4]

Following the press conference, Roosevelt maintained a public silence regarding the Court, but in private he continued to express his fears. After a Cabinet meeting in December, Secretary of the Interior Harold Ickes noted in his diary: "Clearly, it is running in the President's mind that substantially all of the New Deal bills will be declared unconstitutional by the Supreme Court. This will mean that everything that this Administration has done of any moment will be nullified."[5] On January 6, 1936, the Court by a vote of six to three overturned the AAA, depriving farmers of billions of dollars in benefits. The previous August FDR had told a member of his Administration: "If the Court does send the AAA flying like the NRA there might even be a revolution."[6]

While bullets did not fly, words certainly did. Throughout all the turmoil, the President maintained his public silence, though he continued to explore with his Attorney General and others means of reforming the Court. Hopes were raised in February when the Court validated the right of the Tennessee Valley Authority to distribute power generated by the Wilson Dam, then were dashed in the spring by a series of decisions striking down several pieces of New Deal legislation and overturning the New York State minimum wage law. "The sacred right of liberty of contract again — the right of an immature child or a helpless woman to drive a bargain with a great corporation," Secretary Ickes fulminated in his diary. "This is positively medieval, and I am frank to say that if this decision is constitutional, we need either an entirely new or a radically amended Constitution. If it isn't constitutional, then we need a different Supreme Court."[7]

The President was increasingly reaching the latter conclusion: that the problem lay not in the Constitution but in the Supreme Court. On June 2 he spoke of the creation by the Court of a " 'no-man's-land' where no Government — State or Federal — can function," but refused a reporter's invitation to say what should be done about it.[8] While the 1936 Democratic platform called vaguely for an amendment if the constitutional problem could not be solved by legislation, FDR, though clearly worried that such reforms as the Social Security Act and the National Labor Relations Act as well as his relief agencies and such regulatory bodies as the Securities and Exchange Commission were in jeopardy, remained silent on the issue throughout the 1936 campaign. Once reelected, he turned his full attention to the Supreme Court. At his first postelection Cabinet meeting, he referred to the fact that the present Court was the most aged one in our history, with six judges over 70, remarking that he expected the arch-conservative Justice James C. McReynolds to still be on the bench when he was 105, to which his Solicitor General laughingly responded that McReynolds appeared to be in the best possible health. FDR resented the fact that he was the first President in American history to go through a full term without having an appointment to the Supreme Court and had suffered more severe defeats at the Court's hands than any of his predecessors. As far as he was concerned, the Court already was packed — with elderly conservative Republican Justices who, he was convinced, clung to their places "to block our social and economic progress." He now sought to remedy that situation.[9]

Throughout these months, there was a sense of growing anxiety. According to the future Supreme Court Justice Robert H. Jackson, the problem plaguing the New Deal was that if the Court continued to make it impossible for a popularly elected government to regulate capitalism, anarchy and ultimately revolution seemed inevitable.[10] Roosevelt was convinced that democracies abroad were "yielding place to dictatorships because they had proven too weak or too slow to fulfill the wants of their citizens."[11] In his Annual Message to Congress on January 6, 1937, Roosevelt invited the Supreme Court to join him and the Congress in the attack upon the Depression and advised it that "the process of our democracy must not be imperiled by the denial of essential powers of free government." He added pointedly that cooperation could only be based upon "mutual respect for each other's proper sphere of functioning in a democracy."[12] But FDR was not about to wait for the Court to reform itself. His fear that the potentially excrutiatingly slow process of amending the Constitution would squander precious time needed to combat the Depression, and the great popularity he enjoyed following his extraordinary electoral victory emboldened him to attempt a legislative solution.

The notion of appointing enough new Justices to the Court to alter its spirit of constitutional fundamentalism had been discussed since 1935 and was advocated by Attorney General Homer Cummings. The bill crafted by Cummings and Roosevelt, without consulting other members of the Cabinet or of Congress, was cast as a general reform of the federal judiciary, with its extremely crowded dockets and need for greater efficiency. The main provisions of the judiciary reorganization bill FDR submitted to Congress on February 5, 1937, provided that when a judge of a federal court who had served ten years or more did not resign or retire within six months after his seventieth birthday, the President might name an additional judge to the court, but in no case should the Supreme Court have more than six added Justices nor any lower federal court more than two.[13]

The instant furor this proposal generated is demonstrated by the letters below.[14] In spite of the deep divisions in the country, at the outset it was taken for granted that the President, with his control of both Houses, would prevail. But it was not to be. Although the number of Supreme Court Justices was set by legislation and not by the Constitution and had varied — with six in 1789, five in 1801, seven in 1807, nine in 1837, ten in 1863, eight in 1866, and nine in 1869 — it seemed impossible to shake the deeply ingrained belief that nine Justices had been the norm from the beginning and that in changing the number FDR was tampering with sacred tradition. Polls taken throughout the period of contestation over Roosevelt's plan showed a consistently negative majority. In May, a Gallup poll found 54 percent opposed, and by September less than one voter in three thought FDR should continue his effort to enlarge the Court.[15]

Paradoxically, this was in part the result of the fact that while Roosevelt was losing the battle he was winning the larger war, which in the eyes of many rendered his proposal less and less necessary. FDR's Court-packing threat stimulated one crucial swing vote — that of Justice Owen Roberts — to change direction, and in a series of decisions in the spring of 1937, the Court validated the Social Security Act and the Wagner Labor Relations Act and reversed its recent decision against a minimum wage law in New York by upholding a similar law in the state of Washington. One wry comment summed up the Court's reversal: "A switch in time saved nine."[16] At the same time, Willis Van Devanter, one of the more conservative Justices, announced his retirement, allowing FDR to make his first appointment to the Court — he was ultimately to make eight — and change its balance and its approach so that no New Deal statute was found unconstitutional for the remainder of his presidency.

While Roosevelt's Court plan did help to initiate what William Leuchtenburg and other scholars have called "the Constitutional Revolution of 1937," resulting in a Court that took a much broader view of the powers of the central government to regulate business and dispense social welfare, the President did pay a political price.[17] As the letters below also demonstrate, he disillusioned and bewildered significant numbers of his constituents. More than that, he helped consolidate a coalition of conservatives in both parties destined to frustrate many of his future reform attempts, and the constitutional debate with its fear of encroaching presidential power worked to undermine the remarkable pragmatic acceptance of the New Deal that had marked FDR's first term. Nevertheless, until the final defeat, FDR remained convinced that his Court plan was essential for the effective functioning and even the survival of democracy, and he fought for his doomed bill with all of his formidable powers. "The President felt very confident — almost 'cocky' — that he could win, and was in no mood for compromise," his speechwriter and friend Sam Rosenman commented.[18] Though FDR was apprised of the content of the huge number of letters he received on the Court issue, the majority of which supported him, had he paid closer attention to the *tone* of that flood of letters, his mood might have altered.

On March 4, he addressed a Democratic Victory Dinner in Washington's Mayflower Hotel and roused his large audience by making it clear why the nation could not afford the impasse imposed by the Court:

> Here is one-third of a Nation ill-nourished, ill-clad, ill-housed — NOW!
> Here are thousands upon thousands of farmers wondering whether next year's prices will meet their mortgage interest — NOW!
> Here are thousands upon thousands of men and women laboring for long hours in factories for inadequate pay — NOW!
> Here are thousands upon thousands of children who should be at school, working in mines and mills — NOW!
> Here are strikes more far-reaching than we have ever known, costing millions of dollars — NOW!
> Here are Spring floods threatening to roll again down our river valleys — NOW!
> Here is the Dust Bowl beginning to blow again — NOW!
> If we would keep faith with those who had faith in us, if we would make democracy succeed, I say we must act — NOW![19]

Five days later, FDR took his case to the American people in his first Fireside Chat since his reelection.[20] He reminded his listeners of the conditions that prevailed when he had taken office just four years earlier. "In 1933 you and I knew that we must never let our economic system get completely out of joint again . . . that the only way to avoid a repetition of those dark days was to have a government with power to prevent and to cure the abuses and the inequalities which had thrown that system out of joint." The Court, however, has "cast doubt on the ability of the elected Congress to protect us against catastrophe by meeting squarely our modern social and economic conditions."

> We are at a crisis, a crisis in our ability to proceed with that protection. It is a quiet crisis. There are not lines of depositors outside closed banks. But to the far-sighted it is far-reaching in its possibilities of injury to America.

He repeated the homey metaphor he had used in his Mayflower Hotel speech calling the U.S. government "a three-horse team . . . the Congress, the Executive and the Courts. Two of the horses, the Congress and the Executive, are pulling in unison today; the third is not."

When the Congress has sought to stabilize national agriculture, to improve the conditions of labor, to safeguard business against unfair competition, to protect our national resources, and in many other ways to serve our clearly national needs, the majority of the Court has been assuming the power to pass on the wisdom of these Acts of the Congress — and to approve or disapprove the public policy written into these laws.

The Supreme Court, he charged, "has improperly set itself up as a third House of the Congress."

We have, therefore, reached the point as a Nation where we must take action to save the Constitution from the Court and the Court from itself. We must find a way to take an appeal from the Supreme Court to the Constitution itself. We want a Supreme Court which will do justice under the Constitution and not over it. In our Courts we want a government of laws and not of men.

In this Chat, as well as in earlier pronouncements, FDR committed what he himself later thought was a blunder by stressing not only policy but age — which older Americans, in and out of Congress, resented and which many of all ages thought disingenuous. He praised his plan as a system that would bring into the judiciary "a steady and continuing stream of new and younger blood, . . . younger men who have had personal experience and contact with modern facts and circumstances," thus saving "our national Constitution from hardening of the judicial arteries." He went out of his way to inform his listeners that Supreme Court Justices could retire on the generous pension of $20,000 a year for life. He struck an uncharacteristic defensive note in his refutation of the charge of "packing" the Court, invoking his record as Governor and President, which had proved his "devotion" to liberty. "You who know me can have no fear that I would tolerate the destruction by any branch of government of any part of our heritage of freedom." He explained in detail why a constitutional amendment would not solve the problem. There was vast disagreement on what kind of amendment was needed and the process of amending the Constitution was too cumbersome to meet the nation's current needs:

No amendment which any powerful economic interests or the leaders of any powerful political party have had reason to oppose has ever been ratified within anything like a reasonable time. And remember that thirteen states which contain only five percent of the voting population can block ratification even though the thirty-five states with ninety-five percent of the population are in favor of it.

He concluded by invoking the Constitution itself:

During the past half century the balance of power between the three great branches of the Federal Government has been tipped out of balance by the Courts in direct contradiction of the high purposes of the framers of the Constitution. It is my purpose to restore that balance. You who know me will accept my solemn assurance that in a world in which democracy is under attack, I seek to make American democracy succeed. You and I will do our part.

MARCH 13, 1937

Respected President: I have written both of our Iowa Senators urging them to oppose you in your effort to bend and shape the Supreme Court to your liking and thus in the future if not at once make it possible for a president and a Congress to pass any law that appealed to their ideas — The very Supreme Court and Constitution that makes it possible for me as a citizen to write and urge you to Stop — Look — Listen is the very Court and Constitution that you with your fine mind but human seem determined to undermine —

I love my freedom and realize that did I live in Russia, Spain, Italy or many another country where the court is subservient to the ruler that this frank yet respectful letter would probably mean the loss of my physical freedom if not worse —

I along with 99% of the Iowans who voted for you did not give you a mandate to change the Constitution or Supreme Court — You have made a wonderful record for yourself as President and I am urging our Iowa representatives to save you from yourself in this crisis. . . .

The Supreme Court is highly respected in Iowa as are you — All this from a democrat —

Very respectfully,

Mrs. N. E. Richardson
Delta, Ia.

* * *

Dear Mr. President:

Never before have I written to a President of the United States, but never before have I been so strongly moved by a pending measure as the Judicial Reform Bill proposed by you.

I have not the slightest idea that you will see this letter, but it will act as a safety valve for me any way.

Surrounded as you are by "yes" men — and fawning subordinates — I wonder if you are really able to discover what the sentiments of the people are on this measure? Would it not be a wonderful thing for you to have honest, frank, disinterested and intelligent people to turn to for opinions — rather than to rely upon politicians & dependant office-holders?

I have been a great admirer of yours in the past, Mr. President, altho' not a Democrat. You probably realize that you would never have been elected by the votes of dyed-in-the-wool Democrats alone & it seems to me that you should be interested in the views of that great body of independent voters, of the middle class, who hold the balance of power.

The small merchant, the small professional man, the small salaried man, the small farmer were largely with you in the past, but they are not with you on this Supreme Court issue. Because the classes I have enumerated are not organized and are not particularly articulate — does not mean that they are not thinking. The Labor unions constitute a minority, but a very noisy & powerful one. Same with the farmers — But the hard back-bone of the country belongs to neither group.

We are not willing to turn over to you the dictatorship of the Supreme Court. You now have Congress under your thumb, in spite of us — but that has happened before & probably always will happen with a popular & powerful executive. We have been told by professors that a benevolent despotism is the best form of government — but we do not want despots — benevolent or otherwise.

Oh! Mr. President you have an opportunity to go down in history as one of our great presidents — along with the Great Theodore. Do not throw it all in the discard because of a personal pique & a personal quarrel with the Supreme Court. If you can trust the people — & you always have said you did — why not submit the question in an open way to the people & accept the verdict. Why descend to the contrivances of the petty politicians to gain your desires?

The elderly people will not soon forget your cruel flings at old age. They notice that you do not suggest that the elderly statesmen — such as Borah, Norris, McAdoo, Robinson & others retire. They wonder at your inconsistency.

They believe, as I believe, that the three co-ordinate branches of our government should be retained in their original dignity & power — until such time as the people decide otherwise.

In other words, however desirable the enactment of your social legislation may be, & I do not dispute that at all, it should not be accomplished by trampling on the Constitution.

The people will support the Supreme Court. In North Dakota & Wisconsin all through the years that the liberals have had control of the executive & legislative branches — the people have stood by the old judges & re-elected them in spite of the attempt made by partisans to control the judiciary.

Now, I have had the pleasure of writing this & you will never be bothered by having to read it.

I wish you well — I respect & admire you greatly — do not spoil it all now — do not give way to partisan motives in a matter so fundamental.

Respectfully yours,

W. H. Gurnee
St. Paul, Minn.

MARCH 10, 1937

Dear Mr. President:

. . . The desirability of obtaining expeditiously the social legislation which the President has in mind cannot in my opinion compensate us for the price we would be paying. In our zeal to accomplish what we may consider advantageous or important now we should not scuttle the American system, destroy our checks and balances, and throw overboard the protection of a free untrammeled Supreme Court.

I once heard you say very aptly, Mr. President, that you laid no claim to infalibility, but what you strove for was a good high batting average. You surely have that. What if the umpires have given you some unfavorable decisions, and even though you feel that they may continue to cut the corners against you, don't throw down your bat and demand the privilege of appointing your own umpires. That isn't cricket, it isn't baseball, and it is not American. Such procedure might improve ones batting average, but it would also kill the game.

There is no clear outspoken command from the people to accomplish this thing. Even the tremendous personal popularity of the President, which would write a blank check for him on most issues, is apathetic and in many cases revolted by this proposal. The President himself must have been surprised at the lack of spontaneous support which this issue has evoked. The reason is not difficult to find, the people don't want it.

I think it is very regretable that in placing this issue before the people it was found expedient to cast an unfavorable light on our Supreme Court. The spectacle of the Nine Silent Men, striped of the traditional reverence with which we have been accustomed to regard our highest tribunal, and held up to public disesteem, is to me a sorry sight. I venture to believe that there are other Americans who feel as I do.

Respectfully yours,

Lewis W. Berghoff
Chicago

MARCH 12, 1937

Mr. President: —

I understand that the right of sorvegnty [sovereignty] in this cuntry belongs to the People. Not to anney or part of the constuinal goverment That the constunial goverment is the President, House of Representives, Sennet, and the Surpream Cort. Now the point I can not understand is how the surpream coart came to the right to declair anney act of congress unconstutinal. as they are only a part of the constutinal Goverment. Rising themselves above congress and usupering the Sorvergn rights of the people is I think going beyond thire juresdiction. The people of this cuntry do Not send over 500 of thire best talanted peopel to Washington to make Laws for them jest to have a Dictorial supream cort knock them out the First round.

When a constutinal Goverment makes a Law it is constutnial. The surpream cort has Nothing els to do onley to see that it is put into use when or where Needed. Would you point out whire I am Rong thanking you in advance I remain a citisen by Berth.

Charles A. Nelsen
San Pedro, Calif.

MARCH 15, 1937

Pres. Roosevelt

I am just a poor uneducated farmer but want you to know I am with you on your changes on the Supreme Court it has always been constitutional when the government helps the industries or Big Business But when we have a president and congress that want to help and serve people the court says unconstitutional.

. . . it seems that some of our officials are crooked and some crippled in the head when you are just crippled in your legs Hats off to the greatest president we have ever had. . . .

Very Respectfully,

R. T. Hanners
Hartselle, Ala.

MARCH 11, 1937

Dear President Roosevelt:

I am for your plan all the way. Those men on the Supreme Court never were hungry. That's why they have no feelings for the lower third of our population.

Good Luck

Daniel Geller
Cleveland, Ohio

MARCH 10, 1937

My dear President Roosevelt:

I want to write and thank you for the enjoyment and satisfaction I derived from your "Fireside Chat" last night.

My husband and myself have supported you from the beginning. Altho' we have not suffered greatly from the depression, we have seen and feared the danger to our beloved country. . . . from the greed and increasing misuse of power by intrenched wealth; also the dishonesty, political bias and inefficiency of our Courts and lawyers. I have been a legal stenographer for many years and have seen many things in the courts and legal procedure which has disturbed me greatly. My husband's employment brings him into contact with every type of people, from bank presidents to janitors and elevator men, and he sees misery and injustice on every hand. . . .

Therefore, you can see why we are your ardent supporters in your war against special privilege which is creating a deadly hatred among the people, and which condition inevitably leads to serious consequences to the nation involved.

. . . I believe you are exactly right and that it is intolerable for a lot of prejudiced, jaundiced old men to nullify the wishes of the people. We will never have any progressive legislation if they are left in power, and Heaven only knows what an incensed people will do under the circumstances. We surly do not want conditions here to be as they are in Europe, but that is exactly what we will get if the majority of the people cannot have the necessities of life and some of the luxuries. . . .

Hoping God's blessing may rest on you, and that you may be able to keep our country intact without bloodshed, I am

Very Sincerely

Ethel H. Smith
Walworth, N.Y.

MARCH 17, 1937

My Dear President:

I am taking this opportunity of giving you some facts in the middle west, which I presume are true all over the country, showing the absolute necessity of some kind of government action in regard to the labor situation. I have read of the sit-down strikes in the east and if conditions there are as they are here, I cannot blame them one bit, and you would not either if you were placed in a like position. We, here in the middle west, whenever we are in a gathering of working people, the story is the same, viz: "I am being driven like a slave, made to do two mens work and receive one man's salary." Unless someone can get industry to awaken itself, there will be a revolution in United States, just as surely as the sun comes up in the morning, Men are being driven to desperation. For instance; . . .

I am working in the law office of one of the most influential firm of lawyers in Northeast Kansas. There are four lawyers. We have one stenographer who does nothing else; I am the Chief Clerk, and supposed to take all the responsibility of the outer office, keep about four sets of books, take dictation for two of the lawyers, etc. etc. We are compelled to work from 8 to

10 hours a day 6 days a week, and then we alternate on Sundays. She draws $105.00 a month and I get $165.00 a month. We are driven so hard that finally we are exhausted and have to go to bed and be out of the office from a week to 10 days resting up. These men draw all the way from $10,000.00 to $15,000.00 a year. You may say, "why dont you quit"? I have a family to support and where could I go to better myself. It is the same all over. This young lady has an aged father to help support. These lawyers seem to think you should be satisfied and glad that you have a job. Perhaps that is true, but they are not satisfied with what they are making.

I am hoping and praying that you will be successful with your Supreme Court fight and get men in there who will be a help instead of a hinderance. The only objection that I have to the whole thing is the fact that they would retire on full pay. I ask you this question: Why should they be pensioned anymore than the man who does any other kind of work. What act of God entitles these men to an easy seat the rest of their lives? If they can't save enough from their salaries of $20,000.00 a year while they are on the bench, to take care of them the rest of their lives, then how can a man drawing $100.00 or $150.00 be expected to save up enough to take care of him when he gets to be 70 years of age. Is it any wonder that we are having these uprisings. I am not a radical, a red, or an agitator, just an honest, hardworking American Citizen who would like to see a semblance of a square deal to the middle class of people. . . .

They can call you a Dictator if they want to, but if you are a DICTATOR then power to you.

If I can give you any further information as to the conditions in this state, I shall be only too glad to do so.

With the kindest personal regards, I am

Very sincerely,

Eugene S. Simmons
Atchison, Kansas

MARCH 11, 1937

Mr. President: —

After listening to your talk last night I just have to write you a note telling you how much I really appreciate your talks, and your courage. I no you are gaining thousands of friends daily. At the plant where I work The Sinclair Refinery East Chicago Ind. Conditions are 90% better since you came into office and gave us the write for collective bargaining. And the men in that plant are 97% for you. We talk of you often. Many remarks are made as to your fearless courage and your continued fight against organized capitalist. We no it is a hard uphill fight but we are with you. We are all for your Supreme Court change and several of us have written our representatives to vote for it. I am encouraging them to do this. . . .

The workers of America are praying for your success and your health so you can carry on to free the white Slaves of America.

There is lots I would like to tell you but I can't take up your valuable time explaining it in a letter. Sure wish all of us workers could no you personally. We all no you are our friend.

So we will continue to hope and pray for your success.

If there is any thing I can do to help in any way please let me no. I will be happy to do any thing in my power.

Thanks a thousand times for all you have done and for what you will do. May God bless you and keep you well.

Wishing you all the luck in the world.

I am
A Born American

Clyde Lowrance
and wife Bessie
Hammond, Indiana

MARCH 10, 1937

our President Mr. Roosevelt Dear Sure I lisen in to your wonderful speech on the 9th of March and i think they was the wonderfuls speech off our history your problum should have tuch the hart of all worker & men and women Just as it Did mine. We have neve befor had a president to take any step to help the progress of the worken class and it looks like it is un posable for you to pull us up buy the head when the Cort pull us Dawn buy the feet you are only one man and there is nine holding us Dawn We working class was with you in the start and we are with you to the ind in any under taken that you think will make the standed of liven better for us working class it is Just left up to you to Do your will we workers are with you from start to finish what wood we Don from 33 untell now if it had not been for you so i wish you all the sucsess from Richard. Cruse. Col.[ored] Chicago, ill

MARCH 26, 1937

Dear Mr. Franklin D. Roosevelt
Hon. President of the U. States.

As a citizen of this Country permit me to voice my opinion in favor of your plan in regard to the Supreme Court.

Every worker in this Nation is eagerly anticipating legislation to protect his right to live decently according to the present standards of living.

I work for a railroad 7 nights per week, 10 hrs. per night, a total of 70 hrs. per week, and watchmen for the same railroad work 84 hrs per week. There is no sunshine, no recreation of any sort for us, and millions of others like us throughout the Country. In face of so much unemployment this is intolerable.

Only the Federal Government can put a stop to such abuses, and may God give you strength to conquer all opposition.

We workers are with you to the bitter end of this fight. Wherever a group of citizens is found, no other topic interests them so much as this, and the dissappointment would be great should you fail in your great endeavor to protect the American people.

I am sending a similar letter to Senator Wagner of New York urging him to use his influence in this matter.

Yours Sincerely,

Manuel Mendes
New York, N.Y.

MARCH 12, 1937

Dear Mr. President:

I am writing you to say that the working men of California and of the Nation are behind you just as strong now as we were when we elected you to your high office. We elected you by an overwhelming majority and we feel that we are paying you a good salary to work for us and we feel that you are working for us but we did not vote for nor appoint the Supreme Court and we do not feel that they have worked for us but, rather have worked for the newspapers and the corporations that told us that if we voted for you that we would not have any jobs. The vast majority of working men have learned that we can produce everything in abundance that is needed for human welfare and if this Supreme Court and the corporations do not care to co-operate to this end we are willing to do without them and work for the federal government and the nation but we demand a few of the necessities of life.

I attended a meeting of 350 oil workers last night who are just 100% behind you and your plans to reorganize the Supreme Court. We admit that we are dumb but we know enough to know that this court has over ruled everything that would be of any benefit to a worker. . . . You do not have to be very smart to see that these recent decisions have nothing to do with the constitution but rather are the results of the private thoughts of these men who have been raised up under the false theory that the wealth of the nation is produced by the corporations instead of the workers.

Mr. President we are behind you. If you do not think so just send agents out into any bunch of working men and let him ask.

Very truly yours,

L. A. Duncan
Long Beach, Calif.

MARCH 13, 1937

My Dear Sir.

The English vocabulary fail to contain sufficient words to express our gratitude to you, for your great leadership.

We are hoping and praying, that congress may see the wisdom and abide your judgement; in the reorganizing the "Supreme Court."

The world has changed, and the onward march of civilication necessetate a change in laws, homes and most every pursuit of life.

We nine millions of Negros down South have watched your move from the first year you was elected President of these United States, we find that you emulate the Blessed Savior, when He was on earth You have fed the poor, clothed the naked and establish away by which those that are born afflicted could be healed. You have healed broken hearts.

I have in mind, the "Infantile Paralysis institutions" establish in a way that every loyal citizen can help. Its miraculus. We Negroes see things in the Democrat party, that we had never seen before. . . .

You have done more for the Negroes since you have been elected President, than the Republican did in a quarter of a century. You are the next "Moses" that "God has sent to lead the country to the promise land. There are no other country in this World, that gives the privilege to their minority and exslave race, as this country of ours; gives us. (No kick due us.)

Why, I write, you, I dreamed, that I saw you standing on a high mountain. You were called a Shepherd, there were millions of sheep down in the vally in a pasture. Some were White and some were black. as you stood with a staff in hand, you gave orders to the men to drive them all to the right. You was ask "must we separate them," You said no. They are all sheep; put them togather in this larger pasture; to my right. This point, I awoke and it bothered me. I promised myself to write you and express our thanks for your kind deeds done for our race.

I am an old school teacher, teaching now in the public Schools of Natchitoches Parish. I am in my sixties. Finally, Mr. President go on, God is leading you. . . . The unborn athousand years from now; will see your foot print on the sand of time by reading your history.—Your obedient Servant.

Matthew C. Harrison
Natchitoches, La.

MARCH 10, 1937

Dear Sir:

You want six extra judges so the court will interpret the Constitution and give your social laws a clean bill. . . . You talk about helping the lower third but the people worst off in the United States are the Southern Sharecroppers. I haven't heard you speak about the situation or do anythink about it. Talk about the workers in the factories, they get 600 to 700 dollars a year while down south 150 to 300 dollars is very common. Of course with Southern Senators being the main support of the Democratic party and they being elected by the Southern version of the "Economic Royalists" as only 30% of the southern people vote you cant do anything for the share-croppers without stepping on your southern friends toes. And talking about liberty as you did last night the Southern Democrats have always been the ones who took away the right to vote of about 70% of the southern voters. If you appointed six democrats some would be southernors and the southern courts have a nasty habit of taken away the liberties of a man and we can assume that any of them appointed are liable to bring the habit to the Supreme Court of the United States. This court is the only court that has stood between the southern citizens and unjust laws and trials. . . .

Yours for a court that will say what it thinks and not what you think.

Tom Stryker Rice
Oshtemo, Michigan

*   *   *

My Dear Mr. President —

May I introduce myself to you as a man of about your own age raised on a corn farm in Nebraska and now farming in California. I am registered a Democrat and my entire education was acquired in a Little Red School House 14′ × 22′ located in the country. . . .

The use of your "three horse team" as you used it was wrong, which you would have known if you had ever been a real dirt farmer and not a gentle-man farmer. You know you hitch the three horses to a three horse evener so that each horse has to do its part.

The Supreme Court as I see it corresponds to the horse in the furrow or the horse in the middle which keeps the other two bronchos going straight and also keeps the two mavericks from running away with the plow and breaking things up.

Please look into the working of a three horse team before you make an-other talk because any real farmer knows that your example of a three horse team really proves that the Supreme Court the odd horse or the horse in the furrow is the most important animal in the team.

Please get right on this Supreme Court and Federal Judiciary question. You are more often right than wrong. Get right on this question. You will be the greatest man in history. Do not listen to the politician. He has his ears to the ground for reelection.

Trusting you will get right on this question and make it an even 100%. I am

Very respectfully yours

D. E. Wilson
Chatsworth Park, California

MARCH 11, 1937

Mr. President

Too bad your fireside speech of last night didn't fall into the fire before you got a chance to deliver that masterpiece of hypocracy and deceit!

Yes our government is DIVIDED into 3 branches, but they are not supposed to PULL TOGETHER — that is the very thing they are not supposed to do if they are going to achieve the purpose of the framers of our constitution. What sense would there be in dividing the government into three branches if those branches are going to work in collusion???

. . . may I suggest that your reference to our revered elderly Justices who have given their best to the service of our country, as old foggies with "HARDENING OF THE ARTERIES" comes with exceedingly bad grace from one who can't stand on his own two feet unassisted!!! Shame on you, Mr. President! That remark hurt me more than anything you have ever uttered. How about making a MUST·LAW which will require candidates for the presidency to be physically and mentally fit for the high position?

Sincerely yours

Leo P. Hansen
Democrat
Lacey, Washington

* * *

My dear Mr. President,

I, at least, am not of the number who can follow you in your assault on the Supreme Court. In fact, while a Democrat, the things you are now proposing and trying to rush through a "yes-man" Congress are so dangerous that I now have reluctantly to regard you as the most dangerous man who has ever been president. Nor am I a man out of touch with the common people. I know farmers and men of other businesses all over this county and in many other places, — and I know that I am not the only man who is now desperately afraid of you.

Yours, with sadness,

Daniel S. Gage
Fulton, Missouri

* * *

FRANKLINSTEIN 1937
By, Erwin Clarkson Garrett.

They raised them up a towering form —
A fearful Frankenstein;
They placed him in the highest seat —
All powerful — divine.

He bore a hypnotizing smile —
(That many called absurd) —
And tossed his chin with sparkling glance
And sweetly crooning word. . . .

Twain hands — that have with tyrant grasp
Choked Senate — crushed the House —
Till manhood and initiative
Bespeak the frightened mouse —

Twain hands are reaching now to raze
Democracy's last tower,

Which through the storm and stress of years
Has stood in righteous power. . . .

And you men call "Americans,"
And heroes' praises sing,
Will ye stand idly by and let
Him do this fearful thing?

Erwin Clarkson Garrett
Philadelphia, Pa.

MARCH 10, 1937

Dear Sir:

As a plain American citizen (I was not born an economic royalist on a Hyde Park estate) I think your attacks on the Supreme Court the most contemptible speeches ever uttered by a President of the United States. . . .

I understand on good authority that your speeches are written by a clever Jew and I can well believe it for only a shifty Oriental could write such a tissue of distortion and, in my opinion, only a traitor could get up and mouth it.

We, who know you, know that your purpose is unholy and that you lust for ever greater power. As a demagogue and as a dispenser of patronage you are without equal but no American President should be proud of these attributes. . . .

I am a Democrat and my father who is now 70 years old has been a Democrat his entire life (would you like me to chloroform him as an obsolete dotard?)

In my opinion, your undemocratic proposal has, indeed, rendered you unfit for the honorable office you hold. I cannot remain in any party that deliberately seeks to undermine our American system of government.

Karl Young
New York, N.Y.

MARCH 14, 1937

Pipe down, you with the Julius Caesar complex.
You may be MUSSOLINI, but we, thank God, <u>ARE NOT WOPS!</u>

Decent American
New York, N.Y.

MARCH 11, 1937

Mr. President:

Keep right on giving 'em hell. The great majority are with you in your attempt to put some much needed new blood in the Supreme Court.

. . . I have a wife and 3 fine, healthy children and fire a boiler for a gas company for our living. . . .

I am not alarmed in the least about a dictatorship because the American people just aren't, "built that way." I have previously mentioned having 3 children (from 3 yrs old to 12 yrs.) and I am firmly convinced that your course is the only one that will save America for them.

In my humble opinion the worst dangers in America today are the large corporations and I know you are handicapped now by the court in your effort to bust 'em up.

I want to congratulate you on your 2 fine speeches on the court issue and with the help of God I hope you succeed.

Very truly yours,

W. W. Boals
Pavonia, O.

MARCH 10, 1937

My Dear Mr. President: —

I listened to your chat last evening and I quite agree with your conclusions, action is necessary and leave the past dead bury the dead. . . .

We must have reform along with recovery otherwise we will go stumbling along until we go head long into the ditch.

Frankly if I were in your place I would have this reform at all cost, in other words I would put this Nation under martial law and remove all those old fossils from the bench the Country over, and with them gather in all the International Bankers, and big industrialists and if need be stand them up against the wall and shoot them.

I believe in constitutional Government and real Democracy and not a Democracy of special privilege which is slowly but surely bringing us to a revolution. and believe me Mr. President that if it comes to that point wher we have once more to fight for our freedom, I will be on the side for freedom.

Yours respectfully.

M. A. Cypher
Butler, Pa.

MARCH 15, 1937

Dear Sir. I am heartily in favor of your plan to curb the Szarist policies of the Supreme Court, the opponents of curbing them argue that we had just as well do away with the court as to curb it on the other hand if the present policy is continued we in reality have no Congress, no Senate, no President, and in reality have already an absolute monarchy, composed of nine men who are not the real rulers in fact. the real rulers are the heads of the big corporations for whom they formerly worked in fact J. P Morgan aught to be called Emperor, for he is the real ruler and these old men always do his will regardless of the constitution. for in fact the constitution is not the complicated document these hired spellbinders claim it to be any tenth grade schoolboy can understand it and any adult who cannot comprehend it has no business on any court bench and any nine men who cannot agree unanimously when the facts are squarely before their eyes should be impeached for they have made up thier minds before the case comes before them. . . .

You have been too fair to these men by inferring that they are old fashioned and cannot change with the times. if those consistently stubborn members of the court were investigated you would find that their relatives are holding highly paid corporation jobs who would be fired if the Judge decided against them. in fact we have a Nazi or Facist government here now. and if something isnt done to curb the infallible, omnipotent pose of the Judges trouble is sure to come. . . .

Your friend

T. W. Howell
Okolona, Miss.

MARCH 12 AND 13, 1937

Dear Sir —

I listened carefully to your speech on Tuesday, and read carefully the one of last week, and have waited to cool off before writing. You may never see this, but I hope you will know what people are thinking, probably not the majority who usually follow the crowd without thinking but the thinking minority who seem to have little to do with your thoughts.

Naturally things should be better in a few years, no matter who would be president, so you could not possibly brag about that. But are they so much better? Many are still on relief and it seems in the present order of things they will forever be. . . . You had a landslide election, not because of your popularity, but because of all the benefits the so-called "poor working man" and laborers received and which they credited you for. Men think more of their pocketbooks than of principles. Who wants to get paid high wages by the hour to strike a small tree in the ground or wave a red flag of danger on a road being built? I mean who wants to live that way who is honest? No one. . . . Why are you always for the employees, never for the employers? Don't you sometimes wonder how long people will be so dumb as not to see through what you are doing? Whoever heard of a "free?" country allowing strikers sitting down in a plant owned by the ones who pay them, and wrecking it unless their wants are satisfied? Who has ever heard of so many strikes and so very much unrest as there is now? The unlawful element in the country have found they can almost get away with murder and nothing is done about it, so they go ahead and do almost anything under the sun. You can thank yourself, and no one else for the bitter class hatred you have stirred up. And what for? Popularity? Votes? And you are in the Capitalist class yourself! That is what makes it so funny if it were not so tragic! To think you always pose as being for the poor man and what do you know about being poor! You have never had to earn a dollar in your life and never will have to. Your sons have done many unlawful things and seem to be able to get away with them because they are your sons. What kind of example is that for the young people of the country? Where is your idea of fair play?

And now you are after the Supreme Court. . . . Why not think of the men who own small business places or the much maligned white collar man who has his Social Security money taken from him when he is earning less than the poor working man, but has no union to help him strike? I'd call him the "forgotten man" and not the strikers. . . . how can you pose as being for the "poor under dog" when you take money away by taxes from honest, hard working people who are middle class (so called) the backbone of the country, to pay for some of the worthless ones who get their money from those taxes? And they are even getting so they won't work otherwise knowing they can get government jobs from the Alphabet Soup and not have to hurt themselves working for it. We are getting to be a nation of spineless saps, and when I think how our forefathers worked to make this country what it has been and may never get to be again, I simply boil! . . .

Yours truly

(Mrs. C. O.) Mabel Young King
Berkeley, California

MARCH 10, 1937

Dear Friend: I am writing this letter to let you know that I agree with you in all you said last night about the supreme Court. . . .

It is said that you are causing class hatred but you are not. Class hatred was started before you were born. The very ones who are fighting you at every turn: such people as J. P. Morgan Rockefellers etc etc are the ones who are causing class hatred. There is class hatred most of us poor folks hate the rich class with a bitterness that hurts. You are doing more than anyone I know to do away with this feeling. You are trying to get them to stop doing the things which cause us to hate them. . . .

As I see it the supreme Court as it now stands is just like Old King George of England only there are nine Kings instead of one.

I sincerely hope you can win in your fight to subdue them. No one should be appointed for life and they certainly should not have power to overrule elected representitives of the people. . . .

Yours truly,

Ruskin Tansel
Swanton, Ohio

MARCH 10, 1937

Dear Sir;

I was somewhat uncertain as to the advisability of the proposed change in the Supreme Court, but after hearing you talk on the radio Tuesday night, I am convinced that such a change would be a disaster to the American form of government.

. . . You know as well as I do that it was only those millions who are on your pay roll in some way or another who re-elected you and not the popular vote. I do not know of any one person who voted for you who was not receiving money from some source or other or were promised money or jobs by the government.

Your talk of child labor makes me tired. My father died when I was four and my mother when I was eleven years of age. A maiden aunt, my brother who was two years older, and my self worked to keep the home to-gether. My brother worked in a grocery store after school, Saturdays and vacations, and I cared for babies, ran errands until I was thirteen and then worked during vacations in a shoe factory at Nyack, N.Y. which was our home town then. We both graduated from High school, and both upon graduation went to work in a large bank in N.Y. City. I was seventeen at the time. My brother is now an official of that same bank. I worked there for years and then became a reporter for some of the largest newspapers in New Jersey. . . . Had you been president at the time of my mother's death we would probably have been placed in an institution and to-day I would probably be on your relief rolls.

It is sad but true that you who would have been one of the most beloved of presidents, has brought so much sorrow and sadness on the middle class, that now the mere mention of your name sends the chills down our spines. Both my father and mother's families came here a hundred years or more before the Revolution, I am a member of the Society of Mayflower Descendents in the State of New Jersey, the D.A.R. and the New England Women, and I weep for the future of my beloved country. Fortunately I leave no children behind me who will not be able to enjoy the freedom of the loved country, as I knew it, but who would live and serve a Dictator in a Communistic Country, for as you say "we are on our way."

Very truly yours.

Edith H. Frank
Chicago, Ill.

* * *

President Roosevelt —

Who do you think you are to undertake disrupting our Supreme Court which has rendered unquestionable service to the public for 150 years, while you in four years have brought nothin but distruction, poverty, and misery of all kinds upon the Nation with the exception of the thousands and thousands of paid parasites which you unnecessarly mentain at Washington at the expense of the tax payer. . . . Like Hitler you imagine you know more than God Almighty. — You are crazed from the effects of the rotton disease your old carcass has been carrying around for the last fifteen years. — Now you want to dictate to, and dominate the nation at large. — The American people have tolerated you too long, you will get your desert one of these days. You damn traitor, liar and hypocrite of the deepest dye. — The very knowledge that you had the audacity to place your hand on the Holy Bible and swear allegiance to your country and people, which you failed to do is enough to disgust even Stallan. There is nothing too base for an animal like you to do.

. . . We are thoroughly disgusted with your whole tribe. You and your family have been a menace to the American standard of cilivization. Your son and daughter with two wives and two husbands. What an example placed before a Nation. Never have we had such rubbish in the White House.

Think of the condition of the country today from strikes and you don't say one word. Why? because you are a coward, you are afraid of John L. Lewis. I hope he will lick hell out of you before he gets through. You are nothing but a dirty lowdown Communist of the lowest grade. You, Farley, Wallace, Hopkins, Tugwell and the whole ring of vampires at Washington should be tared, feathered and set on fire. You are a marked man, you won't escape much longer. The dungeon of Hell will never be filled until you and your diabolical gang are dangling on pitchforks over the flames. It would be a real pleasure for the people whom you have deceived, ruined financially and physically to witness the scene which will surely take place. — You pretend to be a great philanthropist. You are worse than a highway robber stealing the hard earned pennies from the poor under the guise of your deceitful Security Act.

Not being satisfied with all this damage, you now want to regiment the children like Hitler and Stallan.

We all know your Communistic aims. — You old feather duster.

These are the sentiments of every decent American today, which you are not.

[unsigned]

MARCH 11, 1937

Dear Sir, I am now past 61 and have supported the Democratic ticket about all my life. . . . all the people I talk to say they think Judges on the U.S. Supreme Court should be retired at 70 but seem to feel that $20,000 a year is a big Pension to grant to men that have a plenty when there are so many old folks that are half fed and half dressed through the Country to day I have talked to a good many farmers and Factory workers and they tell me that the AAA and the N.R.A. was the only thing that ever done anything for them. . . . Economic Royalists who say that a Judge is in his prime of life when he is past 70 are the same boys who throw there own workers on the scrap heap at 40

Frank Deacon
Belding, Mich.

MARCH 11, 1937

THE SUPREME COURT IS PULLING OFF THE BEST SIT-DOWN STRIKE. THE
COUNTRY OFFERS THEM 20 GRAND TO GO HOME PERMANENTLY. STILL
THEY SIT.

> JOE FERGG
> CHICAGO

MARCH 16, 1937

Dear President: —

. . . You are the finest President we have ever had since Lincoln, and all
the poor people love you dearly and have complete faith in you. If it were
not for that love and faith, I believe America would have had a revolution
before this time. We may have it yet if your hands are kept tied by the Conservative Supreme Court. I think the old Grandpas ought to be sent home
to their rocking chairs where they can learn to knit stockings. It would be
of more benefit to humanity than what they are doing now.

. . . I cannot agree with you about paying them for retiring. They have
been dictators in this country too long, and should be retired forcibly. If
they do not know how to knit let me know, and I will instruct them by mail
free of charge. There is nothing like knitting to keep hands out of mischief
and minds out of politics. Wouldn't dear old Willy Van Devanter look com-
ical with a bunch of yarn held in his 77 year old Tory hands? How in the
world do you suppose he could ever be comfortable in Heaven, associating
with millions of poor trash like the common people? Or do they have a separate, exclusive heaven for conservative lawyers?

. . . God bless you always dear Mr. President, and may He comfort,
guide and protect you in your hours of need. I send you also my deepest
gratitude for the work you have given my husband on the W.P.A.

> Mrs. Frank Taylor
> Portland, Ore.

MARCH 10, 1937

Dear Mr. President,

Enjoyed and approved every word of your masterful "fireside chat" last evening. . . .

I am enclosing some nonsensical little nursery rhyme parodies I thought you might be able to put in the hands of some clever cartoonist, who would be in a position to capitalize on them.

Again assuring you of my complete approval of what you are trying to do for our Country, I remain,

Very respectfully yours,

H. C. Brown
San Diego, Calif.

"GRANDFATHER GOOSE RHYMES"

Hickery-dickery-dock
Old Age holds back the clock,
By votes of one, are laws undone,
Hickery-dickery-dock

. . .

Fe-fi-fo-fum
Judges as old as Methuselum,
Cast their votes as in days gone by,
Viewing tomorrow with yesterday's eye.

. . .

Ancient Judges, sat in the Hall,
Ancient Judges, due for a fall,
Our country's Great Leader thinks some younger men,
Would see that the Court gave us justice again.

. . .

MARCH 5, 1937

Mr. President;

Not knowing the correct form one addresses the Cheif Executive which I believe in this instance to be a fortunate one as my thoughts will not be stilted or modified by form. . . .

I feel secure in asking the folowing question and your answer will be highly appreciated and considered personal. Would you consider the appointment of a Negro to the Supreme Court and is there one to your knowledge possess of the necessary qualifications?

Perhaps I should have stated before that I am a Negro and beleiving Democracy being a Government representative of all the people. Having faith in your fairness I submit this question without qualms.

The fact that I am writing this will show I hope, the gap you have bridged when a member of a minority group can with confidence submit this question and be correctly understood more especially so when the question is address to one who occupies the highest post civilization can offer. I feel you are interested in problems that confront a large group of American citizens.

Thanking you for this privilege and wishing you continued strength and sucess to carry on.

Truly yours,

Leon Wadlington
Philadelphia, Penna.

MARCH 16, 1937

Honorable President Roosevelt:

Your idea to increase the No. of members in the Supreme Court, if the Justices over 70 years of adge will not retire, is a very good idea.

All over the world it is known, the unjustice, done by the American court, to the american common people, cries to the heaven.

It is a nessesety to get more justice in the court. . . .

New blood shall fill the arteries of the Justice-Department. to change the condition. But honorable Mr. Roosevelt please do not fill this arteries with Jewish or Negerblood.

We are 100 Millionen Arier [Aryans] in this country and I think these 100 Millionen Arien should have the right they claim, neamly to be ruled and justivied by Ariens. Don'd you think so too?

Respectfully signed by an American Citizen

Marta Schmidt
Philadelphia, Penn.

MARCH 19, 1937

Dear President Roosevelt!

The statement was made here at the A.A.U.W. National Convention by Mary Ritter Beard that more women than men were writing to you in protests against changing the Supreme Court.

For some weeks I have been thinking I should like to write & say that I am with you. Moreover, many of my friends, all college women are with you.

We do hope however, that you put a woman or two on the bench.

Very sincerely yours,

Sonia Pickett
Kirkwood, Missouri

MARCH 11, 1937

Your Excellency:

The logical argument in the matter of the Supreme Court is not that it is composed of nine old men, but that the Document they are called upon to interpret and apply is outmoded and no longer suits the conditions prevailing in the United States. This has been partially recognized by various amendments.

When the Constitution of 1789 was adopted:

The land of the country was practically unlimited and free for use to all who desired to settle upon and till it. . . .

There were no huge Corporations with "plants" in various States, employing hundreds of thousands of citizens, exceeding in some instances the population of certain States, and forming Industrial Empires within a Republic.

There were no huge Department Stores absorbing all the business of small independent Store-Keepers, and turning those independent dealers into employees.

There were no Bankers, National or International, having sole control of what is called the "circulating medium", the money of the country. . . .

To day there are few independent workers; the mass of the people are dependent on these huge Corporations for the privelege, and the right, of working to gain a subsistence.

And where does the profit earned by these great Corporations go? As huge salaries to the high officials. The common stockholders, the real owners of the Plants, may, or may not, get a trifling dividend.

Is it any wonder that men shut out from independent means of support should turn to criminality?

The logical need of the Country is a new Constitution that will make the People of the Country, and not the individual possessors of its money, supreme; and to that end the Government, representing the people, should own and control the industries of the Nation that are not strictly personal; and be the sole owner of the circulating medium, Money. And no individual should be allowed to accumulate money for the purpose of loaning it out at interest. . . .

When industry gets to the stage that the co-operation of thousands of men is required to produce the things desired, the Government should take it over. The welfare of the people as a whole is dependent upon it, and through its intimate relations with other and equally large industries the welfare of the Nation is affected.

As matters stand now there is a contest being waged for mastery between Capitalists and the so-called Labor leaders, while the Government stands by as a spectator having no interest in the conflict, or making feeble attempts at conciliation. But its own existence is at stake whichever of the constestants wins, for the victor will be the ruler of the people, a function that belongs solely to the Government as the representative Executive for all the people and their manifold interests.

Respectfully submitted.

Gustavus Harkness
Spring City, Pa.

MARCH 10, 1937

Dear Mr. Roosevelt,

... You complain that the Constitution, as interpreted at present, blocks "the modern movement for social and economic progress through legislation." But after all, the method of that modern movement, a strong centralized government, is one that its framers thoroughly distrusted; and so not only did they grant to government a minimum of specified powers, but made restrictions, in the form of a Bill of Rights, on the use of those powers. The fathers of the Constitution looked upon governments as potential tyrants. They established a system of checks and balances, so that one branch could not dominate the others, or a majority oppress a minority. They did not intend that the three branches, like three horses, should pull in unison.

You may sincerely believe that government is competent to direct a planned economy in the general interest. But that cannot be done without distorting or amending the present Constitution. The course of candor would be to submit the question to the people for their decision.

You have not done this, I take it, because you do not see the issue clearly. The choice is between historic liberalism and collectivism of one form or another. The record of your administration has shown that you want to combine incompatible elements of each. . . . Sooner or later, one or the other method must give way. We must either have an authoritarian state, with destruction of civil liberties, subverssion of democracy, and economic nationalism; or we must return to the methods of liberalism, which seeks prosperity by favors to none, rather than favors to all.

It is a tragic bit of irony that the party of Jefferson should be the party that has betrayed the principles he stood for.

Sincerely,

Conrad Wright
Cambridge, Massachussetts

MARCH 11, 1937

Your Excellency,

. . . I didn't think it necessary for ordinary folks to write to you. However, I learned my husband had written a very disrespectful letter to you and I feel it my duty to write that our daughter (a voter) and I are entirely in favor of this reform. . . .

Respectfully yours,

(Mrs.) Katharine Kandler
Chicago

MARCH 10, 1937

Sir — Attached copy of telegram sent you I as the telegrapher at the railroad station had to handle this in as much as it was against my will.

I cannot picture in my mine a woman so low in her walk of life lowering herself to stoop to such a cowardly act to belittle her President of her United States.

Never the less please confide in me when I say that I and hundreds of other railroad men are back of you one hundred percent and hope you remain in your present office the third term.

We appreciate you as a true friend of labor.

Most respectfully yours.

Charles E. Freeman
Beverly, Mass.

MARCH 10, 1937

IT IS COWARDLY TO TAKE ADVANTAGE OF YOUR POSITION TO BROADCAST STATEMENTS AGAINST THE JUSTICRATS OF THE SUPREME COURT TO WHICH YOU WILL REALIZE THEY MAY NOT REPLY BECAUSE OF THEIR RESPECT FOR THE OFFICE YOU OCCUPY IT IS AN INSULT TO EVERY CITIZEN

GRACE UNDERWOOD PERRY
IPSWICH, MASS.

MARCH 10, 1937

Dear Mr. Roosevelt I am the Hotel Man that wrote you good letters while you was a candidate for the Presidency You remember sending me a picture of you and your good Wife.

Mr President We are for you 100% for your Court change and dont weary you will get it all OK.

Now Mr Roosevelt I notice in the paper a few days ago that you was the best dressed man in the land I have always noticed you was so well dressed I am just a little Hotel Man but I am a real Roosevelt man and always speak a good word for you how about you sending me a suit of your clothes that you have discarded it would make me dressed up.

You owe it to me for all that I have done for you and you dont know how it would be appreciated.

We are the same size and the same age.

Your best friend.

J. C. Winder
Sulphur Springs, Texas

MARCH 9, 1937

Beloved President:

. . . I have never voted for you, though my wife has. When you were elected President the first time I obtained one of your pictures and rolled it up — I had seen the workers fooled SO many times — and said to my wife "put this picture away in a secure place and if and when this man has done half what he has promised the people I shall have it placed in a frame suitable to a great man and the accomplishment of a heroic undertaking and it shall be given an honored and conspicuos place in our home." I shall have it framed tomorrow; for I am convinced that under your leadership and with the cooperation of a liberty loving people, "It Can't Happen Here." May God Bless, strengthen and continue to guide you.

Most sincerely yours,

James W. Miller
Eldon, Mo.

BALANCING THE "HUMAN BUDGET": OCTOBER 12 AND NOVEMBER 14, 1937

FDR DELIVERED TWO MORE Fireside Chats during 1937.[21] The first came on October 12. Earlier that day, the President called for a special session of Congress to convene on November 15 to consider passage of legislation made necessary by the Supreme Court's nullification of several of his basic reform measures. That evening he spoke to the American people about the nature of the proposals he would place before Congress in the hope that his listeners would exert pressure for reform on their Senators and Representatives, who, with Congress adjourned, were then in their home states and districts. Indeed, Sam Rosenman called this Fireside Chat "an appeal to the people over the heads of the Congress."[22]

Roosevelt began by explaining — and defending — his decision to call for an extraordinary session: "I have never had sympathy with the point of view that a session of the Congress is an unfortunate intrusion of what they call 'politics' into our national affairs. Those who do not like democracy want to keep legislators at home. But the Congress is an essential instrument of democratic government."

Considering that the nation was on the brink of a recession which would plunge it into conditions not seen since the beginning of the New Deal, FDR spoke more prophetically than he knew when he warned of the dangers of "a merely temporary prosperity" and proclaimed: "The kind of prosperity we want is the sound and permanent kind which is not built up temporarily at the expense of any section or group." Without mentioning the Supreme Court, he made it clear that their recent decisions had undercut efforts to create a stable prosperity:

> The people of the United States were checked in their efforts to prevent future piling up of huge agricultural surpluses and the tumbling prices which inevitably follow them. They were checked in their efforts to secure reasonable minimum wages and maximum hours and the end of child labor. And because they were checked, many groups in many parts of the country

still have less purchasing power and a lower standard of living than the nation as a whole can permanently allow.

Therefore, in spite of the fact that 1937 had thus far been a good year with steadily returning prosperity, the people didn't want the government to stop governing. Americans, he asserted, "do not look on Government as an interloper in their affairs. On the contrary, they regard it as the most effective form of organized self-help."

> Sometimes I get bored sitting in Washington hearing certain people talk and talk about all that Government ought *not* to do — people who got all *they* wanted from Government back in the days when the financial institutions and the railroads were being bailed out in 1933, bailed out by the Government.

FDR had just returned from a trip to the Pacific Coast, and he was impressed by how well the "average citizen" understood the issues before the nation: "They want the financial budget balanced, these American people. But they want the human budget balanced as well." They "want a national economy which balances itself with as little Government subsidy as possible. . . . They are less concerned that every detail be immediately right than they are that the direction be right." Even though he himself proclaimed a third of the American people "ill-nourished," he remained concerned about agricultural overproduction. He criticized those who charged that he had created an "economy of scarcity." If Americans kept their shoe factories running twenty-four hours a day, seven days a week, they would duplicate the conditions now prevailing in agriculture. Those businessmen who condemned crop control "never hesitate to shut down their own huge plants, throw men out of work, and cut down the purchasing power of the whole community whenever they think they must adjust their production to an oversupply of the goods that they make. When it is their baby who has the measles, they call it not an 'economy of scarcity' but 'sound business judgment.'" He called for legislation that would protect farmers and consumers from alternating crop surpluses and crop scarcity. He advocated policies "to stop soil erosion, to save our forests, to prevent floods, to produce electric power for more general use, and to give people a chance to move from poor land to better land by irrigating thousands of acres."

His recent trip led him to stress again the interdependence of the entire nation. In the Boise Valley of Idaho, he visited a newly irrigated district being farmed by families who had recently been displaced by the dust storms that had affected ten states. "And, year by year, we propose to add more valleys to take care of thousands of other families who need the same kind of a second chance in new green pastures." He had also visited the Grand Coulee Dam in the state of Washington, where he learned that "almost half of the whole cost of that dam to date had been spent for materials that were manufactured east of the Mississippi River, giving employment and wages to thousands of industrial workers in the eastern third of the Nation, two thousand miles away." He called for legislation that would create seven planning regions — quickly labeled the "little TVA's" — in which local people would originate and coordinate recommendations as to what types of development and projects their areas needed. "To carry out any twentieth century program, we must give to the Executive branch of the Government twentieth century machinery to work with." Thus he called for the reorganization of the executive branch of the federal government.

On his trip, he learned of "the millions of men and women and children who still work at insufficient wages and overlong hours." Business had it within their power to improve their condition by paying better wages: "A few more dollars a week in wages, a better distribution of jobs with a shorter working day will almost overnight make millions of our lower-paid workers actual buyers of billions of dollars of industrial and farm products." Adequate wages and fair hours had to spread throughout the entire country if the demand for industrial and farm goods was to be revived and that spread was not the sole responsibility of business but also of the executive branch and the Congress as FDR made clear when he sent a minimum wage and maximum hours bill to the special session. While he believed in adequate pay for all labor, he explained to his listeners, "right now I am most greatly concerned in increasing the pay of the lowest-paid labor, those who are our most numerous consuming group but who today do not make enough to maintain a decent standard of living."

Whatever danger there was to property and profits "comes not from Government's attitude toward business but from restraints now imposed upon business by private monopolies and financial oligarchies." Thus the government was studying means of strengthening antitrust laws in order "to free the legitimate business of the Nation."

He closed his October 12 Fireside Chat by acknowledging that the prosperity of the United States was deeply affected by outside events: "we know that if the world outside our borders falls into the chaos of war, world trade will be completely disrupted. Nor can we view with indifference the destruction of civilized values throughout the world. We seek peace, not only for our generation but also for the generation of our children." ·

> We seek for them, our children, the continuance of world civilization in order that their American civilization may continue to be invigorated, helped by the achievements of civilized men and women in all the rest of the world.
>
> . . . In a world of mutual suspicions, peace must be affirmatively reached for. It cannot just be wished for. And it cannot just be waited for.

It was a theme he was to return to again and again in the coming years.

A month later, on the evening of November 14, he returned to the air with a Fireside Chat that was brief and on the surface narrow in scope. From the outset, one of the prime difficulties in combating the Depression was the appalling ignorance concerning how many Americans were actually unemployed and underemployed. In the initial years of the crisis, President Hoover provided a classic example of how ideology can rearrange facts to confirm one's sense of the way the world works. He ruthlessly edited the latest unemployment figures to reach his desk, cutting those workers he decided were jobless only temporarily and those he somehow convinced himself were not seriously searching for work. Even after he left office, Hoover continued to maintain that the apple sellers, who quickly became a familiar sight on street corners in cities throughout the nation, represented not the unemployed — even though many of them placed signs reading "UNEMPLOYED" on their box of fruit — but rather those who had "left their jobs for the more profitable one of selling apples." As late as 1936, Harry Hopkins, FDR's chief welfare adviser, conceded that his information on unemployment was not "adequate," and admitted that whether there were eight million or eleven million jobless depended on whose figures were consulted.[23]

To end the confusion and gather reliable figures, Congress decreed that a National Unemployment Census should be undertaken. In his Fireside Chat, FDR appealed to those who were unemployed or "insufficiently employed" to respond to the Unemployment Report Card they would receive in the mail the following Tuesday. If they would "conscientiously fill out these cards and mail them just as they are, without a stamp, without an envelope, by or before midnight of November 20, our nation will have real facts upon which to base a sound reemployment program. . . . we will know not only the extent of unemployment and partial unemployment, but we will know also the geographical location of unemployment . . . what age groups are most severely affected . . . we will know the work qualifications of the unemployed . . . in what industries they are suited to function, and we will be equipped to determine what future industrial trends are most likely to absorb these idle workers."

The President went beyond this appeal to discuss unemployment itself.

> Enforced idleness, embracing any considerable portion of our people, in a nation of such wealth and natural opportunity, is a paradox that challenges our ingenuity. Unemployment is one of the bitter and galling problems that now afflicts mankind. It has made necessary the expenditure of billions of dollars for relief and for publicly created work; it has delayed the balancing of our national budget, and has increased the tax burden of all our people. . . .
>
> It is a problem of every civilized nation — not ours alone. It has been solved in some countries by starting huge armament programs but we Americans do not want to solve it that way.

As a nation, "we adopted the policy that no unemployed man or woman can be permitted to starve for lack of aid." Nevertheless, unemployment relief was a temporary cure. The permanent solution lay in cooperative effort and planning involving industry, agriculture, and government. He expressed his conviction that the United States had "the genius to reorder its affairs" so that "everyone, young and old," could "enjoy the opportunity to work and earn." There was neither logic nor necessity "for one-third of our population to have less of the needs of modern life than make for decent living." Our "far-sighted industrial leaders," he said with perhaps more hope than conviction, "now recognize that a very substantial share of corporate earnings must be paid out in wages, or the soil from which these industries grow will soon become impoverished. Our farmers recognize that their largest consumers are the workers for wages, and that farm markets cannot be maintained except through widespread purchasing power." Unemployment, thus, was a problem "in which every individual and every economic group has a direct interest."

The President's attitudes toward unemployment reflected those of an increasing number of Americans. In July 1935, *Fortune* magazine, in the first of its influential series of quarterly national surveys, asked: "Do you believe that the government should see to it that every man who wants to work has a job?" It is not surprising that 88.8 percent of poor, 91.1 percent of Black, and 81.1 percent of lower-middle-class respondents answered yes. What is striking is that 69 percent of upper-middle-class and almost half of prosperous respondents did the same. Public opinion, *Fortune* concluded, "overwhelmingly favors assumption by the government of a function that was never seriously contemplated prior to the New Deal." National polls taken by the American Institute of Public Opinion (AIPO) in the months before Roosevelt's November 1937 Fireside Chat revealed that 76 percent felt that unemployed persons taken off relief jobs would have a "hard time" finding work (January 3); 67 percent were convinced that private business could not "absorb the able-bodied persons on relief during the coming year" (January 18); 73 percent supported a national census "to find out how many persons are unemployed" (June 20); 57 percent thought "there will always be as many as five million unemployed in this country" (July 12); and 68 percent opposed dropping WPA workers from relief before they have found jobs in private industry (August 9). A month before FDR's Chat *Fortune,* in its tenth quarterly survey, found that 63.8 percent agreed with the President "that one-third of the population of the U.S. has less than a minimum of the necessities for a decent life." More of those polled (34.8 percent) felt the federal government "should take care of relief" than state (17.6 percent) or local (28.4 percent) governments, and only 2.5 percent responded: "none of them."[24]

FDR understood better than any of his predecessors that in the complexities of a modern industrial world full employment could no longer be taken for granted; it had to be achieved. "The inherent right to work is one of the elemental privileges of a free people," he proclaimed in concluding his Fireside Chat:

> Continued failure to achieve that right, that privilege, by anyone who wants to work and needs work is a challenge to our civilization and to our security. Endowed, as our nation is, with abundant physical resources, and inspired as it should be with the high purpose to make those resources and opportunities available for the enjoyment of all, we approach this problem of reemployment with the real hope of finding a better answer than we have now.

OCTOBER 14, 1937

Dear Sir, — Your fireside chat on the evening of Wednesday Oct 13, was by far the most inspiring address of the several we have heard to date. It has proven to me that you are still the popular president of the millions of citizens in these United States. It has also shown that your principles and ideals remain the same as prior to your election which has made you the most popular president of all time. Your waning support and esteem is just so much "newspaper print" which is constantly aiming to hoodwink the public from actual facts. A true census of public opinion would still reveal that you are the same popular president that acclaimed you in 1932. I dare say if a vote were taken in my own little plant which employs approximately 300 people you would be chosen by at least 95% and I am reasonably certain that our plant is representative of the nation.

Your decision to call the Congress into special session on Nov. 15 is a masterful stroke, indeed, and is certainly approved by all fair minded and level headed citizens. Why shouldn't these men work when there is work to be done? You and I pay them to accomplish things, — not dilly-dally and after accomplishing little or nothing, declare a recess. You are the chosen captain and Congress is expected to enact legislation in accordance with your demands. When we, the public feel that your proposals are wrong or ill-timed we will soon put a stop to it at the ballot box. Until then let the work go on without fillibuster and shameful waste of public funds for doing nothing.

The public is still in back of you 100%, honorable President, and welcomes your fireside chats to let them know where you stand on matters of vital interest. We would welcome more such talks, especially now that we are constantly given nothing but biased opinions by our "press".

Yours Sincerely,

Benjamin B. Weiss
East Cleveland, Ohio

OCTOBER 13, 1937

Dear Mr. Roosevelt:

I heard your speech last night and I say right now that I agreed with everything you said. I'm glad that you called a special session of congress and I hope that now that you have the congressmen and women will cooperate with you as they should.

Your speech last night was very thorough, I thought, and one of the cleverest and truest parts about it was when you pointed out that if a shoe factory was faced with over production they would not hesitate to close their doors and then you said why not do the same with farm products. Why not indeed I would like to know.

As for your stand on the international situation — three cheers! I knew when you made your speech one week ago yesterday that you did not mean to imply that we would enter any war wherever it may be unless it was right here on our own shores. After your speech of last week my father, who is a World War veteran, and my Grandfather were sure that we were heading for another war but I told them, without any luck at convincing them, that you had seen war and what it could do. Therefore, I told them that you would do nothing to get us into it. You convinced them last night. Frankly I don't see how they could possibly have had any doubt at all after watching you for almost five years.

I agree, too, with your stand on wages and hours and hope with all my heart that you will be able to get your legislation on that subject passed. As a matter of fact I hope that you will get all your legislation passed for I know that it would be best for the nation and after all you were elected to finish the job you began so splendidly. I still think, and always will, that your Court Reorganization was a fine idea and I hope that you will be able to attain it.

I would be deeply grateful if you would send me a copy of last evenings address.

I noticed that you sounded very tired last night Mr. Roosevelt. Please for your own sake and the sake of the country don't work too hard. I know you are earnestly striving to do the job you were elected to do and you are doing it in spite of all the silly opposition you have met with. Don't strive too hard for that would only lead to illness for you and that of course would never do.

You have earned and will keep forever my sincere gratitude and admiration and I will always do my utmost to cooperate with you in whatever small way I can.

A Sincerely Grateful citizen,

Beatrice Godin
Chillicothe, Ohio

OCTOBER 14, 1937

Gentlemen.

We have had another "Fire side chat" And I cannot help but wonder what manner of man our President really is.

He apparently imagines a great many things and seems to take it for granted that he is really doing some thinking. When in reality he is just letting his imagination run riot. A restless soul.

Nothing but "Front page Headlines" meets his ideas of life. So we must have another session of Congress. For no particular reason only his restlessness.

It is unfortunate that the idea of "Crop regulation" cannot be applied to the doings at the White House.

Very truly yours,

Robert Burgess
Brookline, Mass.

OCTOBER 14, 1937

Dear President Roosevelt:

My family and myself wish to write you a line to thank you for what you said in your recent fireside address.

I was not fortunate enough to hear it on the radio but I have just finished reading it in the Minneapolis Star.

We liked what you said about agriculture. As farmers we do not want doles, but we want to find our rightful niche in the economic plan of this nation. The Agricultural Adjustment Act was a great guide in that direction until it was taken away from us.

... The immediate concern is to get Congress to useful work. A subcommittee of Senators from the Agricultural Committee are holding hearings in St. Paul tomorrow. A number of us farmers are going down to ask for enactment of the ever normal granary, crop insurance, etc. ...

We are glad for the guidance and the courage generated in all of your addresses. We hope that many, if not all, of the objectives you seek will be attained soon. But if they are not we desire that all of your addresses be compiled in convenient form for coming generations to study. They are fountains stirring new hopes and new ambitions in the people down and out.

In closing will say that we have had a fairly good year. We have nothing to complain about, since we are comfortable. The only thing that worries us is that we can not see any program of national scope enacted thus far to prevent a debacle like the one in 1932 and 1933. But we shall tell the Senators tomorrow of that fear. Perhaps they will go then to the special session of Congress and work for such programs as will assure to all of our people, — laborers and farmers alike, — a sense of security in this land which is the best in all the world.

Sincerely yours,

Mr. and Mrs. J. Edward Anderson
Buffalo, Minnesota

OCTOBER 16, 1937

Dear Mr. Roosevelt:

I take this means to extend to you my appreciation of your speech the other night. I assure you it gives me a feeling of the greatest security to know that we have a President that has the foresight and wisdom that you have shown.

Please understand that I am an ex-service man and in a CCC camp drawing thirty six dollars per month and that before I came here have worked for three bushels of turnips per day boarding myself. Might I add that I am the father of six children, three of which are in high school. Of course I am not satisfied with the condition we are forced to live in because of the depression. Having been fortunate enough to have been with a firm for some eleven years previous to 1932 my family was used to the average standard of living, (1800. Annually). This is mentioned that you might know the drop in our living condition.

If we were to be faced with the continued circumstances we find ourselves in, life would be hopeless indeed BUT what cheers us is the thought, not of the petty errors of petty politics, but the splendid vision you have and the progress you have made. It is very easy to visualize what would have happened these past years when at the time you took over the ship of state the waves of dispair was washing over the whole country, had we not some one with courage enough to do the things you have done.

Your speech encourages us to "saw wood" and pull for the future you so courageously plan. It seems very dark indeed to us at times and personally I would like to hear you broadcast more often. It brings us out of the "Blues".

May our God watch over your every move and word and be with the leaders of our Nation.

Very respectfully,

Lawton L. Brown
Miller, Missouri

OCTOBER 16, 1937

My dear President Roosevelt:

Shades of Woodrow Wilson! The poor fellow must have stirred in his grave in efforts to warn you not to make the same mistake he did. He wanted to "make the world safe for Democracy" — you want to make the world safe for "civilization." Heaven preserve us from our heroes! I'm rapidly coming to the conclusion that this country, at least, is in far greater danger from people who want to be "noble" than from rascals.

If one can help to avert hostilities of any kind before a shot is fired, no one should refuse to negotiate. But after the conflagration has started then there is little one can do but try to keep it from spreading to one's own shores.

Haven't you heard that one must never argue with those who are angry, when they are angry? Always wait until they've cooled down, my teacher used to tell me. That applies to nations, I'm sure. Japan and Spain are already warring savagely. Do you really think you, or the rest of the world, or both, can shake a finger at them and say: "You naughty children, stop fighting at once. If you don't, I'll spank you; if you do, I'll give you a lollipop." — and presto! the wars will stop!? It's by far more probable that the harrassed warring nations will turn on their admonishers.

What possible harm could come to this country if it sat tight within its shores and attended to it's own domestic problems (numerous enough, as you know)? Under those circumstances, can you picture an enemy sending ships, planes or troops to molest this country? On the other hand, I can imagine so many complications arising out of a positive policy such as you advocate that I shudder away from really contemplating it.

After listening to your speech Columbus Day I'm sorry, for the first time since your election, that you are at the head of the government of this country. Fear shakes my heart at the thought that one with your views of the subject should hold the most important and influential position in the United States at this serious and turbulent time. And this fear will be my most constant companion unless something — perhaps Congress — checks your too ambitious course. Maybe neutrality laws should be mandated after all!

I'm not impugning your motives, which I still respect, your personality being such that one is somehow emotionally loyal even at a time when reason refuses to be loyal! (Of such personality stuff are dictators born, I suppose, even benevolent dictators such as you would be — not that I think you want to be. But I, and "the four million" like me who would suffer most in the cataclysm, pray that you have a change of heart. You have enough on your hands taking care of America — a job which, barring a few errors like the Supreme Court bungle, you are doing well. Please don't try to "save the world!"

I hope you will pardon this outpouring from an admirer, on the grounds of sincere anxiety which would not be stilled.

Respectfully,

Brownie Dressler
New York, N.Y.

OCTOBER 13, 1937

Dear President Roosevelt:

. . . Last night you sounded so weary, so different from the time before, when you sounded so proud to be able to tell the American people that you were protecting them, and when I saw you on the screen, (and for once they really let us hear your whole speech,) you looked so proud and sounded so happy, that last night I could have cried when I heard you sound so terribly weary — weary with the weight of having to actually use a sledge hammer to knock simple truths into the American people — who think they are so wise. — weary with constantly having your speeches misconstrued, deliberately misunderstood — weary with the WHY of it all. I felt so sorry for you — wished I could ease your burdens — wondered how you keep on — where you get the power to keep your vitality from being drained by an ungrateful populace. Glad — with a fierce gladness for the powers that be that gave us a MAN who could and would face the world for a CAUSE that HE KNEW was JUST & FAIR.

You promised America a NEW DEAL — well, you sure gave it to us. While so-called Brainy and highly educated people are really small-minded — you have taught others to THINK — you have succeeded, even if at times you may think it is useless — You HAVE given American people a NEW DEAL. . . .

I've wished many times there was some job I could fill to help you with your wonderful work, to be a part of the greatest thing in the world, to be able to feel that I was helping GOD'S MAN, then I realize I am a nonentity, just a scrub oak, looking up at the mighty great Oak. I realize you don't need my help, that you are backed by splendid people — first of whom are your Wife and Mother, and then I'm glad — but, still, I want to help.

Don't ever let them lick you — Always keep your smile — and lets hear from you more on the radio — and may God keep you in strength and health to finish the marvelous task you set out to do, for your pattern is so beautiful, some day, I know it will be hung in THE HALL OF FAME — finished — lovely — and INSPIRATION.

Sincerely,

Emma E. Wright
Roosevelt, N.Y.

* * *

Dear Mr. President:

I have just listened to your radio address of even date and wish to take this occasion to congratulate you on your talk. I enjoyed it immensely.

I was particularly impressed by the way you brought out the fact that in 1933 certain elements within our borders, and possibly outside our borders, were very happy for the so-called government intervention, which was accompanied by cash, stabilization of credits, and a general reduction in the feeling of fear by the people at large.

To-day, these certain elements would gladly like to take the reins again into their hands. Needless to say, if this should occur, I am of the opinion that within a very short time we would be back to the same condition which confronted our citizens when you first took office as President of these United States.

I believe that the majority of the people see eye to eye with you on your statement that a "reduction in hours, increases in salaries, stabilization of production, and distribution of certain consumer materials, dissolution of trade barriers within our shores" would soon produce such a tremendous market of home consumption that an unbounding prosperity would make us the most envied people of the world.

At the same time such a situation, if properly handled, would not only aid our export as well as import business but would materially decrease international jealousies, and set up a new standard for other nations of the world to follow, and we would still be preserving the great ideals of democracy.

We would move forward with a new spirit of hopefulness because as you expressed it "one part of the country cannot have prosperity if the other part of the country is exploited;" This cannot be stressed too often, as I believe there are certain elements still with that "rugged individual" strain running through them who believe they are not interdependent upon the prosperity of others for their own share of worldly goods.

Again I wish to state, believe me, when I wish you good health to carry on for democracy.

Sincerely,

D. P. Alterman
Mount Vernon, N.Y.

OCTOBER 12, 1937

SHOE PRODUCTION CAN BE CONTROLLED BY HUMAN HANDS. CROPS ARE
CONTROLLED BY NATURE AND SHOULD BE LEFT ALONE. . . .

> HILDA ARIAS
> NEW YORK, N.Y.

OCTOBER 12, 1937

IN YOUR SPEECH TONIGHT YOU FORGOT TO TELL US HOW YOU ARE GOING
TO CONTROL THE WEATHER AND INSECTS. I SUGGEST YOU DEVELOP A
PLAN TO GROW HAIR ON BALD HEADS.

> J. D. GOODMAN
> PHILADELPHIA, PENNA.

OCTOBER 12, 1937

PLEASE SPEND YOUR EVENINGS ATTENDING "I'D RATHER BE RIGHT" THAN
MAKING FIRESIDE CHATS AND POSSIBLY YOU MIGHT LEARN SOMETHING.

> H. S. BABCOCK, STILL A REPUBLICAN
> MYSTIC, CONN.

OCTOBER 12, 1937

MY REACTION: THIRTY MINUTES WORSE THAN LOST.

> W. A. BLACK
> OAKLAND, CALIF.

OCTOBER 13, 1937

Dear Mr. President:

For sometime I have wanted to write and tell you that I am very much in
accord with your entire program and after your speech of last night I could
not resist the impulse.

I suppose that if any one [of] my elders knew I was doing this they would advise me not to waste your time because they feel that I am too young to know much about politics. But on the contrary, I flatter myself that we young people of the coming generation know a great deal. Circumstances have forced us to understand and observe what is going on in the world about us, and I know from my contacts with young people that I am only one of scores who are standing firmly behind you.

While you were in Chicago . . . passing down La Salle Street everyone was at the windows and in the excitement some sneak-thief stole my purse from my desk. This occurrence made me the butt of many of my Republican friends jokes. But I think it was well worth all the tormenting I received, and the loss of my nice new black purse, of which I was very proud, to have been able to see you again.

But be that as it may the important thing which I wanted to convey is that we, the young people are with you all the way up that road which will lead us back to prosperity.

More power to you Mr. President.

Yours very truly,

(Miss) LaVergne E. Hintze
Chicago, Illinois

OCTOBER 12, 1937

Dear President:

I wish to take this opportunity of complimenting you on your radio speech this evening, it was wonderful!

However, there is one slight criticism I have to offer. After your hearty cough you overlooked pardoning yourself. I sincerely trust you will accept this jest in the right spirit.

Yours, as a public spirited citizen,

. Henry Black
Rahway, N.J.

NOVEMBER 16, 1937

Dear Mr. President:

I listened, as I always do, to your radio speech of the 14th. You have a pleasing radio voice.

You are asking, and are going to ask, business to help you in reducing unemployment. Is it possible you have not heard that business is deceased? The death certificate gives "starvation" as the cause. Business had been ailing more or less since the New Deal policies got well under way. At first its health was very good. Your promises, before the election of 1932, to balance the budget, and to reduce government expenses 25% acted like a tonic, and everybody thought the patient was on the way to recovery. I remember your words: "I have a way of getting things done in Washington." But when these promises went sour, the body of the patient became heavily acidulated, aggravated by a malignant infection of taxeatus, the decline set in, which resulted in the recent demise of the patient.

Life might have been prolonged without the budget being balanced; but instead of the government expense being reduced, it has been so drunkenly increased, that the patient became afflicted with high blood pressure and dizzyness, resulting in heart failure.

Had you been willing to take business into your confidence, instead of by the scruff of the neck and the seat of the pants, we feel that the result might have been different. I fear it is too late now, even for resurrection. As the new deal resulted in death, we are looking forward to a new birth three years hence that will give us life again.

Yours respectfully,

W. B. Ladd
Denver, Colorado

NOVEMBER 14, 1937

Dear Mr. Roosevelt:

Five minutes ago you finished your epoch making explanation of the reason and purposes for the Unemployment Census. It was SUPREME! God bless you for it, and all of those who are with you. May you meet with the highest success!

That is the kind of work that will quickly put your knockers and opponents — the enemies of humanitarianism — under the table where they should stay and hide their faces in shame until they will apologize and promise to be good.

I am not one of the unemployed. I am working full time at sufficient pay to keep the wolf from the door, with a little to spare for needy relatives, etc., but I can well imagine the courage and gratitude which your promise of help must have brought to millions of homes this night. For that you have won my gratitude also. If I can be of help to you, just say the word.

Very truly yours,

W. E. Hendrickson
Alameda, Calif.

COMBATTING RENEWED
DEPRESSION: APRIL 14, 1938

NOTHING IN FRANKLIN ROOSEVELT'S second term seemed to rise to the heights of the magnificent electoral victory that so auspiciously placed him in office for an additional four years. The struggle over the Supreme Court was only the first of the setbacks Roosevelt faced after his second inauguration. More troubling for the President and his people was the so-called recession of 1937–38, which was in reality a renewed depression and threatened to bring back the perilous conditions that had gripped the nation when FDR first took office in 1933. The President's opponents were quick to use the renewed economic woes — which began in the late summer, accelerated in the latter months of 1937, and grew worse in early 1938 — as proof of the failure of the approach at the heart of the New Deal. In fact, the severe economic setback — which was indeed largely self-inflicted — was created not by Roosevelt's reform program but by his ambivalence toward that program.

FDR liked to see himself as a bridge between traditional America with its ethos of individualism and a modern America characterized by huge organizations and enterprises and the new spirit of collectivism. Spanning two historical stages, the first of which was not yet completely erased from and the second not yet completely born in the popular consciousness, may have been a necessary role but not an easy one. It was particularly difficult for Franklin Roosevelt, who, as flexible as he proved to be, was himself in many ways still in the grasp of the assumptions and beliefs of traditional America. As FDR's adviser Rexford Guy Tugwell said of his chief: "And yet he too had not been immune to our national myths. He, like others, would spend a lot of time in the coming years planting protective shrubbery on the slopes of a volcano which was by no means finished with eruption." Roosevelt, Tugwell maintained, "like all of us, had a weakness for what was familiar and trusted which led him to overestimate their sufficiency and to underestimate their irrelevant antiquity." Tugwell, who often understood FDR more profoundly than most of his other advisers, thus comprehended more acutely than they the price the President paid for deviating too sharply from tradition.

The serious student is forced to conclude that this man deliberately concealed the processes of his mind. He would rather have
posterity believe that for him everything was always plain and
easy, that he undertook all his projects with certainty and pur-
sued them serenely, than ever to admit to any agony of indeci-
sion, any serious study of alternatives, any misgiving about mistakes. But it was not so. Not less for him than for others, his
burdens were burdens, carried with pain and endured with fa-
tigue.[25]

FDR's actions prior to the economic crisis of 1937–38 bear out Tugwell's
insight. Roosevelt's policies during the early months of his first term, as
necessary as he conceived them to be, had left him uneasy. That disquiet
was manifest as early as the summer of 1935, when the President responded
to a letter from the publisher Roy Howard warning FDR that business was
becoming edgy in the face of all the New Deal's reforms and asking him to
grant "a breathing spell to industry, and a recess from further experimentation." Roosevelt responded by assuring Howard that the New Deal's "basic
program . . . has now reached substantial completion and the 'breathing
spell' of which you speak is here — very decidedly so." That FDR was no
enemy to the fundamental structure of the American economy is revealed
by the fact that he liked one of Howard's concluding sentences so much he
repeated it in his own letter: "With all its faults and with the abuses it has
developed, our system has in the past enabled us to achieve greater mass
progress than has been attained by any other system on earth," and agreed
with the publisher that what the New Deal was about was not "revolution"
but the "orderly modernization of a system we want to preserve."[26]

The confusion, vacillation, and meandering that often characterized
New Deal economic policies was produced by the tension created between
what Roosevelt believed in and what he found himself having to do to bring
about recovery. Much of Roosevelt's heralded pragmatism stemmed not
from an absence of a prior faith but rather from the fact that the prior faith
he held was inadequate to deal with the situation he found himself in, and
he was constantly searching for solutions that would alleviate the situation
and do the least violence to those things in which he believed. Thus, as we
have seen, FDR never went as far as he could have in those crucial early
days of the New Deal. Thus many of the steps he took — such as his support of labor legislation and Keynesian pump-priming — he took with

some reluctance. Thus he did not give up on business support until it gave up on him — and he never gave up on it entirely. He made this clear in a speech in Chicago during the campaign of 1936 when he insisted: "It was this Administration which saved the system of private profit and free enterprise after it had been dragged to the brink of ruin by these same leaders who now try to scare you," and then turned to humor to deepen his point:

> Some of these people really forget how sick they were. But I know how sick they were. I have their fever charts. I know how the knees of all of our rugged individualists were trembling four years ago and how their hearts fluttered. They came to Washington in great numbers. Washington did not look like a dangerous bureaucracy to them then. Oh, no! It looked like an emergency hospital. All of the distinguished patients wanted two things — a quick hypodermic to end the pain and a course of treatment to cure the disease. They wanted them in a hurry; we gave them both. And now most of the patients seem to be doing very nicely. Some of them are even well enough to throw their crutches at the doctor.[27]

While Roosevelt's statement to Roy Howard was premature in 1935, the relative prosperity of 1937 seemed a more propitious time to act as if the New Deal were in fact complete. The economy had made an impressive recovery, with industrial production almost 80 percent greater than it had been in 1932 and agricultural income almost matching that of 1929. "The emergency," Senator James Byrnes of South Carolina announced in May, "has passed."[28] Although FDR was reviled by conservatives for reckless and irresponsible spending, and although he did proclaim that a "balanced economy rather than a balanced budget" was his goal, at no point did he accept deficit spending as normal policy or abandon his desire to balance the budget. He promised to do so during the campaign of 1936, and early in 1937 he reiterated his desire. "I have said fifty times that the budget will be balanced for the fiscal year 1938," he exclaimed to his conservative Vice President, John Nance Garner. "If you want me to say it again, I will say it either once or fifty times more. That is my intention."[29] He took an important step in this direction by substantially reduced funding for work relief, cutting the number of people working on WPA projects in half. In addition he decreased farm subsidies and encouraged the Federal Reserve to tighten credit, thus further reducing the circulation of money in the economy.

The times proved to be less propitious than FDR — and many of his supporters and opponents — had assumed. Indeed, while production, income, and profits had increased, the fact that 1937, with its seven million unemployed women and men — representing some 14 percent of the workforce — could have been considered prosperous in the first place, is a testament to the lowered expectations of the period and the deepening resignation that the United States would never again regain the buoyant abundance of the past. In his 1936 book *Spending to Save,* Harry Hopkins, the nation's relief administrator, wrote: "Intelligent people have long since left behind them the notion that under fullest recovery, and even with improved purchasing power, the unemployed will disappear."[30] In July 1937, 57 percent of those polled by the American Institute of Public Opinion agreed that "there will always be as many as five million unemployed in this country."[31]

By August 1937, the effects of FDR's policies of reducing the federal government's role in the economy were felt dramatically. Although many businessmen had called vigorously for a diminished federal presence, they proved unwilling or unable to step into the gap left by the withdrawal of government monies from the economy. The results were inevitable: the stock market plunged, along with production and sales, while unemployment soared to 20 percent of the workforce. Roosevelt, reluctant to increase government spending and debt, chose to wait the recession out, but waiting availed him no more than it had Herbert Hoover after the crash of 1929. He was besieged on all sides with contradictory advice: retrench further urged the conservatives; increase government spending counseled avid New Dealers; attack the trusts suggested the old Wilsonian progressives among his advisers. During his press conference of October 29, 1937, FDR told reporters of letters he had recently received from two distinguished economic experts: "One says the entire question is one of the velocity of capital turnover credit, so do not pay any attention to purchasing power. The other one says: forget all this algebraic formula about the velocity of capital turnover credit; the whole question is purchasing power on the part of one hundred and thirty million people." "It is," the President concluded wryly, "a fascinating study."[32]

It was not doctrines but circumstances that determined the President's course. He might have been ambivalent about unbalanced budgets but never about human suffering and want. Unlike his predecessor, he could find no rationale for tolerating the misery of his fellow citizens or blinding himself to their ordeal. He had been visibly moved when he told Secretary of the Interior Ickes that during his 1936 campaign stops in the West he heard voices from the crowds that lined the streets exclaiming: "He saved my home," "He gave me a job," "God bless you, Mr. President."[33]

When in March 1938 stocks took a frightening plunge, business conditions deteriorated further, and there were several million newly unemployed workers, FDR's decision was made for him. On April 14, he sent a message to Congress urging the appropriation of billions of dollars for work relief agencies and farm subsidies, which, along with more liberal policies governing credit, would help restore the economy and diminish the massive new suffering.

These were difficult days for the President. The day before he was to send his message to Congress, his Secretary of the Treasury and old friend, Henry Morgenthau, told him, "if you insist on going through with this spending program I am seriously thinking of resigning." In an emotional scene, FDR was able to dissuade him, but this encounter typified the pressures he was laboring under; pressures that emanated not only from his opponents but from within his own Administration and party as well. Not long after his confrontation with Morgenthau, he met with a group of his advisers and read them a first draft of his message to Congress, and then with a group of his speechwriters he worked on the final version until one o'clock in the morning and announced his intention to go to bed. His secretary, Missy LeHand, reminded him that he had scheduled a Fireside Chat for the next evening. "Oh, I'm tired, let me go to bed," he responded, but LeHand insisted: "You just have to get something down on paper tonight." Sam Rosenman, who was present, described what happened next:

> He leaned back on the sofa with an air of resignation and shut his eyes for a long time. We sat there very quietly; after a while we thought he had actually fallen asleep. But finally he opened his eyes and, starting to dictate, said, "Mah F-r-a-a-nds" in such an exaggerated drawl of "My friends" (with which salutation nearly all his fireside chats started), and with such a comic expression, that we all broke out laughing. That perked him right up, and he dictated steadily until 2:15 A.M., when we let him at last go to bed.[34]

That afternoon he joined Rosenman, Harry Hopkins, and Thomas Corcoran and worked on the final draft until six. He then took a nap, as he often did before a radio speech, had a light dinner in bed, and at ten-thirty in the evening, in his twelfth Fireside Chat, he addressed a beleaguered, apprehensive American people in an address that the *New York Times* found "strikingly reminiscent . . . of the dark days of 1933, when Mr. Roosevelt first came into power and in rapid-fire fashion set in motion a series of governmental actions to halt the economic depression which started in 1929."[35]

He opened by apologizing for intruding upon Holy Week but explained that what he had to say "to you, the people of the country, is of such immediate need and relates so closely to the lives of human beings and the prevention of human suffering that . . . I have been strengthened by the thought that by speaking tonight there may be greater peace of mind and that the hope of Easter may be more real at firesides everywhere."[36] In the past seven months, he said, the country had suffered a "visible setback." He had waited "patiently to see whether the forces of business itself would counteract it," but it had become apparent "that Government itself can no longer safely fail to take aggressive Government steps to meet it." He assured his listeners that the nation had not returned to the disastrous conditions that had prevailed when he first took office: banks were safe, stock speculation was minimized, farmers and workers had greater income, government had "an established and accepted responsibility for relief."

> But I know that many of you have lost your jobs or have seen your friends or members of your families lose their jobs, and I do not propose that the Government shall pretend not to see these things. . . . I conceive the first duty of Government is to protect the economic welfare of all the people in all sections and in all groups.

He spent a good part of his hastily prepared Chat quoting and summarizing passages from the message he had sent to Congress earlier that day. At the heart of his message and his thought were the people's "human problems of food and clothing and homes and education and health and old age." He had told the Congress that neither it nor the Chief Executive could afford

> to weaken or destroy great reforms which, during the past five years, have been effected on behalf of the American people. In our rehabilitation of the banking structure and of agriculture,

in our provisions for adequate and cheaper credit for all types of business, in our acceptance of national responsibility for unemployment relief, . . . in our encouragement of housing, and slum clearance and home ownership, in our supervision of stock exchanges and public utility holding companies . . . in our provision for social security itself, the electorate of America wants no backward steps taken.

On the contrary, the federal government had to move forward, and he proposed three groups of measures for Congress to act upon. First, to appropriate a billion and a quarter dollars more than he had asked for in January for the Works Progress Administration, the Farm Security Administration, the National Youth Administration, and the Civilian Conservation Corps. Second, to make some two billion dollars of gold reserves and bank reserves available for the credit needs of the country. Third "to make definite additions to the purchasing power of the Nation" by enabling the United States Housing Authority to undertake the immediate construction of three hundred million dollars worth of additional slum clearance projects; to renew public works projects by making one billion dollars worth of needed public improvements in states, cities, and counties; to add to his original requests an additional one hundred million dollars for federal aid to highways, thirty-seven million dollars for flood control and reclamation, and twenty-five million dollars for federal buildings in various parts of the country.

In recommending this program I am thinking not only of the immediate economic needs of the people of the Nation, but also of their personal liberties — the most precious possession of all Americans. I am thinking of our democracy. . . .

History proves that dictatorships do not grow out of strong and successful governments but out of weak and helpless governments. If by democratic methods people get a government strong enough to protect them from fear and starvation, their democracy succeeds, but if they do not, they grow impatient. Therefore, the only sure bulwark of continuing liberty is a government strong enough to protect the interests of the people, and a people strong enough and well enough informed to maintain its sovereign control over its government.

We are a rich Nation; we can afford to pay for security and prosperity without having to sacrifice our liberties into the bargain.

As he often did, Roosevelt assumed the role of historian and teacher, explaining that during the first century of our existence the federal government had distributed its vast holdings of land, timber, and other resources to the American people in order to promote business and economic growth. "Thus, from our earliest days we have had a tradition of substantial Government help to our system of private enterprise." It is therefore "following tradition as well as necessity, if Government strives to put idle money and idle men to work, to increase our public wealth and to build up the health and strength of the people — to help our system of private enterprise to function again." It was crucial that these public expenditures be fairly distributed among all the people. "Consequently, I am again expressing my hope that the Congress will enact at this session a wage and hour bill putting a floor under industrial wages and a limit on working hours — to ensure a better distribution of our prosperity, a better distribution of available work, and a sounder distribution of buying power."

He reminded his audience that the increase in the national debt of some sixteen billion dollars included billions of dollars worth of assets: "schools, roads, bridges, tunnels, public buildings, parks and a host of other things that meet your eye in every one of the thirty-one hundred counties in the United States." Government spending not only added wealth, it also acted "as a trigger" to stimulate private spending of vast proportions. He concluded with what he called "a personal word to you."

> I never forget that I live in a house owned by all the American people and that I have been given their trust.
>
> I try always to remember that their deepest problems are human. . . . I try not to forget that what really counts at the bottom of it all, is that the men and women willing to work can have a decent job, — a decent job to take care of themselves and their homes and their children adequately; that the farmer, the factory worker, the storekeeper, the gas station man, the manufacturer, the merchant — big and small — the banker . . . that all of these can be sure of a reasonable profit and safety for the earnings that they make — not for today nor tomorrow alone, but as far ahead as they can see.

. . . I always try to remember that reconciling differences cannot satisfy everyone completely. . . . But I know that I must never give up — that I must never let the greater interest of all the people down, merely because that might be for the moment the easiest personal way out.

I believe that we have been right in the course we have charted. To abandon our purpose of building a greater, a more stable and a more tolerant America, would be to miss the tide and perhaps to miss the port. I propose to sail ahead. I feel sure that your hopes, I feel sure that your help are with me. For to reach a port, we must sail — sail, not lie at anchor, sail, not drift.

"I heard Roosevelt deliver this speech," Rosenman has written. "His voice seemed to reach out right into every home in the United States. Those paragraphs, spoken badly, could have sounded very 'corny'; but, as he delivered them, they expressed the deep, sincere, warm emotions of a leader who was terribly concerned about the millions of human beings whose welfare was so greatly affected by the policies of the government he led."[37]

APRIL 14, 1938

Dear Mr. President,

My wife and I stopped in the middle of drying our dinner dishes tonight to sit down in the kitchen beside the radio to hear your talk. I know the many hundred men who work where I do have also listened.

We cannot afford telegrams and too many of us feel that letters are of no consequence. Yet knowing how you have been harrassed by the loud voice of a selfish minority I am certain that a word of warm encouragement is not amiss.

You have not let us down. We know that. All the forces of propoganda in the world can't keep from us that knowledge. We know that you have kept the pledge you gave us. That you have justified the faith we have placed in you. We aren't very articulate about it. The men at my plant like men elsewhere were beginning to take you for granted — sort of the way a man takes health for granted until he gets sick. But it's now become obvious that the fight wasn't over with our 27 million votes in 1936 — it's obvious that we must make our voices heard again. We know that you are carrying on the program we voted for — and we mark well those delegates of ours who are letting us down, who are blocking our program and our will.

We have gained a better life — we mean to maintain this better life and extend it to others. Our wishes that you have so persistantly fought for have materialized. We used to leave work at nine o'clock in the evening. Now every day we go home at five! We used to live in a one room shack. Now we live in a flat with a kitchen, living room and bedroom — and best of all — with plumbing! Before we didn't dare hope for children. Now it's not such a bad idea as we can afford orange juice and cod liver oil. We even have a few extras such as a pork roast some Sundays and perhaps ice cream.

It's not important that this has happened to just us. But it is important that this has happened for so many millions of us, important that you are trying to extend this to many millions more.

And we do not forget that we have these things only because you did not let us down!

How necessary it is that you know these things. You have hurled at you every day the clamoring voices of self seeking individuals. How often, though, do you hear the voice of the people? Believe me, Mr. President it is the people speaking now. You must know that we are for you and with you.

Sincerely,

Mark F. Hawkins
San Francisco, California

APRIL 15, 1938

Dear Mr. President as a Citizen and a Colored American of this Country; also a veteran of the World War and an earnest listner of all your chats especially the last one made. In this regard I am attempting in these lines to express my sincere feeling toward you as a leader. I first wish to state I am unable to say to you and about you in words what is in my heart toward you. But as a man you are human, kind and sympathetic; as a Leader, you are Courageous Fearless and yet Gentle; and as an excutive thou art full of thoughts and masterful. God has truly sent you to the Seat of this Government to preside at such a times as these.

I am praying that you overcome oppositions confronting you and accheive in your efforts, that from 1933 until now, can be clearly seen have all been based on the needs of the people. May God Bless you and your household.

A true friend.

Rev. William White, Sr.
Venice, Ill.

APRIL 17, 1938

Dear Sir:

I want to register my emphatic protest against your proposed program.

Your policies have already begun to undermine the most precious possession of a people — its morale. They are stultifying the ideals of individual independence and integrity which gave this Nation whatever leadership it had. They are reducing the people to shame-faced alms-takers and grafting idlers. Your leadership along the lines you are following are deleterious.

I write only because of an earnest desire to arouse you from your error. . . .

The production and distribution of wealth, supply and demand of commodities, rent, wages and interest; price, etc., are all governed by Natural Laws — Laws which neither Presidents, nor Congress, nor Dictators can circumvent, Laws which are no respecters of men or measures. We may disobey them as we are doing and we can reap the consequent "depressions", "recessions", unemployment, poverty and all the horrors of life by "trial and error" with eventual chaos.

Therefore I beg of you since you have the position of leadership to seek the Law and follow it. It has been discovered and expounded and called to your attention more than once since you became president. You haven't the moral right to neglect it and lead a people to ruin.

Very truly yours,

Olive Maguire
Berkeley, California

APRIL 18, 1938

Dear sir:

I missed listening to your "Fireside Chat" last Friday, so I read it in the papers.

Your alibi for the present "re-cession" may get by a lot of people who dont know what it is all about, but some of us cant swallow it. . . .

Why cant you and your New Dealers recognize the truth that too much of the wealth is concentrated in the hands of the few for any ordinary activity, "pump priming" or what not, to balance our economic system so that human activity can ebb and flow according to the needs, desires, and aspirations of humanity. . . .

Your "pump priming" plan now, if it goes thru, will have the same effect as your first one — it will set the machinery going for a while, how long remains to be seen, but if you and your New Dealers dont do something that MUST BE DONE meanwhile, you will be going out of office about the time when the second re-cession comes along.

If a man has been robbed of everything he has, you cant make him normal economically, nor mentally, spiritually or physically, by giving him a WPA job, or a $30 per month pension. That is not restoration. That is TOLERATION of the crime, especially when nothing is done to make a repetition of the crime impossible. . . .

We dont want fine words, sympathy, and assurance that no one shall go hungry. It takes more than that to make a normal human being. We want RESTORATION of the rights that we know are ours. We want an equitable distribution of the wealth that humanity has produced. . . .

Sincerely yours,

J. EMIL NELSON
Willmar, Minnesota

APRIL 15, 1938

Sir —

I am amazed that after the "pump priming" you have already poured into the Country you should have nothing better to offer than a repetition of the same old dose. Surely it is apparent that this method is no good and cannot possibly take the place of the business methods this country has always followed. This proposed expenditure will bring the U.S. debt above $45,000,000,000. How can any apparent taxation possibly take care of the interest on this amount of money? To say nothing of reducing the principal?

My forefathers fought in the Revolutionary war, my father four years on the Union side in the Civil war and I certainly am opposed to the prospective ruin of this country by such methods as you are pursuing. There is no doubt that our present depression has been brought about entirely by your own false measures in combatting business with one hand while distributing political largess with the other.

I am 63 years old; have been out of work for several years, but my wife and I have managed to get along on a little tea-room business without one cent from the Government at any time. You are making it increasingly hard for every one in any small business to exist: to say nothing of what you are doing to larger businesses. Of course there is lack of confidence; how could it be otherwise with your vacillating policy?

It was a sorry day for America when you were elected. You will go down in history as the man who ruined America.

Yours.

Harry H. Rung
Waynesville, N.C.

APRIL 28, 1938

Dear Mr. President:

I should like to voice my humble approval of your plan for recovery as expressed in your recent radio address. Such forward-looking, courageous words seem to me in the best traditions of American leadership.

This plan must be put into immediate action. The plain people of America, and especially those whom you have designated as the ill-clothed, ill-housed, ill-fed "one-third" — these people cannot wait. The farmers cannot wait. The youth of the land cannot wait. None of us can hold out very long in the face of this devastating new recession.

That is why we urge you, Mr. President, to act upon your words. That is why I and the majority of my friends promise you our utmost support in your program.

I am not interested in balanced budgets and government interference in business. I am asking to see America — including myself — at work once more, if not in private industry, then on WPA. I am not interested in "rugged individualism". I am interested in the life and health of the average person — and that includes myself.

Sincerely yours,

Hellen Tenney
New York

APRIL 15, 1938

Dear Mr. President:

This being our 25th Wedding Anniversary I would like to celebrate it by doing something so different, that even to me it seems just a little forward and brazen.

But lets forget it at the present, for after hearing you talk last night over the radio, I made up my mind that I could talk to you as sincerely as to my own brother. Do you think Mr. President, that if you appealed to the people of our country, to play fair in every respect, I mean this, that if every man financialy independent and holding a job some other man could fill (propably just as good) would give this said job up, and if every woman employed that really does not have to work, would stay home and raise a family or take up some hobby (she would be much happier too) Im positive there would be plenty of work to go around and hence end the depression. Im not saying this to criticize any of your work, for to my estimation, there is no person living or dead that has accomplished as much as you have, you have saved our home from foreclosure, and helped us throu direct relief in 1933 and even now my husband got a job on the W.P.A. after being off steady employment 6 years, so you see, dear Mr. President, there's no one more gratefull than I am, but Im a woman past 45 and mother of 7 children, — ranging from 23 to 10 years of age — 5 of which are boys, so naturally Im a little concerned about their future, and also the future of all the younger generation.

Forgive this letter dear Mr. President, I just had to do it.

Sincerely and
Humbly
yours

Mrs. Agnes Drufke
Chicago, Ill.

*   *   *

Dear Mr Presdent

After listening to you speach over the Radio I have allways said You cant borrow you self out of debt, as I never buy enything unless I have the money or know where its coming from. Credet is the Curse of this country as its over done

As there is no steady work in the factory any more

Working man buys Cars on time Elec stove etc. and then the're laid off, and they cant Pay and the man take his car or what ever he cant pay for after he has Put $100.00 or more into it. . . .

Real astate Insurrince & the Auto Business are three of the crookest business in this country All these things should be controlled by the Government as this is part of Wall St. dirty work on the poor working man. . . .

Stop the Recession

by

No. 1 cut White House expenses and do away with strikes all over the country. . . .

No. 3 stop married Women from working when there husbands are working. Put more men to work. let the Women stay home where they belong. . . .

No. 5 Welfare is demorolising the hole country give us work. not Welfare let keep our honer & Liberty. . . .

No. 7 Pass the Townsend Plan to take the old men out of factory and give the young men a chance to work. . . .

These are a few things for you to think about to make it a better country in which to Live

a good Citizen

Your. Truly

Wm. Mackintosh

Mt. Morris, Mich.

APRIL 16, 1938

Dear Sir: I heard your fireside chat and it made me sick at heart, to think you have nothing on your program only the same old thing you have had for 5 yrs. just giving to those who will take it. You have tried nothing else for 5 yrs and we are worse off then we were before. You speak of another depression. We have never been out of the first one and anyone knows it. The people around here have just been living off the Government, and the rest of us people ever since this started. You spoke of certain businesses making more. Yes the car business is making more because you are giving W.P.A. workers and others our money to buy them with, the mail order houses are making more because you are giving people money to order, the saloons and pool halls are flourishing because that is where the W.P.A. workers spend their time only what few hours they have to works. None of these wouldn't sell much if it were left up to us who just have what we make ourselves. The reliefers and W.P.A. workers and Farmers who draw big checks just laugh when we cant have the things they have. . . . You have enough bribed to put over anything you wish for they have come to the place where they wont vote against a dollar but God only knows what is to become of us few who aren't getting anything. It is taking all we have for taxes to just exist. We have little children ready for high school we cant send them for we haven't the money. We cant do anything the governments favorites are doing and yet I guess we will have to drag along for we wont sign a paper and say we are destitute, can't make our way, can't get any credit, to get on the W.P.A., till you take everything we've got.

Yours

Mrs. A. M. Jones
Inka, Ill.

APRIL 14, 1938

Dear Sir:

We heard your radio address and have concluded that we're all out of step but Jim.

I travel the state of Georgia continuously and if your ideas of recovery are right all of us down here are crazy.

Did it ever enter your head that the country ran before your time and will after your gone? Try dipping your head in a pail of water three times and just bring it out twice. Then the country will really recover.

Yours truly,

Harry Spencer
Atlanta, Ga.

APRIL 15, 1938

AS A NATIVE BORN AMERICAN WHO FOUGHT FOR 18 MONTHS IN THE FRONT LINE TRENCHES TO PRESERVE WHAT I CONCEIVED THEN AND NOW ASSERT TO BE OUR TRADITIONAL SYSTEM OF REPRESENTATIVE GOVERNMENT I

WISH TO SAY THIS. I WOULD RATHER HAVE DIED BY AN ENEMY BULLET THAN TO HAVE LIVED TO SEE THE DAY WHEN THE PRESIDENT OF MY COUNTRY CAN SERIOUSLY ADVOCATE DOCTRINES AS EXPRESSED IN YOUR FIRESIDE TALK TONIGHT WHICH ARE SO COMPLETELY OPPOSED TO THE THINGS FOR WHICH I FOUGHT THAT I SOLEMNLY PROMISE YOU THAT I WILL GIVE WITHOUT STINT OR LIMIT ALL OF MY FREE TIME AND ENERGY TO DEFEAT AT ELECTION YOU AND ALL CANDIDATES FOR OFFICE WHO SUBSCRIBE TO YOUR SPECIOUS DOCTRINES.

DONALD A. HOBART
BRONXVILLE, N.Y.

APRIL 14, 1938

Dear Mr. President.

Your talk over the radio Thursday was wonderful. . . .

We should have a "Wage and Hour" Bill by all means. Right here in Dade County, the richest county in Florida where millions are spent every winter for pleasure there are many families living in one and two room huts with no electric light or bath. A little woman whose child I teach in Public Schools works six days a week for 6.00 and seems glad to have the work. She is a nice sensible woman too, not much education, but an honest upright person trying to rear three children. It is a shame yet nothing is done about it. There are men with families working for 1.50 to 2.00 per day. They cant live decently or give their children proper food. It must be changed by Congress and those who have the authority to do it.

Your friend & supporter,

Sarah M. Cobb
Miami, Fla.

APRIL 14, 1938

My dear President: —

. . . The night before your radio talk, while sitting in a restaurant, I listened to such unjust criticisms of your theories and policies by some of my friends, most of them quoting your personal enemies, that I resented them as tho they were criticising me personally. I thought to myself, "What a fool our president is to be working so hard to please such ingrates." But to-night, as I listened to your words which I know and feel come from your heart, I was again moved as I was on that famous night in March 1933.

Carry on, in spite of the fools who know not what is good for them. May God bless you and yours.

Very humbly yours,

Nat Baumann
New York, N.Y.

*   *   *

Dear President Roosevelt:

As staunch believers in your interpretation of the American way, We, the undersigned, feel it to be our duty to leave the vast ranks of the inarticulate and give voice to our approval of your humane program.

We have followed with admiration your capable leadership in lifting the nation from the gloomy depths of despair into which it had been plunged by the laissez-faire policies of a decade.

We have witnessed the tragic destruction of the earning power of many — either from technological inroads, or because of other factors — and have seen men so displaced, unceremoniously thrown into the lap of Government for food, clothing, and shelter, and, for the first time in our history, have seen Government accept that responsibility by creating "W.P.A." "P.W.A." "C.C.C." and other worthy work-relief agencies.

We have witnessed, too, the most vociferous criticism of such Government action emanating from those who were instrumental in creating the burden. Even during the period of recovery, the destruction of earning power, through the installation of labor-saving devices, goes feverishly on aiding in creating a recession, because the ability to produce exceeds the ability to consume because the ability to buy has been destroyed, and always the Government has been required to shoulder the added burden.

Needless to say, we wholeheartedly accept Social-Security; visualizing the economic security and attendant contentment it will afford us and millions like us, who otherwise, in an age where the productive years of the average worker is gradually diminishing, would be forced to face an insecure old age not pleasant to contemplate.

We have recently had occasion to witness the wisdom and soundness of "F.D.I.C." when an economic setback has failed to follow historical precedent, in that it failed to produce long lines of panic-stricken, desperate, people; storming the doors of failing banks, and in its stead, see complete confidence existing in the security of insured deposits, speaking eloquently of the fact that "F.D.I.C." is a perfectly functioning being.

We are convinced that the inexorable hand of time will bring into full view the magnificent import of the reform and social legislation enacted by your administration whereby the common man, championed as never before, will have the opportunity to share equitably in the bountiful beneficence of a kindly provider.

The tortured interpretations presented to the public, through the misuse of the Freedom of the Press, and through other sources, seeking to belittle your sound program, has reacted quite favorably from many, for it has spurred us to seek and find more reliable channels of information in quest of the facts, and the result is the greater ease with which to recognize propoganda.

Accordingly, we feel that we owe you and your administration a deep debt of gratitude for what has been achieved, and a pledge of our unwavering loyal support in your splendid objective to rid our country of the stigma that one-third of our population is still ill-nourished, ill-clothed, and ill-housed.

We are confident that when the true history of our generation has been written and the names of your detractors will have disappeared in the maw of mediocrity, yours will stand immortalized as a true friend and leader of man, as one, indeed worthy of his generation.

It is our sincere hope that you may enjoy continued good health, and retain your indomitable courage to chart our course along the road that you have so ably mapped out.

> [signed by Henry G. Steinbrenner and
> forty-one other men and women]
> Chicago, Illinois

APRIL 17, 1938

Dear Mr. President:

Your splendid talk given on the evening of Holy Thursday cannot but make the working man feel secure as long as you are in the White House. In a very small but temporary job as claim clerk with the Unemployment Compensation Bureau, I can see the suffering in the faces of the men and women who are receiving their small checks.

The Collins & Aikman Corp. where most of these people have been working have enough orders to work twenty four hours a day, just as they have been doing for years; but I know that they are purposely closed in an attempt to break the spirit of the people, and to embarrass your administration. They are attempting to impress the public that you and your Congress have imposed too many taxes on them, and that shall stay closed unless you lessen their burden of taxation.

I want you to know Mr. President that the workers still have faith in you, and that they do no believe the bunk handed to them by Charles B. Rockwell and his Collins & Aikman Corp. I do not know how much longer they can endure it. The compensation checks they are receiving weekly are diminishing, and the Lord only knows what will happen to them.

Please Mr. President do not let them down, If big business is retarding your program, crack down, and crack down hard. I feel certain that most of them could open their factories to-morrow, but they purposely are trying to make the people lose faith in you, don't let them do it.

Call me a Fascist, Bolshevist, Anarchist, Socialist, or a nut (one of your secretaries will probably call me that anyhow) my solution would be for you to declare that an emergency exists, take over all the mills and factories and have the government run them. If you had a few more able men like my Senator Green to help you I believe you could do it. Although it may be unconstitutional, when a man and his family is hungry, get him a job, he doesn't care how you do it. . . .

Sincerely yours,

Dominic J. Langello
Bristol, R.I.

APRIL 28, 1938

Honorable Sir:

For the last thirty years I have been actively engaged in the Real Estate business in this section, and I am addressing you as disapproving the $4,500,000,000 relief expenditure which you propose to make. . . .

If I had you out here for an hour, I could show you miles and miles of river and creek beds where W.P.A. workers spent millions of our hard earned cash on putting in inadequate, poorly constructed, poorly planned flood control work, and what is left to show for all this time, labor and money? Nothing! Miles and miles of river bank covered with rock work laid in sand, when concrete was absolutely necessary. Any eleven year old child could have predicted it would go out with the first hard rain and it did. No wonder we are all heartsick.

Another point I wish to get across to you, is that you can never win, barter or steal the confidence of thinking people in this country as long as you try to fool them. Some Americans may be dumb, but not the large majority of them. You can't take the laboring man with his limited mental capacity, and put them over or on a par with live thinking, brainy business men. If you don't play ball with business men who furnish labor with jobs you are due to learn a harder lesson than you have already learned. . . .

Thanking you, I am

Respectfully,

Colin Stewart
Pasadena, Cal.

APRIL 14, 1938

Dear Sir:

. . . In June, 1935, my husband and I motored from Portland through Washington, Idaho, Montana, North and South Dakota to St. Paul, Minn., and returned home by way of Iowa, Nebraska, Wyoming, Idaho, into Oregon. It was hot and dry even then in most of the states just prior to the drought spell. In everyone of the most insignificant, barren little towns, the only work that appeared to be available was a WPA project and every one of these projects was a most necessary one and perhaps the outstanding civic accomplishment in that particular place. Without these, I doubt if people could have carried on. In Portland, we have many wonderful projects that have been accomplished through the WPA throughout the state of Oregon. The CCC boys have beautified natural scenic points of interest by their handiwork almost unbelievably and it is a joy to all who have the privilege of using these facilities. I have an elderly Uncle, and if it wasn't for WPA work, he and his wife would be without funds and would lose their home. So with any criticism that comes, you will know deep within yourself the goodness you have wrought.

Your devoted and humble servant,

(Mrs. E. H.) Marguerite McMahill
Portland, Oregon

APRIL 15, 1938

Dear President Roosevelt:

. . . I believe your speech was most helpful and inspiring at this time. How can anybody be against you?! You have kept so many parents and children together through W.P.A.

My husband is working under W.P.A. and what would we, including two small boys, four and three years, do without it! My husband is a strong, healthy man used to outside work. As you know all the work, outside, not under W.P.A., is or has all the men they want.

You have made it possible for us to lead a respectable life. We live in four rooms upstairs which I try to keep clean and orderly by using plenty of soap and water freely. I try to buy and prepare good food so that we stay healthy and strong.

My husband helps put up small bridges over creeks in this county. He enjoys the work very much.

I think your ideas and plans are very good if you only can carry them out. You have my loyal support as everyone I come in contact with I am in your favor.

May W.P.A. continue for a long time!

Yours very truly

Mrs. Albert Downs
Rochester, N.Y.

MAY 10, 1938

Dear Mr. Roosevelt,

. . . I am a student on the W.P.A. Music Project I am also a wife & a mother of a high school son.

Ive wanted to play the piano since I was a child I could only take a few lessons when I could afford them that was rarely.

When I heard of the W.P.A. Music Project I immediately joined one of the classes It has given me hope Art helps one to live.

The art projects should be broadened The American people should be made art concious No wage cuts The 25 dollars the artist gets is far too little My husband makes 25 dollars a week Its a terrible struggle to live Its borrowing here & borrowing there, then the worry of how to give back

One consolation We have these days is that we have a president that is fighting on the side of the have nots.

Friends & I are looking forward to hearing more of your fireside chats Its the only way that you can get the American people to understand what you are trying to do The newspapers generally distort the news to suit certain interests and play down your effort on behalf of the people.

Wishing you and Mrs. Roosevelt the best of health

I am

Yours sincerely

Etta Rich
New York, New York

APRIL 21, 1938

Your Excellency:—

After hearing your "Fireside talk" over our local station W.S.M.B. on Thursday evening, I feel privileged to write to you. . . .

We are indeed indebted to you to the fullest extent for enabling us to lead a useful, pleasant and normal life. For instance, what should I do, if it were not for the W.P.A. A woman past middle life, lately widowed, and with no income other than my salary as Senior Translator and research worker? I have been assigned to one of your projects at our local "Historic State Museum" in the heart of the "Vieux Carre" I spend six hours each day, delving in old documents, yellow with age, moth eaten, water stained, partially burned in a fire which threatened to destroy Our City in 1788 — reading the history of our Metropolis in the French vernacular, and translating it. These hours which I spend in quaint surroundings, in an environment replete with historic relics and memories, are in contrast to my home where I repair every evening to a comfortable, well kept house, to be greeted by my Mother and Sister who are ever gracious and happy to welcome my return to the fireside. Incidentally those ladies feel very much indebted to you for the joy and pleasure they enjoy.

. . . There had been propaganda talks of a depression worst in it's effects and ravages than the one from which we were emerging; and no words of encouragement, comfort and solace were ever spoken until you delivered your address Thursday night. I was enveloped so to speak in a mantle of insecurity and mental anguish until you lifted the pall from my shoulders. . . .

With the assurance of my deep appreciation for all you have done for me, and asking God to bless and protect you Our Beloved President, I remain,

Very respectfully yours,

(Mrs.) Marie Louise Charbonnet
New Orleans, La.

APRIL 15, 1938

My dear President Roosevelt:

You have just finished your 'Fireside' talk over the radio. Somehow, since your voice came out so clear and distinct it seemed as though you were speaking individually to me, hence to each of the millions listening in! individually!

Your message had an especial message to me, since my work as an Investigator for New York City Relief, in what might be termed one of the worst housing sections of this city. Most of these buildings are condemned and will come down, and as you spoke and have spoken before — I realized afresh that you are the first President we have ever had who has been so thoroughly awakened to the situations that exist to-day, among and in the under-priveleged classes.

. . . I have been since the begining deeply interested in your program —

saw you at the first Inauguration within the Capital, as I also saw your wife — and I felt then as I still do that both of you were sent by an all wise Providence to help this country and its people to a new and better and more unselfish day!! One of the reasons also, that I think you must have been a great men even in your youth, was that you had the vision, perception and intelligence to choose Elanore Roosevelt for your life-partner!! She is certainly a great spirit and a great soul, unselfish with a big and noble heart. . . .

I do not know exactly where you and Mrs. Roosevelt get all your broad and basic understanding and philosophy from, coming from the homes you both did — but to me it is remarkable you have the character and insight and understanding to stand up (despite many of your wealthy friends) and say and plan and do as you both have since you came to Washington! . . .

With my social-work case load I see only the poorest and the unskilled but their families are large and increasing, even tho' men have not had work for many years — these large families fostered from relief and other charity organizations. If these people could grow up to be rugged and healthy citizens I would not care, but the health conditions even with better housing will never fully take care of the rapid increase in the birth-rate! When will Birth-Control have real planning thru' the Government so as to reduce the population in these quarters. . . . I can see where Birth-Control Clinics have already helped many plan for and 'space' their children, but this is not carried to those among the very poor and less intelligent groups — many of whom are in fear of the laws of their Catholic Church! You have been so wonderfully forceful and creative in going ahead with your program in face of opposition; perhaps you may be able later on to give this issue some of your attention!! . . .

From one of many who sends out a prayer for renewed strength and courage, for the daily battle! to go on, despite all adversity and opposition. These are sincere words.

Janet Speakman
New York, N.Y.

APRIL 20, 1938

Dear Mr. President Roosevelt: —

After hearing your radio address to the public and pondering it a few days I am impelled to write you . . . not since Abraham Lincoln have we had a president with such zeal behind his efforts to help the enslaved man. To be sure it's a different form of slavery but non the less tyranneous.

. . . I am a Sunday school teacher in a local church here in Detroit and was endeavoring to teach one of my 5 year old boys about Moses and the children of Israel in their pilgrimage through the Red Sea. Later during the week the little fellow, who lives near me, was playing in the street with another neighbor boy. They came dashing in to me to settle an argument they were having. Frankie said to me, "Auntie, was it Moses or President Roosevelt who led the children of Isabel through the Red Sea? Freddie said it Moses but I said it was President Roosevelt." So you see even the little children have the greatest confidence in your ability and we larger children pray that you will be successful in leading the children of this great Democracy through the great sea of labor's troubled waters. May we all pull together and reach the shore in safety.

Thank you and sincerely
Yours

Mrs W. E. Lange
Detroit, Michigan

GOOD FRIDAY, 1938

My dear Mr. President:

I am only one of the hundreds of thousands of ordinary people for whom you are striving so nobly. But your fire-side talks have come to our home and made us feel that you are not only a great leader, but a friend as well.

Last night it seemed to us that, in spite of your superb courage and gallantry, there was a note of weariness and a trace of discouragement. I should think this might well be so, and I felt that we, for whom you are fighting, must some how reach you quickly with a word of faith and encouragement.

I am the mother of a family of growing boys, and I would give my children something even more important than food and good physical care. They need faith and ideals of service, and examples of heroism. To them you are a great living hero, fighting against the tremendous forces of greed and fear and tyranny. For them your struggle has all the poetic glamour of the old epics, as well as the fascination of an actual contest in which some day they must take part. The contest which will mean the life or death of democracy. And they feel for you all the whole-hearted loyalty a boy gives to a great warrior.

My husband is a newspaper man, whose task is studying foreign affairs. Sometimes, I am afraid, the world looks to him like a quaking bog of deceit and hate and lost illusions.

To him you are a beacon of light. You have given him something much finer even than economic security. You have given him back a faith in decent, sane government — a faith which he lost somewhere in France during the war.

I hope you will forgive my writing to you of my family, but I'm sure the same things are true in many, many families, from whom you never hear.

The newspapers are full of bitterness and criticism. The columnists scream with hate. But I'm afraid you don't hear from all the little homes where you are loved and honored, and where your cheerful courage is an inspiration.

This is Good Friday and we are recalling the supreme sacrifices of the Great Leader, who was betrayed and crucified for our sake.

May Easter time bring you renewed strength and courage to carry your great burdens. You have our gratitude and love.

Very sincerely yours,

(Mrs. James H. Powers) Anne Campbell Powers
Sudbury, Mass.

APRIL 15, 1938

Dear Mr. Roosevelt,

In listening to the opening words about Holy Week in your radio speech last night, I felt sorry that you had not also recognized that your Jewish listeners were celebrating Passover. Mention of their Holiday would have included instead of excluding a large group of your people and would have added to the sense of unity which your talk stressed.

Very sincerely yours,

Caroline F. Ware
Vienna, Virginia

EPILOGUE

AFTER 1938, Franklin D. Roosevelt faced two challenges, in a country divided on both: he needed to preserve the New Deal and simultaneously maneuver to keep out of the coming war. First the threat and then the reality of World War II increasingly drew his attention and efforts. But the President continued to be confronted by domestic problems, and he continued to have to depend on a fractious Democratic Party for support of his reform program. In the midst of the extreme crisis of 1933, he had generally received what he wanted from a compliant Congress. Nevertheless, he understood that the nature of the American party system constituted a potential obstacle to political innovation. In a country as large and heterogeneous as the United States, Democrats elected from different geographic regions, different states, and different counties or cities often had little in common, representing divergent constituencies, cultures, and belief systems. Because of his tendency to seek advice from both conservatives and liberals, and by insisting that party labels were less important than others contended, FDR had established a binding hold on the American people, but he still needed the support of his party in the Congress. Although the need for restructuring the Democratic Party had been clear to the President from the beginning, he was loath to confront southern whites directly. Southern Democrats, stalwarts of the party and chairmen of many Senate and House committees on whose votes the President depended, saw themselves as defenders of states' rights and were unhappy with efforts by the federal government to right the economy or take on other domestic issues. They also opposed legislation in support of African Americans, many of whom had shed their loyalty to the Republican Party of Lincoln and voted Democratic for the first time in the congressional election of 1934.

The final major social reform of the New Deal—at least until the GI Bill of 1944—was the Fair Labor Standards Act of 1938, which abolished child labor in interstate commerce and established minimum wages and maximum hours. Despite overwhelming Democratic majorities in both houses, this important bill passed only after conservatives had weakened many of its provisions. As President Barack Obama had to contend in 2009 with Blue Dog and other conservative Democrats who opposed essential features of his effort at health care reform, Franklin Roosevelt could not prevent conservative Democrats of his day from watering down important provisions of his labor reform. In fact, the Democratic Party appeared as inherently unstable and as prone to ideological and political stalemate in the late 1930s as it had been when Roosevelt became its leader. That FDR desperately wanted to avoid leaving that kind of legacy became clear when he decided to oppose conservative fellow Democrats in the 1938 party primaries. He sided with the liberal school of thought that "recognizes that the new conditions throughout the world call for new remedies" and complained about attempts to "reawaken long slumbering racial and religious enmities which should have no place in this country." FDR's attempt to purge his own party won him more publicity than success, and all of the most conservative Democrats he most openly opposed were renominated, which in the South of that time was tantamount to reelection.

The outbreak of World War II in Europe in September 1939 shifted the focus to foreign affairs. Although he shared many of the hesitations, concerns, and confusions that the American people had about the impending war, the President spent much of his energy fighting the U.S. tradition of evading entanglements with other countries and the pacifism generated and reinforced by the negative experience of American participation in World War I. The country was deeply divided, and despite the preference of the majority for Britain and France, Americans made it clear that they desired no direct involvement. A series of Neutrality Acts between 1935 and 1939 banned sales of arms and supplies to belligerents, forbade Americans to take passage on ships of belligerents, prohibited American vessels from carrying arms and munitions, and barred even loans and credits. The President was unhappy with the inflexibility of this legislation but signed the various acts into law. By the spring of 1940, however, when Germany invaded Denmark and Norway and swept into Holland, Belgium, Luxemburg, and France—with Britain now left "alone to face the terror"—an increasingly large number of Americans had come to see their fate as tied to that of the Allies. Yet despite increased pressure to come to the aid of Britain after the fall of France and the entry of Italy into the war on the side of the Axis during the summer of 1940, Americans still remained reluctant to get involved. Six days before the November 5 election, FDR felt obliged to assure the public that our "boys are not going to be sent into any foreign wars."

After election to his third term in November 1940—with the territories under Nazi siege now including Greece, Yugoslavia, and North Africa, and the President insisting that under the circumstances of modern warfare the Atlantic and Pacific oceans no longer provided protective barriers—formidable opposition to U.S. intervention continued from a strong contingent of congressional isolationists, among them midwestern progressives who had supported FDR's domestic reform. Roosevelt found himself having to reassure his supporters that there would be no rollback of the New Deal while simultaneously pleading with Congress for authority to supply the Allies with needed implements of war that the United States could produce. In March 1941, Congress passed and the President signed the Lend-Lease Act, which authorized sending war materials to Great Britain and Greece. Yet the signals from the public continued to be mixed, and Roosevelt had to continue his efforts to persuade Americans to confront the danger facing them. In the end, it was the Japanese attack on Pearl Harbor in December 1941 that decided the issue of America's entry into World War II. Germany's declaration of war against the United States four days after Pearl Harbor necessitated fighting a two-front war, in Europe and in the Far East, but at least away from American shores. Throughout the following years, FDR had to work to maintain the American people's support for the war effort.

Both before the war and as it unfolded, the President remained ever mindful of the need for policies and actions to secure a stable domestic postwar future. In his January 1941 annual message to Congress, Roosevelt formulated his vision of the world that he wanted to emerge from the carnage of war. That world would be founded "upon four essential human freedoms": freedom of speech, freedom of worship, freedom from want, and freedom from fear. The first two of these are enshrined in the Constitution. The latter two reflected FDR's conviction that, like the war against fascism, the struggle against want, destitution, and economic demoralization was a fight for the survival of democracy and that the survival of democracy demanded economic and political fairness and stability. In July 1943—at a time when victory by the Allies seemed assured, though the war was not yet over—he called for what came to be known as the GI Bill to ensure that returning servicemen would not be demobilized in an environment of inflation and unemployment. He outlined six parts of his proposed legislation: mustering-out pay to cover a reasonable time between being discharged and finding a job; unemployment insurance for those who could not find jobs; funding for further education or training for those who had served their country; credit for unemployment compensation and old-age and survivors' insurance for the period of service; improved hospitalization, rehabilitation, and medical care; and adequate pensions for the disabled.

The rapid concentration of economic power required to meet the accelerated production of war materials had resulted in allowing business to make large profits out of defense and war contracts that led to unjust disparities between the very rich and the very poor. Insisting in January 1944 that "out of this war we and our children will gain something better than mere survival," FDR asked for a national service law to equalize the burdens of war. Moving beyond the reforms of the New Deal, he enumerated an economic bill of rights to determine the strategy for winning a lasting peace:

> the right to a useful and remunerative job in the industries or shops or farms or mines of the nation;
>
> the right to earn enough to provide adequate food and clothing and recreation;
>
> the right of farmers to raise and sell their products at a return which will give them and their families a decent living;
>
> the right of every businessman, large and small, to trade in an atmosphere of freedom from unfair competition and domination by monopolies at home or abroad;
>
> the right of every family to a decent home;
>
> the right to adequate medical care and the opportunity to achieve and enjoy good health;
>
> the right to adequate protection from the economic fears of old age and sickness and accident and unemployment; and, finally,
>
> the right to a good education.

These were FDR's most radical proposals. The conservative Congress elected in 1942 had eliminated a number of New Deal programs, including the popular Civilian Conservation Corps. The loss impelled FDR to propose his economic bill of rights to secure the achievements of his presidency and to reassert his commitment to have government serve the common good and ensure a safe future. He died before economic justice was realized, but his vision lived on. Like Franklin Delano Roosevelt, Martin Luther King, Jr.—the civil rights leader who came to oppose the Vietnam War—expanded his fight for equality to include economic rights in his Poor People's Campaign. Assassinated in 1968, King too died before these rights could be achieved. And still the struggle continues. Sixty-five years after FDR's failure and forty-one years after King's, President Barack Obama fights to provide health care for all Americans.

Not fully three months into his fourth term, Roosevelt died suddenly of a cerebral hemorrhage at his cottage in Warm Springs, Georgia, on April 12, 1945. His funeral train wound its way slowly from Warm Springs to Washington, D.C., as crowds of people, many crying openly and many more standing in silence, lined the tracks along the train's route through Georgia, the Carolinas, and Virginia. In Washington, tens of thousands of grieving, often sobbing, people stared in disbelief as FDR's flag-draped casket traveled from Union Station to the White House for a funeral service. Then, the President left on his final train trip—once again with women, men, and children gathered along the tracks all through the night —to his ancestral home in Hyde Park, where he was buried in a simple ceremony. "I never realized the full scope of the devotion to him until after he died," his wife Eleanor reported.

Franklin Roosevelt used the medium of radio to forge a relationship with millions upon millions of Americans. The closeness of this relationship would have been difficult to predict given the President's aristocratic background and demeanor and the fact that, for all his abundant charm, he was, as the historian Bernard Asbell has written, "a singularly private, unintimate man." But the journalist Anne O'Hare McCormick was also correct in writing at the time of FDR's death: "The crowds in the streets felt close to the President. They felt they knew him intimately. He had that rare faculty of communicating himself to masses of people, so that millions who had never approached him knew he was approachable."[1]

The radio expanded the ballot box. It enabled Roosevelt to come into people's homes, workplaces, automobiles; into many sites of leisure activity; even into houses of worship. It helped FDR and his audiences transcend boundaries both spatial and social. It enabled large numbers of Americans to feel themselves part of the political process, to imagine themselves in intimate contact with their President. It stimulated them to think carefully and often deeply about the issues that confronted them and their nation. It stirred them to action, led them to pick up pens and pencils and fill sheets or even scraps of paper with their feelings and opinions for the edification of the President, their representatives and senators, their local newspapers. It brought them out on the street to talk with neighbors and friends, to sign petitions and telegrams to officials of all kinds. In our day, the President can communicate with the people over the Internet with even greater reach and flexibility.

We can see in the letters people wrote to FDR how his radio talks buoyed them even though, when his voice faded from the air, they remained poor, unemployed, undernourished, unfulfilled. The letters reveal the myriad images Americans had of him. His very lack of intimacy allowed people to write to the President they imagined and molded to their own needs: FDR as father, brother, neighbor, friend, fellow Christian, leader, protector, crusader and, to a considerably lesser extent, FDR as power-hungry traducer of America's sacred political traditions, incompetent bureaucrat, relentless enemy of American business, reckless destroyer of sound economics, fomenter of war, dictator, Antichrist.

A substantial number of the letters conveyed a sense that Franklin Roosevelt was a kindred spirit, an approachable being eager to hear from his fellow Americans. But communicating with the President was not invariably an easy act. Lack of money or time, lack of education or writing ability, the perception of being insignificant or not worthy to take up the President's time found expression in some of the letters and must have prevented others from being written. What is striking is how many Americans, from the beginning of Roosevelt's first administration, overcame these inhibitions. "I don't just know, possibly I shouldnt have written this letter, because my education is very much limited and I know that my English is not correct," William Kinzell wrote from Oregon, "but . . . I just had to express my true opinion." Those three-cent-stamped letters, penny postcards, and telegrams that now reside so quietly and neatly boxed in the FDR Library were, in the 1930s and 1940s, dynamic instruments that gave voice to those who had been rendered inarticulate even in the ballot boxes, where the reasons for their votes, the hopes and expectations they attached to them, and the future they imagined by casting them remained mute.

NOTES

————⟪❈⟫————

FOREWORD

1. Lizabeth Cohen, *Making a New Deal* (Cambridge: Cambridge University Press, 1991), 327.

2. Denis Mack Smith, *Mussolini: A Biography* (New York: Knopf, 1982), 127; Coughlin quoted in Michael Kazin, *The Populist Persuasion: An American History,* revised edition (Ithaca, N.Y.: Cornell University Press, 1998), 124.

3. See Ira Katznelson, *When Affirmative Action Was White: An Untold History of Racial Inequality in Twentieth-Century America* (New York: W. W. Norton, 2005).

4. Millworker quoted in David M. Kennedy, *Freedom from Fear: The American People in Depression and War, 1929–1945* (New York: Oxford University Press, 1999), 297.

5. Rogers quoted in Kazin, *Populist Persuasion,* 110.

6. A good study of this subject is Paul Ryscavage, *Income Inequality in America* (Armonk, N.Y.: M. E. Sharpe, 1998).

7. Stephen Skowronek, *The Politics Presidents Make: Leadership from John Adams to George Bush* (Cambridge, Mass.: Harvard University Press, 1993), 36–39; Skowronek, "The Presidency," in *The Princeton Encyclopedia of American Political History,* edited by Michael Kazin, Rebecca Edwards, and Adam Rothman (Princeton: Princeton University Press, 2010).

8. Lawrence W. Levine, "The Historian and the Culture Gap," in Levine, *The Unpredictable Past: Explorations in American Cultural History* (New York: Oxford University Press, 1993), 14–15. The article was originally published in 1970, which accounts for the exclusive use of the male pronoun.

9. E-mail message from Cornelia R. Levine to author, June 17, 2009.

10. www.neh.gov/news/humanities/1997–01/levine.html.

INTRODUCTION

1. Margaret Atwood, *The Robber Bride* (New York: Doubleday, 1993), 4.

2. Hadley Cantril, *The Invasion from Mars: A Study in the Psychology of Panic* (1940; New York: Harper Torchbooks, 1966), xii.

3. Anne O'Hare McCormick, "Radio: A Great Unknown Force," *New York Times Magazine,* March 27, 1932; "Radio's Audience: Huge, Unprecedented," ibid., April 3, 1932; "The Mind Behind the Radio Broadcast," ibid., April 10, 1932.

4. Hadley Cantril and Gordon W. Allport, *The Psychology of Radio* (New York: Harper and Brothers, 1935), 14, 19.

5. Lew Sarett and William Trufant Foster, *Basic Principles of Speech* (Boston: Houghton Mifflin, 1936), 561.

6. Maxine Kumin, "Remembering Pearl Harbor at the Tutankhamen Exhibit," in *Our Ground Time Here Will Be Brief* (New York: Viking, 1982), 73–74.

7. Oral interviews in Ray Barfield, *Listening to Radio, 1920–1950* (Westport, Conn.: Praeger, 1996), 16–17.

8. Myra King Whitson, Houston, Texas, to FDR, March 13, 1933.

9. F. L. Brewer, Richland Center, Wisconsin, to FDR, March 13, 1933.

10. Nathan Weldon, Brooklyn, New York, to FDR, April 28, 1935.

11. Florence Gunnar Nelson, n. p., to FDR, May 26, 1940.

12. James W. Ceaser, Glen E. Thurlow, Jeffrey Tulis, and Joseph M. Bessette, "The Rise of the Rhetorical Presidency," *Presidential Studies Quarterly* 11 (spring 1981): 158–71.

13. McCormick, "Radio's Audience: Huge, Unprecedented."

14. Leila A. Sussmann, *Dear FDR: A Study of Political Letter-Writing* (Totowa, N.J.: Bedminster Press, 1963), 14.

15. Orrin E. Dunlap, Jr., *Radio in Advertising* (New York: Harper and Brothers, 1931), 67.

16. Orrin E. Dunlap, Jr., "Mail Reveals America's Reaction to Politics on the Air," *New York Times*, Sunday, July 17, 1932, 8:5.

17. Ira R. T. Smith, with Joe Alex Morris, *"Dear Mr. President . . .": The Story of Fifty Years in the White House Mail Room* (New York: Julian Messner, 1949), 156, 213–14.

18. Hugh Johnson, *The Blue Eagle from Egg to Earth* (Garden City, N.Y.: Doubleday, Doran and Company, 1935), 260.

19. *New York Times*, December 27, 1933, 1.

20. Smith, *"Dear Mr. President,"* 151.

21. Louis McHenry Howe, "The President's Mail Bag," *American Magazine*, June 1934, 23.

22. Ben Whitehurst, who was the chief of the Correspondence Division of the FERA and WPA during FDR's first administration, claimed that 60 to 70 percent of all White House mail was routed to and answered by his division (Ben Whitehurst, *"Dear Mr. President"* [New York: E. P. Dutton, 1937], 12).

23. Smith, *"Dear Mr. President,"* 189–91.

24. Howe, "The President's Mail Bag," 118. For FDR's treatment of the letters, see also the *New York Times*, May 1, 1938, 4:7.

25. Lela Stiles, a White House assistant who conducted many of these briefs, spoke about them in an interview with Leila A. Sussmann, on December 2, 1954, discussed in Sussmann, *Dear FDR*, 66–69, 84 n. 33.

26. Eleanor Roosevelt, *This I Remember* (New York: Harper and Brothers, 1949), 97–99; Bernard Asbell, *When F.D.R. Died* (New York: Holt, Rinehart and Winston, 1961), 161.

27. Quoted in Robert S. McElvaine, ed., *Down and Out in the Great Depression: Letters from the "Forgotten Man"* (Chapel Hill: University of North Carolina Press, 1983), 5.

28. Albert Moreau, Sr., North Adams, Massachusetts, to FDR, 1937.

29. Margie DeBett, St. Joseph, Michigan, to FDR, June 28, 1934.

30. C. V. Easterwood, Memphis, Tennessee, to FDR, May 28, 1941; Edwin M. Watson to C. V. Easterwood, June 3, 1941.

31. Charles Fisher, Chicago, Illinois, to FDR, December 29, 1940; Stephen Early to Charles Fisher, January 13, 1941.

32. Edwin M. Watson to Mrs. Mary L. Jester, Springport, Indiana, December 29, 1943.

33. Velma Hess, Martinsburg, West Virginia, to FDR, October 12, 1942; Grace G. Tully to Velma Hess, October 19, 1942.

34. Robert W. Woolley, Washington, D.C., to FDR, May 28, 1941; Stephen Early to Robert W. Woolley, June 4, 1941.

35. Jack McIntire, Jr., Detroit, Michigan, to Marvin McIntyre, October 24, 1933; Marvin H. McIntyre to Jack McIntire, October 27, 1933.

36. J. T. Cannon, Philadelphia, Pennsylvania, to FDR, September 16, 1941.

37. *One Third of a Nation: Lorena Hickock Reports on the Great Depression,* ed. Richard Lowitt and Maurine Beasley (Urbana: University of Illinois Press, 1981), 215.

38. *New York Times,* Sunday, January 21, 1934, 9:2.

39. *New York Times,* February 26, 1935, 1.

40. Stanley High, "Washington Hears the Voice of the People," *Literary Digest* 117 (February 24, 1934): 37.

41. Hal H. Smith, "A Deluge of Mail Falls on Congress," *New York Times,* Sunday, January 21, 1934, 9:2.

42. High, "Washington Hears the Voice of the People," 37–38.

43. L. H. Robbins, "The Country Writes to the President," *New York Times Magazine,* October 15, 1933, 3.

44. Smith, *"Dear Mr. President,"* 12.

45. Sussmann, *Dear FDR,* 11.

46. *New York Times,* Sunday, December 17, 1933, 1.

47. Howe, "The President's Mail Bag," 22.

48. James A. Farley, *Jim Farley's Story: The Roosevelt Years* (New York: McGraw-Hill, 1948), 79.

49. Quoted in W. Dale Nelson, *Who Speaks for the President? The White House Press Secretary from Cleveland to Clinton* (Syracuse: Syracuse University Press, 1998), 73.

50. Quoted in Asbell, *When F.D.R. Died,* 161.

51. FDR, Address at Chicago, October 5, 1937, *Public Papers,* 6:406–11; and Four Hundredth Press Conference, ibid., 414–25. The thirteen volumes of the *Public Papers and Addresses of Franklin D. Roosevelt* were compiled by Samuel Rosenman, with a special introduction and explanatory notes by the President. Volumes 1–5 were published by Random House in 1938, volumes 6–9 by Macmillan in 1941, and volumes 10–13 by Harper in 1950. Hereafter cited by volume and page number.

52. Samuel I. Rosenman, *Working with Roosevelt* (New York: Harper and Brothers, 1952), 165–68, 195–98.

53. Sussmann, *Dear FDR,* 67.

54. Ibid., 68–69.

55. Charles M. Flaig, Richmond, Indiana, to FDR, April 15, 1938.

56. FDR, Address to the Tammany Speakers' Bureau, January 18, 1929, quoted in Frank Freidel, *Franklin D. Roosevelt: The Triumph* (Boston: Little, Brown, 1956), 31.

57. Jeanette Sayre, *An Analysis of the Radiobroadcasting Activities of Federal Agencies* (Studies in the Control of Radio, June 1941, no. 3) is a detailed account of the New Deal's use of radio from which all the data in this paragraph has been drawn.

58. FDR to M. H. Aylesworth, December 15, 1932, quoted in Frank Freidel, *Franklin D. Roosevelt: Launching the New Deal* (Boston: Little, Brown, 1973), 230–31. For CBS's equally accommodating attitude after FDR's election, see Douglas B. Craig, *Fireside Politics: Radio and Political Culture in the United States, 1920–1940* (Baltimore: Johns Hopkins University Press, 2000), 79–80.

59. FDR to Russell C. Leffingwell, March 16, 1942, in *Franklin D. Roosevelt: Selected Speeches, Messages, Press Conferences, and Letters,* ed. Basil Rauch (New York: Rinehart, 1957), 310–11.

60. FDR to Mary T. Norton, March 24, 1942, in *F.D.R.: His Personal Letters, 1928–1945,* ed. Elliott Roosevelt (New York: Duell, Sloane and Pearce, 1950), 2:1300.

61. Belle Conwell, Birmingham, Alabama, to FDR, March 15, 1933.

62. B. J. Campbell, Memphis, Tennessee, to FDR, January 10, 1941.

63. *New York Times,* May 13, 1941, 1, 8; May 23, 1941, 1; May 24, 1941, 11; May 25, 1941, 1–2; May 27, 1941, 1, 4.

64. "World-Wide Radio Coverage Arranged for Roosevelt Fireside Chat on Tuesday," *New York Times,* May 24, 1941, 11.

65. We carefully checked three newspapers — the *New York Times, Chicago Tribune,* and *San Francisco Examiner* — for the editions published before, during, and after each of the thirty-one Chats to get a sense of newspaper coverage. The *Times* especially was a good source for the ways in which other newspapers across the nation treated the Chats.

66. Elizabeth Berg, New York City, to FDR, March 9, 1937.

67. Walter Edison, Oakland, California, to FDR, January 4, 1941.

68. Howe, "The President's Mail Bag," 118.

69. Paul Barrett, Philadelphia, Pennsylvania, to FDR, March 11, 1937; "Two Hundred of Us," n.p., to FDR, n.d.

70. A. M. Tebbetts, St. Louis, Missouri, to FDR, December 29, 1941.

71. William M. Ryerson, Little Falls, New Jersey, to FDR, March 10, 1937.

72. Donald Warren, *Radio Priest: Charles Coughlin, the Father of Hate Radio* (New York: Free Press, 1996), 26.

73. FDR, Introduction to *Public Papers and Addresses,* 1:8–9.

74. FDR, Announcement of First Radio "Fireside Chat," March 11, 1933, ibid., 2:59–60.

75. For the miles FDR traveled, see John Gunther, *Roosevelt in Retrospect: A Profile in History* (New York: Harper and Brothers, 1950), 139.

76. "Common Words Keynote of Roosevelt's Talks," *New York Times*, May 16, 1937, 10:10.

77. See FDR's note in *Public Papers and Addresses*, 2:60.

78. Audio recording of the March 12, 1933, Fireside Chat in the FDR Library, Hyde Park, New York. All quotes and summaries from the Fireside Chats in this volume are from the audio and stenographic records in the FDR Library. Except in the case of three Chats that were not taped, the stenographic records have been corrected to conform with the original recordings.

79. Halford R. Ryan, *FDR's Rhetorical Presidency* (Westport, Conn.: Greenwood Publishing, 1988); Earnest Brandenburg and Waldo W. Braden, "Franklin D. Roosevelt's Voice and Pronunciation," *Quarterly Journal of Speech*, February 1952, 23–30; Robert E. Sherwood, *Roosevelt and Hopkins: An Intimate History* (New York: Harper and Brothers, 1948), 217, 297; Grace Tully, *F.D.R. My Boss* (New York: Charles Scribner's Sons, 1949), 98; John H. Sharon, "The Fireside Chat," *Franklin D. Roosevelt Collector* 2 (1949): 17; Orrin E. Dunlap, Jr., "Roosevelt Keeps the Microphone Talking to the People," *New York Times*, March 19, 1933, 10:8.

80. *New York Times*, January 31, 1937, 11:6.

81. Felix A. Ury, Washington, D.C., to FDR, March 10, 1937.

82. W. M. Holmberg, Birmingham, Alabama, to FDR, October 12, 1942.

83. Quoted in Orrin E. Dunlap, Jr., "When Roosevelt Goes on the Air," *New York Times Magazine*, June 18, 1933.

84. "Roosevelt's Voice Held Radio's Best," *New York Times*, May 16, 1935.

85. "Mr. Roosevelt's Address," *New York Times*, April 30, 1935. For more newspaper focus on FDR's voice and radio style, see the *New York Times* for the following dates: February 9, March 1, September 6, November 8, 1936; January 24, 1937, 4:6; March 4, 1937, 11:12; November 7, 1937, 11:14; May 1, 1938, 8:3; August 28, 1938, 9:10; September 11, 1938, 10:10; January 4, 1942, 9:12; December 31, 1942.

86. *The Autobiography of Eleanor Roosevelt* (1961; New York: Da Capo Press, 1992), 162.

87. A. W. Lehman, the manager of the Cooperative Analysis of Broadcasting, wrote Stephen Early after the Fireside Chat of February 23, 1942, that that Chat, along with the one on December 9, 1941, set records for the size of radio audiences. Compared with the 83 percent of radio set-owners FDR drew on both occasions, the three night-time commercial programs with the largest audiences drew less than 41 percent each (A. W. Lehman to Stephen Early, February 24, 1942, in FDR Papers, Hyde Park).

88. Harry Butcher to John H. Sharon, January 10, 1949, in Sharon, "The Fireside Chat," 6.

89. Richard Lee Strout in *The Making of the New Deal: The Insiders Speak,* ed. Katie Louchheim (Cambridge: Harvard University Press, 1983), 13.

90. Dunlap, "When Roosevelt Goes on the Air," 17.

91. Raymond Moley, *After Seven Years* (New York: Harper and Brothers, 1939), 155.

92. Eleanor Roosevelt, *This I Remember,* 72–73.

93. Sherwood, *Roosevelt and Hopkins,* 212.

94. FDR to Russell C. Leffingwell, March 16, 1942, in *Franklin D. Roosevelt: Selected Speeches, Messages, Press Conferences, and Letters,* 310–11.

95. FDR, *Public Papers and Addresses,* 5:391–92.

96. Charles Michelson, *The Ghost Talks* (New York: G. P. Putnam's Sons, 1944), 12–13.

97. Perkins, *The Roosevelt I Knew,* 113.

98. Tully, *F.D.R. My Boss,* 99; Rosenman, *Working with Roosevelt,* 11–12, 486.

99. E. D. Warren, Jackson, Michigan, to FDR, May 8, 1933.

100. Harry G. Nelson, Ithaca, Nebraska, to FDR, March 10, 1937.

101. Frank A. Mercato, San Francisco, to FDR, April 15, 1938.

102. "The Fortune Survey XX," *Fortune* 19, no. 2 (1939): 108.

103. Lawrence W. Levine, *The Unpredictable Past: Explorations in American Cultural History* (New York: Oxford University Press, 1993), 313, 316.

104. Charles E. Comer, Dayton, Ohio, to FDR, October 22, 1933.

105. C. E. Holiman, Canon City, Colorado, to FDR, October 1, 1934.

106. Bishop R. R. Wright, Jr., Cleveland, Ohio, to FDR, April 29, 1942.

107. Unsigned telegram from Philadelphia, Pennsylvania, to FDR, March 13, 1933.

108. James W. Henley, Chattanooga, Tennessee, to FDR, September 6, 1939.

109. Harry J. Myerson, Chicago, Illinois, to FDR, March 13, 1933.

110. Antonio Carneiro et al., New York City, to FDR, April 14, 1938.

111. Sidney Rothschild, Forest Hills, New York, to FDR, April 15, 1938.

112. Mrs. Cerena Cibolski, Manhattan, Kansas, to FDR, January 11, 1944.

113. Saul Bellow, "In the Days of Mr. Roosevelt," in *It All Adds Up: From the Dim Past to the Uncertain Future* (New York: Viking, 1994), 28–29.

114. Patrick H. O'Dea, Washington, D.C., to FDR, March 14, 1933.

115. Hal Warner, Director of Publicity, Affiliated Theatres Circuit, Philadelphia, Pennsylvania, to FDR, May 26, 1940.

116. Samuel B. Traum, Forest Hills, New York, to FDR, September 14, 1941.

117. Miss Ruth Lieberman, Brooklyn, New York, to FDR, March 14, 1933.

118. "Hutch," New York City, to FDR, March 13, 1933.

119. F. P. McMahon, Omaha, Nebraska, to FDR, March 10, 1937.

120. A. J. Hamilton, Atlanta, Georgia, to FDR, March 15, 1937.

121. W. A. Blees, Galesburg, Illinois, to FDR, March 10, 1937.

122. Paul F. Lazarsfeld, *Radio and the Printed Page* (New York: Duell, Sloane and Pearce, 1940), 204–5, 258–60; Harry Field and Paul F. Lazarsfeld, *The People Look at Radio* (Chapel Hill: University of North Carolina Press, 1946), 99.

123. "The Fortune Survey XXIV," *Fortune* 20, no. 2 (1939): 176. The 1945 poll was conducted by the National Association of Broadcasters and is reported in Field and Lazarsfeld, *The People Look at Radio,* 101.

124. Field and Lazarsfeld, *The People Look at Radio,* 96.

PART ONE: THE NADIR

1. All summaries of and quotations from the Fireside Chat of March 12, 1933, come directly from the audio recording of the Chat in the FDR Library, Hyde Park, New York.

2. FDR, Inaugural Address, March 4, 1933, *Public Papers and Addresses,* 2:11–16.

3. Frances Perkins, *The Roosevelt I Knew* (New York: Viking, 1946), 182–183; Lawrence W. Levine, *The Unpredictable Past: Explorations in American Cultural History* (New York: Oxford University Press, 1993), 262–66; Robert S. McElvaine, *The Great Depression: America, 1929–1941* (New York: Times Books, 1993), 75.

4. Levine, *The Unpredictable Past,* chap. 11.

5. Max Freedman, ed., *Roosevelt and Frankfurter: Their Correspondence, 1928–1945* (Boston: Little, Brown, 1967), 37.

6. FDR, Campaign Address at Fenway Park, Boston, Massachusetts, November 4, 1944, *Public Papers and Addresses,* 13:397–406.

7. FDR to Helen Wilkinson Reynolds, published in *Year Book Dutchess County Historical Society* 18 (1933): 35.

8. FDR, Note to Inaugural Address, March 4, 1933, *Public Papers and Addresses,* 2:16.

9. Will Rogers, *Sanity Is Where You Find It: An Affectionate History of the United States in the 20's and 30's,* ed. Donald Day (Boston: Houghton Mifflin, 1935), 167.

10. Raymond Moley, *After Seven Years* (New York: Harper and Brothers, 1939), 155.

11. Quoted in Arthur M. Schlesinger, Jr., *The Coming of the New Deal* (Boston: Houghton Mifflin, 1959), 5.

12. *The Autobiography of Will Rogers,* ed. Donald Day (Boston: Houghton Mifflin, 1949), 313.

13. Arthur A. Ballantine, "When All the Banks Closed," *Harvard Business Review* 26 (March 1948): 129–43.

14. *New York Times,* March 14, 1933.

15. The estimate was made by *Times* correspondent Charles Hurd. See his *When the New Deal was Young and Gay* (New York: Hawthorn Books, 1965), 247.

16. All summaries of and quotations from the Fireside Chat of May 7, 1933, come directly from the audio recording of the Chat in the FDR Library, Hyde Park, New York.

17. FDR, Inaugural Address, March 4, 1933, *Public Papers and Addresses,* 2:11–16.

18. Quoted in Schlesinger, *The Coming of the New Deal,* 1–2.

19. See the March 5, 1933, editions of the *New York Times,* the *New York Herald Tribune,* the *Washington Post,* the *Chicago Tribune,* and the *Los Angeles Times.*

20. Quoted in Schlesinger, *The Coming of the New Deal*, 3.
21. *Barron's*, February 13, 1933.
22. For a discussion of these comparisons with fascism, see Levine, *The Unpredictable Past*, chap. 12.
23. Rexford Guy Tugwell, *The Democratic Roosevelt: A Biography of Franklin D. Roosevelt* (Garden City, N.Y.: Doubleday, 1957), 11.
24. Perkins, *The Roosevelt I Knew*, 330.
25. Eleanor Roosevelt, *This I Remember* (New York: Harper and Brothers, 1949), 346.
26. Quoted in Bernard Bellush, *Franklin D. Roosevelt as Governor of New York* (1955; New York: AMS Press, 1968), 134, 147.
27. FDR's statement about being left of center is quoted in Perkins, *The Roosevelt I Knew*, 333.
28. Moley, *After Seven Years*, 281.
29. FDR, Address Delivered at Democratic State Convention, Syracuse, New York, September 29, 1936, *Public Papers and Addresses*, 5:389–90.
30. Eleanor Roosevelt, *This I Remember*, 347–48.
31. Moley, *After Seven Years*, 189.
32. Because no audio recordings were made of the Fireside Chats of July 24 and October 22, 1933, all summaries of and quotations from these Chats come directly from the stenographic copy in the FDR Library, Hyde Park, New York.
33. The lyrics are printed in Guido van Rijn, *Roosevelt's Blues: African-American Blues and Gospel Songs on FDR* (Jackson: University Press of Mississippi, 1997), 75.
34. Eric Barnouw, *The Golden Web: A History of Broadcasting in the United States* (New York: Oxford University Press, 1968), 8.
35. "President Explains Plan," *New York Times*, July 25, 1933, 1; "Roosevelt Gets 20,000 Messages," *New York Times*, July 28, 1933, 9.
36. Hugh S. Johnson, "The Nation Responds," *New York Times*, July 30, 1933, 4:4.
37. Rexford G. Tugwell, *Roosevelt's Revolution: The First Year — a Personal Perspective* (New York: Macmillan, 1977), 188.
38. For these complaints, see *New York Times*, October 24, 1933, 20; October 29, 1933, 4:4.
39. FDR to Edward M. House, May 7, 1934, in *F.D.R.: His Personal Letters, 1928–1945*, ed. Elliott Roosevelt (New York: Duell, Sloane and Pearce, 1950), 1:400–401.
40. Because no audio recording was made of the Fireside Chat of June 28, 1934, all summaries of and quotations from the Chat come directly from the stenographic copy in the FDR Library, Hyde Park, New York.
41. Quoted in James MacGregor Burns, *Roosevelt: The Lion and the Fox* (New York: Harcourt, Brace, 1956), 317, 203–204.
42. George Wolfskill, *The Revolt of the Conservatives: A History of the American Liberty League* (Cambridge: Houghton Mifflin, 1962), 35, 106, 108. For the League's campaign against FDR, see chap. 5.

43. Moley, *After Seven Years*, 291–92; FDR to Edward M. House, May 7, 1934, in *F.D.R.: His Personal Letters, 1928–1945*, 1:401.

44. Herbert Hoover, *The Challenge to Liberty* (New York: Charles Scribner's Sons, 1934), 85, 193, and passim.

45. Tugwell, *The Democratic Roosevelt*, 352–53.

46. All summaries of and quotations from the Fireside Chat of September 30, 1934, come directly from the audio recording of the Chat in the FDR Library, Hyde Park, New York.

47. Beard is quoted in Frank Freidel, *Franklin D. Roosevelt: A Rendezvous with Destiny* (Boston: Little, Brown, 1990), 141; the *Times* is quoted in McElvaine, *The Great Depression*, 229; FDR is quoted in Otis L. Graham, Jr., and Meghan Robinson Wander, eds., *Franklin D. Roosevelt: His Life and Times, An Encyclopedic View* (Boston: G. K. Hall, 1985), 117.

48. FDR's remark is in Schlesinger, *The Coming of the New Deal*, 504–5; Perkins's observation is in Perkins, *The Roosevelt I Knew*, 352.

49. Tugwell's comments are in Tugwell, "The Preparation of a President," *Western Political Quarterly* 1 (June 1948): 138–39; "The New Deal: The Rise of Business," part 2, ibid., 5 (September 1952): 503; *The Brains Trust* (New York: Viking, 1968), xxi–xxiv.

50. Quoted in Robert E. Sherwood, *Roosevelt and Hopkins: An Intimate History* (New York: Harper and Brothers, 1948), 64–65.

51. FDR to Ray Stannard Baker, March 20, 1935, in *F.D.R.: His Personal Letters, 1928–1945*, 1:466–67.

52. All summaries of and quotations from the Fireside Chat of April 28, 1935, come directly from the audio recording of the Chat in the FDR Library, Hyde Park, N.Y.

53. For the latter figure, see George McJimsey, *Harry Hopkins: Ally of the Poor and Defender of Democracy* (Cambridge: Harvard University Press, 1987), 110.

54. John Steinbeck, *The Grapes of Wrath* (New York: Viking Press, 1939), chap. 5.

55. All summaries of and quotations from the Fireside Chat of September 6, 1936, come directly from the audio recording of the Chat in the FDR Library, Hyde Park, New York.

PART TWO: THE CONTINUING CRISIS

1. *These Are Our Lives: As Told by the People and Written by Members of the Federal Writers' Project of the Works Progress Administration in North Carolina, Tennessee, and Georgia* (1939; New York: W. W. Norton, 1975), 210–11.

2. Quoted in Arthur M. Schlesinger, Jr., *The Politics of Upheaval* (Boston: Houghton Mifflin, 1960), 643.

3. FDR, *Public Papers and Addresses*, 2:14–15.

4. FDR, Two Hundred and Eighth Press Conference (Excerpts), May 29, 1935, ibid., 4:200–222.

5. *The Secret Diary of Harold L. Ickes: The First Thousand Days, 1933–1936* (New York: Simon and Schuster, 1954), 495.

6. Quoted in Schlesinger, *The Politics of Upheaval,* 453.

7. *The Secret Diary of Harold L. Ickes: The First Thousand Days,* 614.

8. FDR, Three Hundredth Press Conference (Excerpts), June 2, 1936, *Public Papers and Addresses,* 5:191–92.

9. *The Secret Diary of Harold L. Ickes: The First Thousand Days,* 705; FDR, Introduction, *Public Papers and Addresses,* 6:lxi–lxii.

10. Schlesinger, *The Politics of Upheaval,* 495.

11. FDR, Introduction, *Public Papers and Addresses,* 6:lix–lx.

12. FDR, Annual Message to the Congress, January 6, 1937, ibid., 5:634–42.

13. FDR, Plan for the Reorganization of the Judicial Branch of the Government, February 5, 1937, ibid., 6:51–66.

14. The letters Roosevelt received on the Court issue can be found in President's Secretary's File 165, Supreme Court, January 1937–July 1937, FDR Library, Hyde Park, New York.

15. George H. Gallup, *The Gallup Poll: Public Opinion, 1935–1971* (New York: Random House, 1972), 1:58–59, 70; Hadley Cantril, ed., *Public Opinion, 1935–1946* (Princeton: Princeton University Press, 1951), 148–51.

16. Samuel I. Rosenman, *Working with Roosevelt* (New York: Harper and Brothers, 1952), 161.

17. William E. Leuchtenburg, *The Supreme Court Reborn: The Constitutional Revolution in the Age of Roosevelt* (New York: Oxford University Press, 1995), chap. 5. See also chapter 4 for an excellent discussion of the origins of the Court plan.

18. Rosenman, *Working with Roosevelt,* 160.

19. FDR, Address at the Democratic Victory Dinner, Washington, D.C., March 4, 1937, *Public Papers and Addresses,* 6:113–21.

20. All summaries of and quotations from the Fireside Chat of March 9, 1937, come directly from the audio recording of the Chat in the FDR Library, Hyde Park, New York.

21. All summaries of and quotations from the Fireside Chats of October 12 and November 14, 1937, come directly from the audio recordings of the Chats in the FDR Library, Hyde Park, New York.

22. Rosenman, *Working with Roosevelt,* 170.

23. Arthur M. Schlesinger, Jr., *The Crisis of the Old Order, 1919–1933* (Boston: Houghton Mifflin, 1957), 241; Lawrence W. Levine, *The Unpredictable Past: Explorations in American Cultural History* (New York: Oxford University Press, 1993), 262–66; Irving Bernstein, *A Caring Society: The New Deal, the Worker, and the Great Depression* (Boston: Houghton Mifflin, 1985), 17–18, 276–78.

24. "Fortune Survey I," *Fortune* 12 (July 1935): 67; "Fortune Survey X," ibid., 16 (October 1937): 154–55, 174; Cantril, *Public Opinion, 1935–1946,* 893–95.

25. Rexford Guy Tugwell, "The New Deal: The Rise of Business," part 2, *Western Political Quarterly* 5 (September 1952): 503; "The Preparation of a President," ibid.,

1 (June 1948): 142; Tugwell, *The Democratic Roosevelt: A Biography of Franklin D. Roosevelt* (New York: Doubleday, 1957), 15.

26. Roy W. Howard to FDR, August 26, 1935; FDR to Roy W. Howard, September 2, 1935, *Public Papers and Addresses,* 4:352–57.

27. FDR, Campaign Address at Chicago, Illinois, October 14, 1936, ibid., 5:487–88.

28. Quoted in Robert S. McElvaine, *The Great Depression: America, 1929–1941* (New York: Times Books, 1993), 297.

29. Roosevelt is quoted in *The Secret Diary of Harold L. Ickes: The Inside Struggle, 1936–1939* (New York: Simon and Schuster, 1954), 144.

30. Harry Hopkins, *Spending to Save: The Complete Story of Relief* (1936; Seattle: University of Washington Press, 1972), 180.

31. Cantril, *Public Opinion, 1935–1946,* 895.

32. FDR, Four Hundred and Seventh Press Conference (Excerpts), October 29, 1937, *Public Papers and Addresses,* 6:474–75.

33. *The Secret Diary of Harold L. Ickes: The First Thousand Days, 1933–1936,* 695.

34. John Morton Blum, *From the Morgenthau Diaries: Years of Crisis, 1928–1938* (Boston: Houghton Mifflin, 1959), 423–24; Rosenman, *Working with Roosevelt,* 172–74.

35. *New York Times,* April 15, 1938.

36. All summaries of and quotations from the Fireside Chat of April 14, 1938, come directly from the audio recording of the Chat in the FDR Library, Hyde Park, New York.

37. Rosenman, *Working with Roosevelt,* 175.

EPILOGUE

1. Bernard Asbell, *The F. D. R. Memoirs* (Garden Vity, N.Y.: Doubleday, 1973), 52–53; Anne O'Hare McCormick, "A Man of the World and the World's Man," *New York Times,* April 14, 1945.

ACKNOWLEDGMENTS

The bulk of our research was done during several extended trips to the Franklin D. Roosevelt Library in Hyde Park, New York, where we were treated with courtesy by the knowledgeable and helpful staff. We especially want to thank Lynn Bassanese, Karen Burtis, Bob Clark, John Ferris, Robert Parks, Mark Renovitch, Nancy Snedeker, and Raymond Teichman. We also appreciate the help of the staffs at the National Archives II in College Park, Maryland, and the Division of Prints and Photographs at the Library of Congress. The Doe Library at the University of California, Berkeley, never failed to find the sources and materials we sought. Research funds from George Mason University and the Margaret Byrne Chair at the University of California, Berkeley, benefited our work substantially.

For helping to locate diverse printed materials relating to the Fireside Chats, we are indebted to Gerd Horten, who assisted us at the outset of this project, and Zoe Couacaud, who worked with us during its final stages. Zoe also provided critical aid in getting the letters ready for transcription and helping us proofread them. We thank Louise Mozingo for sharing her father's West Point story.

Robert McElvaine introduced us to the letters the American people wrote to FDR while he was a participant in the National Endowment for the Humanities summer seminar "The Folk in American History," led by Lawrence Levine at the University of California, Berkeley, in 1978. Bob's pioneering work with those letters during and after the seminar enhanced our understanding of the relationship between the American people and FDR and provoked us into asking questions that we have tried to answer in this volume. Our good friend Robert Dallek has taught us much over the years — both personally and in his published work — about FDR and American foreign policy; we trust we have used his lessons well.

Various versions of the materials were presented to an international gathering of scholars at the German Historical Institute in Washington, D.C.; to faculty and students at Arizona State University, Purdue University, The Johns Hopkins University, and Alfred University; to the school teachers participating in the UC Berkeley History–Social Science Project during the summer of 2001; to members of the Berkeley American Studies reading group; and — in what were largely informal, extended conversations — to colleagues and students in the Department of History and Art History and the Cultural Studies Program at George Mason University. The responses we received from these encounters were stimulating and extremely beneficial.

During our work, we have been nurtured and aided by so many people that we cannot begin to list each one here. Let us simply thank family, friends, and colleagues on both coasts who patiently heard us converse about the American people, FDR, and the Fireside Chats and who responded with a generosity and ingenuity that stimulated and informed us again and again. Any successful work of scholarship should involve a certain degree of reciprocity between the authors and their subjects. Ours certainly did. We have learned an enormous amount from the men, women, and children who wrote to Franklin Roosevelt. We recommend their company to everyone interested in the Great Depression.